A COACH'S

Dear Tonia

Thank you so much for
all your Help

Gerard

A
COACH'S
STORY

GERARD O'DONOVAN

bookshaker

First Published in Great Britain 2011 by Bookshaker.com

© Copyright Gerard O'Donovan

Praise

"*A Coach's Story is much more than its title suggests: the experience and expertise of the many coaches who have contributed their stories to this very readable book make it a comprehensive guide to the subject. Anyone who thinks coaching might be for them, either to enhance their lives or as a profession, will find a wealth of information and approaches here.*"

Lucy McCarraher, author of *The Real Secret*,
www.therealsecret.net

"*When asked by new and experienced coaches to recommend a book showing not only how people became coaches but also how they laid the foundations for their business I got stumped. That is until I read Coach's Story. Gerard not only collected a rich collection of tales from different coaches he also shared with openness, honesty and candour his own journey.*

"*A Coach's Story offers a comprehensive range of personal stories that give a real insight into the variety of paths people have taken to become successful coaches. These journeys have not always been smooth or easy, throwing up many unexpected challenges. With resilience, determination and acceptance each coach's story demonstrates both the importance of learning from failure and being grateful for life's opportunities. Each and every coach has been been driven by a desire to improve the quality of their own lives and used this as the means to then support many more people do the same. If you share this desire then I encourage you to read A Coach's Story.*"

Amechi Udo, author of *Choosing A Coaching*
Course That's Right For You and Inspired To Coach

"*This is a really unique book because it's for coaches and clients alike. Anyone exploring a career in coaching will learn a lot about the wonderful coaches who contributed to this book in terms of how coaching not only turned their lives around, but how their careers have blossomed. For prospective clients seeking coaching, it will give them the confidence to make that investment in themselves and hire their own coach because the return is huge. Another successful venture, well done to you all for sharing so honestly.*"

Dawn Campbell, Holistic Health Coach & Living Foods
Practitioner, www.dawncampbellholistichealth.eu

"A Coach's Story is a superb read and an excellent thinking tool for those considering becoming a Coach or taking their career to the next level. The introduction sets the context for this delightful book, with Gerard outlining his personal coaching vision and the revolutionary coaching world that he has worked within for many years. The simple and well laid out sections are thought provoking, interesting and provide inspiration when reading about the experiences and journeys of successful Coaches. I see this book as a priority text for any coaching course and feel enlightened and privileged to have read it. I recommend you buy it as soon as you can – as a gift to yourself!"

Yasmin Mukadam, Life Coach

"It's true - we all love stories. Especially stories about people we admire - from the stories of their life, loves and development we gain a greater understanding about them, and that makes us think about ourselves and our place in the world.

"Gerard has put together a wonderful story book - stories about Coaches. Their ups and downs and how they got to be where they are and each contributing coach tells their own story about their own personal journey. Stories are a wonderful way to illustrate a point. The difference here is that these stories are true. It takes a brutal honesty to tell about the failure as well as the success, the pain as well as the joy and the bad as well as the good. Gerard and the contributors give you clarity and brutal honesty, characteristics that make a good coach.

"From each of these stories we can draw inspiration, education and see and feel the various surfaces others have passed over. The road to success is sometimes hard, sometimes painful and sometimes joyful - just as each of us have found it. We are all different and we each have different stories to tell. What we can all draw from this is the inspiration to go for our goals - to see how others took the action that that was needed. Take inspiration from these stories.

"While you travel on your journey through life, as you develop, immerse yourself in this little book of other Coach's journeys to educate, inspire and encourage you to become whatever you want to be.

"I cannot think of a better companion on the journey of life."

Gordon Piggott

"Gerard O'Donovan has devoted his professional life to helping large numbers of people through the medium of coaching. Having directly coached many individuals himself, he has then gone on to enable others to coach and tells of his journey to achieve this aim.

"In 'The Coaches Story' he has assembled some of his protégés to tell their own personal stories and how they now help to diffuse the overall message; that by helping people realise their dreams and fight their demons from holding them back from achieving their true desires, they are empowered to enjoy greater happiness. In doing so, coaches not only help their clients and bring more light and awareness to the world, but help themselves in this wonderful process of facilitating self accountability. Coaching deals with the now, not dwelling in the past, and helps clients to deliver their own special outcomes.

"Apart from some of the genuinely heart warming stories there are many practical coaching techniques explained and many resources in which to delve, prompting the reader to ask questions of themselves and seek their own coach to help guide them to fulfil their desires."

Scott Milway

Contents

Foreword

THE BENEFITS THAT CLIENTS GET FROM COACHING have hardly changed over the last 20 years since it has become a mainstream profession. True, in past times there have been many kinds of advisers from king's councillors to their jesters. Probably the closest Shakespeare ever got to revealing the concept of the coach is that of the Fool in King Lear, the loyal and intelligent supporter of a deteriorating monarch who, unlike clients today, fails to follow his jester's profound advice. "He's mad that trusts in the tameness of a wolf, horses' health, and the boy's love or a whore's oath" was the Fool's trenchant but rejected advice.

Today, coaching is a truly professional service where clients retain a coach to reach a goal, solve a problem or take advantage of an opportunity. Coaching really does work because the clients get the support they need to make the changes they want.

Coaching also, it is pleasing to record, often brings about profound changes in the people who decide to take up this profession. When I looked through the list of the terrific coaches who have shared their experiences in this book of learning and later serving clients I felt profoundly humble. I have the privilege of knowing several of them personally. One after another they reveal how the process of training to be a coach has uncovered long held desires to serve and help others in a calling which some would suggest is almost as sacred as that of being summoned to the spiritual life.

I have known many coaches who turned with relief to join a coach training school such as noble Manhattan because somehow they knew that there was an occupation "out there" for them but until that moment they hadn't actually realised what it was. In my own case as I was training to be a coach with the late great Thomas Leonard, the acknowledged father of the coaching profession, he once asked me to represent him in a TV interview. I said, "Thomas, as a former PR man, I know a lot about TV but I still know nothing about being a coach." Thomas immediately referred me to an experienced New York coach, Marlene Elliott. "George," she said, "if you think you're a coach -- you're a******* coach!" From that moment I realised that I had actually been a coach in some form or other since my childhood. And so it is with so many of those special people who have ventured to take up this career.

I very much like my coaching colleagues. They genuinely want to do good and help other people. Without doubt, they are the kindness and most generous hearted colleagues, always open to provide help, moral support and even advice and so many of them know infinitely much more than I do! I have probably learned more about the coaching profession (not "industry" for heaven's sake!) from my colleagues who are members of the 800 strong EuroCoach List, which three of us founded some 13 years ago to enable colleagues to communicate with each other over the Internet.

But don't think for one moment that this is an *airy fairy* business. Coaches need to be tough and determined to get and keep new business. Coaching is a "distress purchase", rather like having to replace the tires on a car. No one will invest in paying for a coach just for fun. The coaches who succeed and who are an example to us all in our profession pay particular attention to the need to market their skills. They use the Internet, the social networking sites and they network personally. The great US comedian and film maker, Woody Allen is surely on the right track when he says, "70% of networking is being there." And it is by being *there* that coaches can meet others who will refer business to them on the basis that people will do business with those they know like and trust.

One of the aspects I particularly like about Gerard O'Donovan's Noble Manhattan training process is the extent that it supports those who graduate in the tough task of setting up their businesses establishing a new client base.

As you read the stories of each of the contributors to this significant book I am confident that you will be given a fresh perspective of this useful profession of ours -- and you might even decide to become a coach yourself! Well, if you are already a coach you are bound in any case to learn something innovative and encouraging from these pages.

George Metcalfe
Chairman, the International Institute of Coaching
for Great Britain & Ireland

Introduction

IN A WORLD WHERE SUCCESS IS OFTEN MEASURED by the car you drive, the neighbourhood where you live, the job you perform, and the balance in your bank account, the ability to define and achieve true happiness remains a constant source of concern for millions.

You've probably wondered from time to time why you are here, what you should be doing with your life, and why goals seem so difficult to achieve. Perhaps you long for the days of your youth, when everything seemed so much simpler. Often, you may feel you're missing out somehow on the "good things" in life. If you're feeling trapped, unfulfilled, unhappy, or dissatisfied, this book may provide the answer you seek.

I'm Gerard O'Donovan, founder of Noble-Manhattan Coaching, one of the leading coach training companies in Europe and the only coach training company in Britain to achieve an A* accreditation from the International Institute of Coaching (IIC). Over the last eighteen years, my company has helped people like you discover their hidden talents and achieve peak performance and personal satisfaction.

How have we accomplished this? Through coaching.

Does that surprise you? If so, this book was written for you.

"To put the world right in order, we must first put the nation in order; to put the nation in order, we must first put the family in order; to put the family in order, we must first cultivate our personal life; we must first set our hearts right."

CONFUCIUS

If you feel imprisoned in your life, wishing you could change but unable to break free, working with a qualified coach can offer the personal empowerment you seek to help you balance the pressures and endless tasks in life and work that impede success. Coaching combines ground-breaking techniques, a concrete approach and the forward thinking so necessary in your plan for creating a more satisfying and rewarding life.

I know this first hand. Coaching is responsible for helping me to completely restructure and re-engineer my life, helping me understand that the responsibility lies with me for everything that happens to me. Through coaching, I learned that I can take charge of my thoughts and my feelings, irrespective of what is happening around me. Over the years, this has led me to a deep and profound understanding of what I believe is the nature of life. I have realised that I am in total control of everything that occurs, at home and at work. Through the power of my thoughts and feelings I can create anything I want in my life, using the principles and awesome power of Intention and the Law of Attraction.

Additionally, coaching has helped me to become far less judgmental of others and far more non-directional when dealing with my family, my employees, and my friends. In fact, my current management style is a 180 degree shift from the way I once managed my large insurance company. Back then I was directional, obsessed with being in control, micromanaging the actions of others. Today, I enjoy a high quality peace of mind I never dreamed would be possible.

But I'm jumping ahead before I tell you how I got here.

Humble Beginnings Fuel My Drive Toward Success

I was born in 1958 in the small town of Bantry in southwest Ireland. My family was poor. My father was a fisherman and owned several fishing boats, so when I was young I often accompanied him on fishing trips.

I always imagined I would grow up to become a fisherman as well. Unfortunately, my father died unexpectedly when I was eleven years old. It was a devastating time for me and my family. Because my father left no money to support us and no Last Will & Testament, I had to begin working to help support my mother and younger, two year old sister. So at the tender age of eleven I took on my first job: delivering milk every morning; and my second job, delivering newspapers every evening. On weekends, I worked at my third job, in a shop. Quite a responsibility for one so young.

When I was fourteen, my mother, sister and I moved to Scotland. My mother was Scottish and she longed to be closer to her relatives.

At seventeen I left home and joined the Royal Marines Commandos, where I would soon face an entirely new set of challenges and opportunities unlike anything else I had encountered.

In 1984, at the age of twenty six, I joined an insurance brokerage selling insurance on commission only, which included a great deal of cold calling. I found it very difficult but, I persevered and did quite well, soon achieving the status of most successful salesperson, progressing rapidly into management and eventually becoming Regional Manager then General Manager. Within three years, I was earning a level of money I wouldn't have dared dream of. At this point, I dared to start up my own insurance business linked to Cornhill Insurance and was once more fortunate enough to achieve success. We employed over a thousand people, opened many offices, and became their biggest producer.

Despite this, I was not really fond of insurance, but I had. discovered that there was a lot of personal development training going on within the industry. I was in a position where I had to train, motivate and manage people on a daily basis and soon fell in love with the entire personal growth movement.

I began studying psychology, attending every lecture and seminar I could find on personal development and reading everything I could get my hands on. I studied in earnest, and trained at varying degrees in a number of areas, including psychology, NLP, Gestalt, transactional analysis, occupational therapy, cognitive behaviour, EFT, and Delfin.

In 1993, I sold my insurance company to Cornhill Insurance.

It was time for me to dedicate myself to personal growth.

But all was not well. At this same time I separated from and eventually became divorced from my wife. It was a very unhappy time personally, despite my professional success. I threw myself into my work.

During this same year, I set up a new business, Noble Manhattan Personal Development, specialising in courses and programs on attitude, personal development, self esteem, goal planning and setting, speed reading, mind mapping, and many other relevant topics.

In 1995, I discovered coaching and immediately fell in love with its principles. Everything about the coaching profession was so congruent with my core values. I truly felt as if I had come home.

3

My mind began to work quickly as to how coaching would fit into my current initiatives. In my mind, I pictured the spokes of a bicycle wheel, with each spoke representing Psychology, NLP, occupational therapy, and so forth. Coaching was the hub in the middle, pulling it all together.

At that time there were no coach training programs available in the United Kingdom, so I trained with several American organisations. I then began delivering coaching to individual clients late in 1996. It really was a pioneering movement in those days. Clients had no idea what coaching was, and I found myself having to educate them before I could even dream of asking them for money for my services.

Shortly after this I reconciled with my wife, to my great joy, and we were remarried at the end of 1997. Two years later, I began training coaches through Noble- Manhattan and I am proud to say we have now trained well over 7,000 coaches worldwide since that time. Today, we have students and coaches in 26 countries and growing!

Coaching: Ground Zero For Tomorrow's Leaders

Many individuals who discuss coaching – life, business, executive or other forms -- dismiss it as a passing fad. Nothing could be farther from the truth. Coaching is a billion-dollar industry. Thousands of people, from CEOs of large corporations to women dedicated to caring for their families, have discovered that the strategies and techniques taught and the lessons learned through coaching can be the "magic pill" to effectively unravel years of bad habits that impede one's success. Coaching, when performed by a highly qualified individual, can actually re-teach the concepts, beliefs and principles which form the foundation of personal and professional success and achievement.

Can you read a self-help book and pick up nuggets of wisdom to help you reach your goals? Yes. Can you speak to your peers, or form a support group, to help you get where you want to go? Absolutely. But none of these options compare to the customised experience of working with a trained coach. If it is your aim to firmly plant your feet on a solid journey of self-discovery, self-fulfillment and supreme accomplishment, a coach is the conduit to letting go of your past, enjoying your present, and marveling at your future.

In *A Coach's Story*, you'll hear from qualified coaches at every level, practicing every form of coaching, from far and wide across the globe. As you read and gain a clearer understanding of what coaching is all about, our hope is that you'll also realise that coaching is not a fad. Coaching has been used by thousands to find true happiness in work and life. It's worked for these coaches and their clients and it can work for you too.

As I write these words, it is the start of a new year and another new beginning. It seems the world has changed somehow in the brief transition from one year to the next. People are clamouring for things that are "real"; we're missing the connections, the authenticity that has been reduced by technology and an increasingly smaller global environment. Many of us long to return to the simple life, or at least enjoy some of its elements as a counterweight to our hectic lifestyles. The sad economy and other world events are prompting us to re-evaluate our priorities. We're growing in our understanding of what is important. Coaching fits perfectly into this renewed understanding. Coaching can light the way to reconnect with the people, places and things that have meaning, while making it easier to discard the rest.

In my report, *How Coaching Can Improve Your Life*, I talk about how coaching can help each of us reconnect in a meaningful way. "Coaching is… a way to direct, instruct and train individuals with the goal of achieving or developing specific skills that help the person enjoy greater success, less stress, better organization… Many types of coaching exist, and many methods are available, depending on the type of coaching you choose and the way you wish to receive the information. Busy professionals and everyday people use proven coaching methods to reach life-changing goals and enjoy a fuller, more satisfying existence."

Who can say no to the promise of an existence that is fuller, more satisfying, more meaningful?

My Personal Coaching Vision

I know from many years of experience that one great coach can positively and dramatically impact the lives of thousands of people over the lifetime of his or her coaching career. A highly trained coach can empower clients to achieve mighty things.

So, occasionally, I fantasize a bit about the future of coaching and my role in helping others to enjoy a happier life. It goes something like this:

If I can train more than 10,000 magnificent coaches worldwide and they in turn go forth to massively empower millions of other people – perhaps tens of millions – we could literally create a paradigm shift in the world.

I call it a fantasy but, in truth, it could easily be reality. In the past ten years, my organisation has trained over 7,000 coaches. And we didn't have help from the digital world then. It is entirely possible that we can reach our goal of 10,000 magnificently trained coaches within the next five years.

How fantastic that would be, to help so many people become reacquainted with their true core values!

And that brings me to the next reason for writing *A Coach's Story*.

Einstein Said It Best

*"Not all things that are counted count,
and not all things that count get counted."*

ALBERT EINSTEIN

We've discussed at length the idea of connecting with your own coach. Now, I'd like to turn your attention to becoming a coach.

When we are born, we have no real sense of self. It is not until about age two that we begin to realise that we exist as an individual in the world. This is when the self-discovery journey begins, but for many years we remain selfish in our outlook and dependent on others to do things for us. As we begin to mature we notice there are other people in the world. Soon we discover how different we all are. Some of us are financially needy, others are plagued by ill health, still others seem to have it all. Most of us, as we grow closer to young adulthood, find we have a naturally altruistic side. When we see someone in need, we automatically want to help. This isn't the case for everyone, but for many of us it is.

When I speak publicly I am often introduced and praised with such words as "vibrant", "remarkable" and "inspirational". I'll tell you honestly, it doesn't feel bad. However, I have overcome many challenges on my way to where I stand now. And yet one thing always remains constant: my interest in helping others achieve success.

I have been aware for some time that what I know can help others be happier, more profitable, more grounded. I know this because this knowledge has had that effect on my own life.

So let me ask you: have you ever envisioned what your best life might look like? Did you know you already have within you the skills, qualities and talents to get there? We all do. But life has a funny way of interfering while we're making other plans and most of us become so sidetracked we can't remember where we began, let alone figure out how to get back on track.

I am here to tell you that coach training can help you destroy the roadblocks to your own happiness. Through coach training, you can gain a wealth of knowledge about yourself and, if that's not enough, coach training comes with a special bonus: while learning how to harness your own power, you can use what you've learned to positively affect the lives of everyone else with whom you come in contact. You can truly make a huge difference for yourself and those around you. What better job, award, accolade, or achievement is there?

I'd like you to take a moment to think about that. Then I'd like you to read an excerpt from a book I co-authored with Dr John Lutwitch Clements called *Great Intentions*:

"Few of us will win the lottery in our lifetimes, but visualizing a lottery win is a great exercise in determining whether your life has purpose. Simply ask yourself: If I won the lottery, would I continue my life as it is, or would my life change completely? If nothing would change, you are already living your life with purpose. Your soul is satisfied in a way that goes beyond lottery winnings. But if your first thought surrounds retiring to some remote Tahitian island, you may be suffering from the type of stress overload commonly called burnout, signalling it is time for a change that has nothing to do with money... a spiritual overhaul, so to speak. People who feel connected to a spiritual purpose live more satisfying, more rewarding lives. This type of spirituality is not related to church attendance, but to inner peace that can only come from tapping into your own vital wellspring of internal energy. After all, despite the average person's focus on getting paid to complete certain tasks, payment has nothing to do with one's satisfaction. Finding out what you love to do, then doing it, goes far beyond any payment you might receive. When one is able to follow his or her passion, one is truly living an intentional life."

This is what coaching can do for you, whether you are on the receiving or the giving end.

Don't believe me? The stories in this book, taken from the life experiences of nineteen individual coach-authors, bear testimony to the life-changing nature of coaching. What model car you drive, where you live, your occupation or how much money you have in the bank has nothing to do with it.

Now you know my story. I would delight in hearing yours. I'd like to ask you for a favour. I'd like you to read this book all the way through to the end and think deeply on the experiences described in it. Put yourself in the place of each of these coaches, all of whom have faced overwhelming struggles to become the leaders they are today.

Then ask yourself:

"If I created a wish list for my life, what are the top five things I would want to change?"

Write them down, in as much detail as you like, and send your list to me at my personal email address: md@noble-manhattan.com. If you will promise me you'll do this, I promise to answer you confidentially and explain, in vivid detail, how coaching can bring about positive change for each and every item on your list.

Throughout my career I have enjoyed the extraordinary privilege of being viewed as a visionary in this great movement we call coaching. But you know what? I still get a thrill, a positive charge, with every goal I achieve, and with every coach who goes forth to help others after training with my company. It never gets old!

Now I want you to feel that same thrill, the kick of delight and satisfaction that comes when you mesh your beliefs and desires with your life's true purpose.

Let's get started.

Julie Kennedy

Coaching On The Move

The Butterfly Effect: Building A Coaching Practice From Scratch

WHERE SHALL I BEGIN? If it were not for possible preconceptions, I would probably refer to myself as a Euro-gypsy. I am British, brought up in France and married to a Dutchman whom I met in Spain. I have never lived anywhere more than seven years: Great Britain, France, Holland, and Austria before our marriage; then my husband's diplomatic career took us to Africa for ten years: Cameroon, Uganda and Senegal. Two years ago we landed in Berlin, where we will stay for the next two years. Feeling dizzy? Yes, I sometimes feel it too, though less so since I discovered coaching.

The great side of this lifestyle is the opportunities to visit fabulous places, discover new cultures and people, and feel you are really taking huge bites out of life. I enjoy moving from one exciting location to the next. To be honest, I don't know anything else. I enjoy the discovery, the exhilaration, the feeling one is different and making the most out of life, quite a *leitmotiv* (recurring theme) for me. I settle very rapidly: a whirlwind of activity the first three months till it feels like home for us and our three children. Along the way I have been lucky to master English, French, German, Dutch and Spanish. I was always able to find suitable work wherever we went, in such varied positions as management consultant, development project manager, actress, fashion model, head of sales and PR and, my claim to fame, as President of the Dakar Women's Group. This dynamic organisation, regrouping more than 250 women from all over the world, was a lifeline to many. Together, we got to know each other, the country and its inhabitants better, embarked on self-development and reached out to less fortunate Senegalese women and children.

Fun as it was to be constantly experimenting with new jobs, there was a downside - what I call the "butterfly effect". I was doing a little of everything, hovering a while here and there, yet building nothing, starting from scratch each time. This began to bother me more and more. My restlessness came to a head two years ago upon returning to Europe. I suppose it was a bit of a midlife crisis. I had just turned forty and gone from being an African Queen to a German Cinderella. Goodbye glamorous public speaker with a large backup of household help. Hello Miss Overwhelmed, never having cooked or run a household of five in Europe. The idea of recreating myself yet again and resuming my self- imposed, frantic pace of working, studying, and saying yes to anything on offer suddenly felt pointless. I was running yet never arriving. I assumed I would charge straight back into a serious fulltime job, yet I battled with family values and the not wanting to hand my children over to an au-pair.

To be honest, I didn't know what I wanted anymore.

Coaching: A Brave, New World

In the meantime the synergies of life set in. Whilst talking to the school counsellor about one of my children, I had a wobbly moment and dissolved into tears. She kindly mentioned the idea of being coached, a term I had never heard outside the sports arena. I came home and Googled the term – and beheld a whole new, glittering world which seemed designed for me. A profession I could fully relate to which spoke to the go-getter, no nonsense me as well as the caring, emphatic listener me. I then remembered Wendy, one of my group members in Senegal, commenting that I would be a great coach.

I found a wonderful coach in Germany who helped me untangle many personal issues I hadn't even realised were holding me back and colouring my vision. What a relief after a lifetime of being the cheerleader - Miss Energy and Positivity; what a relief to admit there were things worrying me and to actually have someone listen and question those issues.

Almost immediately, whilst working with Alexandra, I started looking for possible long distance coaching studies. I had an intuition as soon as I discovered the coaching world that this was what I had been looking for. I am naturally blessed with a very dynamic and motivational personality and had for years been looking for the right outlet for all this power. I loved the results side of management consultancy yet missed the human aspect; I loved the development work but felt we were only scratching the surface and failing to make sustainable change. I loved my Presidency of the Dakar Women's Group and my role as motivator, helping women make the most of their posting, yet I missed the financial recognition. Coaching seemed to incorporate all of these, enabling me to make a positive difference in the lives of those around me.

I was at first overwhelmed by the choice of courses offered and, naturally, I wanted the best. By asking around I found Gerard O'Donovan and Noble Manhattan Coaching where all the criteria I needed were fulfilled.

How wonderful life can be: my coach helped me move forward, largely by getting me to examine a series of limiting beliefs I had been carrying around for a while, and helped me fully define who I really am. But most importantly for me, my life purpose was revealed: to coach.

So here I am with a profession I can take with me as we move every four to five years. Through my languages I can reach out to a large audience; in particular, fellow expatriates who do not always enjoy their postings. I can continue learning and sharpening my skills instead of hopping around like a grasshopper with a sugar rush. Very importantly I do not have to choose between professional life and family life. I now have a flexible and rewarding profession which allows me to equally fulfil the family needs and the other dimensions of my life which are important to me, such as sports, cultural outings and taking time for those around me. I have discovered balance.

Coaching: The Vehicle That Moves Lives Forward

I particularly appreciated the structural depth of the Noble Manhattan course and the support offered by the organisation. The modules and tele-classes provided all the learning material and were reinforced by individual mentoring sessions. The essays helped me focus my reading and concentrate on one topic at a time. It was ideal to be able to do this long distance and at my own tempo. However, once we had submitted some written work and completed a certain number of modules, as part of the course students were invited to Oxford for a three day, residential seminar.

This was a fantastic opportunity to meet live, professional coaches as well as fellow student coaches. We worked hard during the day, soaking up all the words of wisdom with enthusiasm and motivation and experiencing many "aha" moments. There was also plenty of time for valuable socialising. Five of us went on to create a buddy group which provided a lot of support and encouragement during the studies, some of whom I am still in contact with now. The residential also gave me the courage to start off with the required pro-bono sessions (where we practise our newly acquired skills in real life scenarios, but free of charge), as I was somewhat frozen before the first leap.

Some parts of the course I found effortless, as if all that information was already deep in me. I realised I had been unofficially coaching for years. Other aspects were more of a challenge; in particular not leading or suggesting. I battled for months with a natural urge to jump in with suggestions in a passionate desire to help my clients. It really took a while for the notion to sink in that each case, each person, is different and, however close another situation I knew of appeared, it was still not the same. This helped me see that by challenging and questioning in an open way instead of serving up pre-conceived solutions, I was serving my client much more effectively: enabling him to take ownership and re-apply what he had learnt about himself to other issues.

My fellow buddies and I went through many personal ups and downs during training, which is to be expected since you cannot help but start with yourself. In some cases we opened cans of worms we had shelved years ago. Yet how can you coach if your own cupboard is full of skeletons? You must be free of your own clutter in order to listen to your client with one hundred percent focus. There were moments when I felt knocked off my balance – not something I was used to – but it was definitely worth it. I emerged much stronger. Perhaps a bit less showgirl, but with a deep, rooted feeling of who I am, what are my values, and what is my mission in life. I felt myself come together. Rather than behaving like a faulty firework exploding in short bursts in all directions, I now had a worthwhile channel for my energy, unleashing a focused, more powerful fire.

All of this self-realisation and actualisation impacted those close to me. Today I am more grounded, a better mother who listens and encourages rather than orders (well most of the time), more generous and supportive as a wife (say I) rather than bitter and aggressive, perceiving household chores as a burden rather than an expression of what they really are - my desire to make our home a place of harmony.

My husband and I also discussed our values. This was a very valuable exercise in itself since we had never really defined the values we shared. Thankfully, after fourteen years of marriage, we discovered we do share a few. This helped us adopt a problem resolution strategy fraught with far less conflict. One of the most profound effects, however, was on the family. The five of us wrote a mission statement outlining who we are as a family unit, what brings us together, what we want to be remembered for, and what we want to do more and less of. The children, aged from seven to twelve years, had as much input as we did and I was really impressed by their ideas. We now also have a logo, weekly family meetings where everyone is free to discuss any issues, and family outings we all decide on together. We speak more about how things make us feel and how we would rather have it instead of just yelling out. Of course, it does still happen every now and then, but we are a much more cohesive group. I am grateful for this opportunity to teach the children already, at a young age, that there is always a choice in our behaviour and a possibility of change. The family unit is all we take with us each time we move and it is particularly reassuring for the children that it is a safe and loving one. I have always been an emphatic, yet challenging, friend but now I have the tools to be even more stimulating.

During the summer of 2009, I graduated from the Noble Manhattan life coach programme with a practitioner degree (with Distinctions I immodestly add) and fueled by a profound desire to help others make a positive difference in their lives. Happily, I set off on my career as a coach.

I cannot over-emphasise the profound, life changing effect of coaching. It is so simple, yet so powerful, that people hesitate to believe it. After seeing people who have been in therapy for years still battling with non-traumatic, paralysing past issues, coaching is like a breath of fresh air. Once these individuals decided to stop looking back, moaning and blaming and decide what they want now while setting themselves clear, measurable goals, coaching moves them forward faster than they would ever have imagined possible.

For some, simply raising awareness of their own life responsibility was enough to get them unstuck. We cannot change the events which happen to us, but we always have a choice in how to interpret them. For some, a negative event will become a huge shackle around their ankle; others will choose to learn from the event, then minimise it and move forward with trust and confidence. To learn from these events and emerge a stronger person, we must take time to examine who we really are deep down inside, to accept ourselves and discover our life purpose.

I have witnessed firsthand the impact coaching can have on so many levels: Feelings of being overwhelmed, time management issues, relationship issues, sports and weight issues, career dilemmas, life-work balance, feeling purposeful... I have had wonderful long term coaching relationships where we have gone to the core and seen the effects snowball on all areas of the client's life. I've also experienced gratifying short term relationships where an issue has been successfully resolved.

One of my favourite success stories is that of a client who found herself having to make a presentation in order to receive funding for her business start-up. She was terrified, felt totally incapable. After two coaching sessions where we focused on her motivation and the dream behind the business, she went ahead, firmly grounded in her vision, and won the first prize and the funding package she needed. Best of all, she feels fundamentally more sure of herself, which is creating an impact in other areas of her life!

A life principle I use frequently, which particularly appeals to me, is that of learning from the past (using failure as feedback and not as an obstacle), planning for the future (being goal oriented), yet living in the present (taking time to enjoy our lives and the people around us).

Despite everything I have revealed up to this point, I'm still fell like a rookie. There is much more work to be done but the feedback so far has been encouraging. My clients tell me my coaching has provided them with much needed focus. Investing time and attention in their issues offers a safe, yet challenging space to think things through. The client is suddenly aware of having the power and responsibility to change. All he or she needs is support as the boundaries of one's comfort zone are moved further out. Several clients have thanked me for helping them to define what it is that they want, to determine if this is in line with their core values and then to be very specific about what needs to be done to achieve that milestone. Coaching has helped to transform the client's dream into a goal and monitor the client's success. Many clients believe the greatest miracle about coaching is the change to individual self esteem, and they often comment on how empowering it was that I, as the coach, believed in them before they actually did.

For now, I have chosen to focus on Motivational Coaching; a form of coaching that seeks the "why" behind the "what" and harnesses that discovery to motivate clients to achieve their dreams with no obstacles hampering the outcome. Alongside motivational coaching, my specific expertise is, of course, Expatriate Coaching. By expatriate, I mean highly mobile clients who need help getting their life back on track after a geographical move. For some, it involves actually defining their lives and how their life purpose can move with them. It is often said that moving is as emotionally traumatic as bereavement, with the physical change, need to adapt to a new environment, sometimes a radically different culture and language. Everything needs to be resettled, from an actual place to live, with all the necessary utilities to set up, to finding new medical care, new shops, a new gym or just simply finding your way around. All of this can be incredibly overwhelming. One can feel very alone and alienated. Often added to this is a feeling of responsibility towards children, helping them adapt to a new school, fit in and adjust. Once the material side of settling in, unpacking, and developing new routines is set, the accompanying spouse (if there is one) often goes through much soul searching to uncover what this new location holds for them. A coach can provide a lot of support, encouragement and clarity in reviewing the new life, gaining closure on the old and enjoying the new posting.

I believe I could coach on any non- traumatic issue (though as coach it is crucial to recognise when the client is outside of the "normally functioning" category and needs appropriate specialist help), as long as the client is committed to doing what it takes to bring about the change. However, the world and the market are big, and I trust the experts when they say you must create a niche.

My coaching journey has just begun. I am sure there will be many more niches to discover along the way. Whomever I coach and whatever topic we discuss, I never cease to be amazed by the huge energy burst it gives me. When the session is over, I am often found to be performing a wild dance in the living room, fuelled by pure exhilaration at having been privileged to accompany a soul towards being a happier, more fulfilled person.

Julie Kennedy

The Never Ending Journey

I, for one, am thrilled, grateful and privileged to be part of this positive, society- enhancing profession. I believe coaching arose to fulfill a cultural need. In most of the Western world, our basic needs are fulfilled. We have no survival purpose. We live in a materialistic society, yet are discovering that material goods alone do not bring fulfillment. The world is suddenly much bigger given the global market. People move around more, weakening the concept of community and traditional family structure. Technological tools, such as the internet, force us to live in a faster world with more stress and an overwhelming amount of possibilities. Our society, especially now in times of financial crisis, is waking up to the fact that we need more than a job and money to be happy. We can run all day long yet at the end still feel unsatisfied. Coaching fills the gap for people who have suffered no serious trauma requiring therapy, yet feel unsatisfied and unable to manage moving forward in life. Coaching responds to a profound need for people to be listened to, to be stretched and shown other ways of viewing situations; of being made aware of who they are and how they fit in to the whole; of being made responsible for taking their own lives in hand and finding inner happiness and balance to be able to reach out to others.

Some say, "But can't people do that on their own?" Yes they probably could, but very often don't, whether from lack space for reflection, time or other reasons. Sometimes, all we need is a little safe haven to explore, together with a professional armed with skills, qualities and a positive mindset, in order to realign ourselves before moving with focus and motivation along our path again.

Through my coaching practice, Kennedy Personal Coaching, I aim to help my individual clients become their personal best by empowering them, inspiring those around them and playing my small part in bringing attention to the importance of coaching to society as a whole. Technology is then a positive factor, as my website can move with me and, thanks to systems such as Skype, a free telephone service via the internet, I can reach out to my clients anywhere in the world.

My path has just unrolled, offering a horizon of future courses to be enjoyed, books to be read and positive differences made in my clients' lives. Coaching synergises for me my results-oriented management consultancy background, multi-cultural understanding and language abilities with a natural positivity and boundless energy, sincere empathy, yet challenging touch, and a profound desire to help.

What better way to live one's life than to work in a profession that not only earns money but also provides me with a meaningful and exciting purpose, helps others, and keeps my life on track?

I feel as though my whole life has pointed me in this direction. All the various jobs I have held, studies I have done, extra activities I have taken on, people I have met... all these things have now come together like many jigsaw pieces, clicking together in one satisfying clunk. No need to keep recreating the wheel at each new assignment; I can take my career with me wherever I go, and be available to help people when they need it most.

Seize the day, hop on board and set off on *your* life coaching journey!

Julie Kennedy

Mike Armour

The Art Of Life And Business Coaching: From Training To Business Start-up

The Journey Begins

DURING A RECENT COACHING SESSION, I had the opportunity to sit for a few minutes and reflect on my life's journey while gazing at the golden sand of Dee Why beach near my home in Sydney, Australia.

The beach stretches in a long curve, from the coffee-filled aromas of numerous cafés at one end to the Long Reef promontory at the other. The rock formation looks like a lion jutting into the sea, exuding an impervious disregard for the Pacific Ocean that daily wears away at the base of the cliff.

The long curve of the beach reminds me of my own journey to become a life and business coach. In late 2008, as the first wave of the Global Financial Crisis (GFC) hit Australia, my role as a project consultant for a large Australian corporate came to an abrupt end. The job market had dried up and I was left wondering what to do next. The defining moment arrived while sipping a glass of bubbles on New Year's Eve, when my daughter pointedly asked, "What do you *want* to do, Dad?"

I had become frustrated with the job search and was not sure which career direction to take.

As it turned out, that was an amazingly powerful question, and one that is not easy to ignore. While I could not immediately answer this question, for the first time in many years I gave myself permission to ponder what I really wanted to do.

As I write this chapter of *A Coach's Story*, I am close to completing my course and gaining a Certificate IV in Coaching for Life and Business, and I have set up my own coaching business. This is my story – only one story – about becoming a Life and Business Coach.

There are many skills to learn when starting out in the business of coaching. From the initial training program to gaining new clients, it takes time for the skills learned in training to become natural and for coaching to become an art. This is something I am still learning. Developing a strong coaching framework, enjoying support and feedback from peers and mentors and developing a business and marketing plan are all part of the challenge.

If you learn anything from my story, I hope you'll take away that coaching isn't a mechanical process; it involves developing a set of skills, continual practice and learning along with the gradual recognition that creating a successful coaching business is like creating an artwork – it takes time and patience.

Why coaching? Well, what other job allows you to work with people to help them achieve what they want in life and ends up as exciting and empowering to your own life at the same time? The notion of making a contribution has been part of my way of doing things for many years and, as I have been discovering, this has also become part of my purpose and mission as a coach.

Training As A Life And Business Coach In Australia

Coaching is a growth industry in Australia. There are many coach training programs available which lead to recognised qualifications.

Most training programs focus on Life and/or Business coaching. I chose to complete the Certificate IV in Coaching for Life and Business, which would provide me with the skills and experience to work in any area I chose. The coaching industry in Australia is currently unregulated; gaining a formal qualification, however, offers the opportunity to undertake further training and ensures that I have recognised skills once the regulation of the industry does occur.

Coming Home...To Coach Training

One of the biggest learning points during my training as a Life and Business Coach was confirmation of my purpose, which is to experience empowerment in all areas of my life. My mission to achieve this is to be a positive force for change, contributing to my own growth and that of others. Training for me was like coming home. I put everything I had into the program and have loved every minute of the journey since then.

Since completing the training, I have set up my own coaching business and currently have fourteen clients who are taking massive action in many areas of their lives from business to health, relationships and career.

I believe coaching is the art of facilitating the unleashing of a person's potential to reach meaningful, measurable goals. Most of my early coaching sessions involved life coaching, which addresses all areas of a client's life, including relationships, career/business, spiritual, financial, emotional and health matters. In the early stages, building rapport with your clients is a key to empowering the change process. Like many success coaches, I use the "Wheel of Life" or Success Map in the initial coaching session to help build rapport and identify specific areas each client wants to address. The focus is on both current and future goals, including developing a compelling vision for the future. Most importantly, this "map" becomes a very powerful way to measure a client's success and propel the client into further action.

No matter the starting point in a coaching session, the discussion often moves to other areas of life or business. As a coach, I need to be ready for anything. Knowing the right question to ask, having a range of tools and models to use, and an understanding of communication styles are essential skills in the coach's tool kit.

One of the great coaching methods I use is called the DRIP method. DRIP is a mnemonic for the following:

D = Delve or Disturb
R = Relax and Relieve
I = Inspire and Integrate
P =Purpose and Plan

The basis of the DRIP method highlights the fact that coaches must sometimes be tough with a client to break through barriers or limiting beliefs – that's the delve and disturb part. There is also a need to help the client move forward to become inspired, determine what goals they want to achieve and what action they are going to take to achieve those goals. That's where the rest of the method comes in. Once you are able to break through with your client, the process becomes one of supporting, encouraging and empowering them to take action towards living on purpose.

The Impact Of Coaching On My Life

One of the major impacts coach training has had on my life is a renewed sense of direction and desire to achieve several large goals. Completing my masters degree, developing photography skills and, even one day, taking a trip into space are among my major goals. And while I don't know *how* I will achieve some of these, I have plenty of new horizons to focus on in the meantime. That has also been true for my clients. They have identified some amazing goals and some little dreams that have been hidden away, and we work together to develop an action plan to turn those dreams into reality. As the sessions progress and the client begins to take more responsibility the focus turns towards empowerment, with the client taking responsibility for achieving their goals and dreams. Each time I have a session with one of these amazing people, I come away more inspired and determined to achieve my own goals. This is the best thing about coaching.

Building A Coaching Business: Getting Started

Starting any small business involves working lots of hours building your business, developing publicity, marketing, networking, gaining new clients and, most importantly, running coaching session with your clients. While I have worked hard, I can honestly say I have enjoyed every moment and have learnt a great deal along the way. The company I trained with runs a monthly Success Club meeting to help their clients stay in the right kind of environment with like-minded people. Each month we focus on one element: perhaps education, health, relationships or other aspects of the Life and Business coaching model. We talk about what we are achieving. Even if I think I know everything about a topic, there is always more to learn. Without this support I might not have had the confidence to keep going when things got tough.

Developing A Niche

A niche is simply the specific market for your product or service. I chose the Life and Career Coaching niche and would undertake Business Coaching as the need or opportunity arose. Life Coaching covers all aspects of the individual, where Career Coaching addresses career goals and aspirations, individual skills and what one must do to ensure career progression. In each case, I strive to help people focus three, five and ten years into the future, to make their dreams compelling, to create words, images, feelings that inspire action. Then my job becomes supporting, challenging and, most importantly, cheering from the sideline.

Sports Coaching is a great example of this idea. The coach does all the lead up work to help the individual or team set their goals and undertake the training (take the actions) they need to succeed. When the game starts however, the coach is always on the sidelines cheering.

Contacting Potential Clients

Here is the exciting part of starting a coaching business. You have done your training; you're feeling confident, ready for anything and eager to get going. So how do you contact potential clients and gain new customers?

What is needed is this:

1. Have a clear intent. Ever since the start of 2009, my intent has been to become the best coach I can be. I wanted this goal more than any other I could think of and I have done everything I could to make this goal a reality, including giving up free time to achieve it.
2. Build a contact list. Even before I finished my training course in March, I had made a list of names, contact numbers, email addresses for as many people as I could think of.
3. Have a big goal, like one hundred people: talk to everyone you know and offer them an introductory coaching session for free. This is where I started to feel more confident in my skills and it became an easy step to move people from a contact to a paying client.
4. Network with as many people as possible and take advantage of every opportunity to gain a potential client.

To illustrate this point, I had to visit my local bank recently to deposit a cheque and get some change. As the Customer Service Officer (CSO) handled my transaction, the following discussion took place:

CSO   "What does Optima Coaching do?

MA   "We work with people to help them focus on their goals and dreams and take action towards making them happen."

CSO   "I think I could do with some coaching, but then I probably couldn't afford your fees."

MA   "Perhaps you can't afford *not* to have me as your coach. What would it be worth to have someone help you achieve all your goals and dreams?"

I use this story for two reasons. First, it illustrates that there are opportunities to gain coaching clients from all sorts of places. Secondly, you must be ready with the right response to create an opportunity for a future coaching session. Make sure you get the other person's business card and can call to offer them a free coaching session – you will be delighted at how easy it is to move someone from a prospect to a customer when they realise how you can help them achieve success in every area of their life.

Developing Your Business

As a new coach, there are lots of other practical things to consider, such as:

- Developing a business and marketing plan.
- Start up costs – what will you need to spend to get started? Computer, printer, internet and email access, publicity material including business cards, brochures.
- Cash flow – how much money you will have each month after costs and expenses? Put aside enough money to cover your tax obligations and, if you are registered for Goods and Services Tax or Sales Tax (GST in Australia), make sure you have enough money put aside for this as well.

Ongoing marketing is also needed to build your client base. Whether by using business cards, brochures, a website or simply handing out flyers at the local train station, (which I did), you need a balance between running coaching sessions and signing up new coaching clients. Every good marketing plan has this balance of supporting current customers and gaining new customers.

There are other tools well worth including in your business and marketing planning such as a SWOT Analysis (Strengths & Weaknesses cover internal factors while Opportunities, Threats identify external factors). Have a look at *www.businessballs.com* under SWOT analysis and consider doing a PEST Analysis, which looks at Political, Economic, Social and Technological aspects of your new business.

Developing Your Coaching Skills – The Art Of Asking The Right Questions

Becoming a successful coach is more than simply developing a set knowledge, skills and methods. Building rapport with your clients is a crucial part of the coaching relationship and understanding your client's communication style is a big part of that process.

Past training in NLP has helped me understand the auditory, visual, and kinaesthetic communication styles and, as a Myers Briggs practitioner, I have come to recognise natural differences in each person as both strengths to be enhanced and challenges to be overcome.

These are all wonderful additions to a coach's overall training. But the art of coaching really involves asking the right questions. This is a huge part of building rapport and getting to know your clients' strengths and weaknesses. As a new coach I found it easy to fall into the trap of giving too much information or proposing my own ideas to the client. Such approaches are better used in training or mentoring. Asking questions, rather than providing the answers, helps the client focus on their own goals and actions.

The real art in coaching comes from asking the right question at the right time to help the client move forward. My experience suggests that asking questions which begin with "what, how and when" are more likely to achieve great outcomes for your clients than "why", an approach which tends to produce more subjective responses.

Coaching questions fall into three main categories:

1. Gathering information
2. Challenging limiting beliefs
3. Empowering change

I asked a number of my colleagues about the art of asking the right questions and received some very interesting feedback.

My colleague Alex Bilbao commented that it depends on the communication style of the individual – are they more visual, auditory or kinaesthetic? Questions, Alex suggests, must focus on the particular style of the individual. My daughter Katie, on the other hand, tends to take the direct approach, cutting through the objections to ask very direct questions such as, "What do you want to do?" or "What do you think you will achieve if you don't take any action?" Another of my coaching buddies, Brent Rowley, tends to be extremely disarming in his questioning style. People end up telling him things they are surprised about later.

Personal style is important and, as a coach, you must develop and be true to your own approach while also communicating in a way that is most effective for your client.

Questions That Gather Information

Closed questions can be used to gather information such as, "Where do you work?", or "How many children do you have?" This type of closed-end questioning is an important part of the early coaching relationship and does tend to break through some of the initial hesitation.

However, the focus of coaching questions to gather information is to help the client take action. For this, open-ended questions are more effective. Some examples of open-ended questions are:

- When do you want to complete that action by?
- What will you do differently in the future?
- What would be the result if you took this action?
- How will your life be different when you achieve this goal?
- What will you do to celebrate when you achieve this goal?

In each case, the question is designed to help the client take responsibility for their choices and actions, rather than the answers coming from the coach. In a recent coaching session with one of my clients, the key goal of the session was to improve health through exercise and changes to diet. During this session, it became apparent that the client generally lived up to promises made to others, but often did not live up to promises to herself. The breakthrough question at this point was, "What happens when you don't follow through on promises to yourself?" The response was both a physical slumping of shoulders and a realisation that keeping a promise to yourself is as important as keeping a promise to another person.

Challenging Limiting Beliefs

Limiting beliefs are messages encoded into our thinking from past experience. These beliefs can affect our creativity and ability to take action towards achieving our goals and dreams. As a coach, one of the main activities I work on with my clients is helping them turn those negative beliefs into empowering statements and actions.

The table below identifies some common limiting beliefs, questions you could use to challenge some of these areas, and the empowering statements that would help bring about change.

Limiting Belief	Questions to challenge limiting beliefs and empowering language
I don't know how…	What would you do if you did know?
	How could you get started?
	I have all the resources I need to get started!
I can't do it…	What can you do? If you could do this, what would you do?
	I can do/achieve anything I want!
I don't have enough time…	What do you need to change so that you have the time you need?
	I have all the time I need to achieve the goals that are important to me!
I don't have enough money…	How much money do you need? What would you do right now if you had some of the money you need?
	I have the ability to earn/save the money I need to achieve my goals!

A recent session with one of my clients demonstrated this in a very powerful way.

My client was talking about a new business opportunity. With many other changes in her life, the client commented that she did not know where to start getting the answers or where to find the right information to get this new business going. An easy approach for me as the coach would have been to provide the information required (that's what the trainer or mentor in me would do). However, a more empowering approach when I am fully in my role as a coach is to help the client focus on the knowledge and resources they already have available to address this challenge.

I asked the client to describe how she undertook a home improvement project, which involved building a brick and concrete fence. As I listened, she described a process that involved thinking through what needed to be done, examining the options and testing an approach, then taking action – a simple, problem solving approach.

Once I recognised this process, I asked, "What would happen if you used that same process to develop your business opportunity?"

At first, the client couldn't grasp what I meant – she had not taken note of how she dealt with practical challenges. When I restated the question so that it connected the two ideas, the change in facial expression was like a light-bulb coming on. This question was framed as follows: "If you were able to apply the same approach to developing your business opportunity (the intangible project) as you have taken to building your fence (the practical project) how would you go about developing your business opportunity?" This turned out to be a breakthrough question for my client and caused a significant transformation. From an initial "I don't know where to start", the client turned this around to "I can do anything I want!" Needless to say, it was a very empowering session for both of us.

As I continue to develop as a coach, the ability to ask powerful questions is a process of continual learning. Questions challenge, confront, and help a client think about things in a new way. Williams and Davis in their book, *Therapist as Life Coach: An Introduction for Counselors and Other Helping Professionals,* devote significant attention to the skill of asking empowering questions.

Questions To Empower Change

A quote that has become a favourite of mine since undertaking the training course is:

*"Our deepest fear is not that we are inadequate.
Our deepest fear is that we are powerful beyond measure."*

By far the most challenging/rewarding aspect of being a coach is empowering clients to take action towards their goals. Asking questions which challenge, not being afraid to delve or disturb and being willing to rattle the foundations to help your client move forward are the most profound actions you can take to help break down the barriers and allow change to take place.

Questions such as:

- What *do* you want?
- What do you *want* to be/do?
- What would your life be like in ten years time if you were to achieve all your goals and dreams?

These look like simple questions, but when used to challenge your client they provoke a reaction and bring about change.

Developing Your Skills: A Process Of Continual Learning

As a coach, I need to stay fresh so that I can continue to be a powerful force for change in my own life and in the lives of my clients. Training for me was just one step along a lifelong journey to become the best coach I can be.

The coaching relationship is unique in that the coach works with the client, helping them take action towards achieving their dreams and goals. Coaching works from the premise that the client has all the necessary information within to determine the best course of action.

The coach is not a counsellor, dealing with problems or issues from the past, nor a mentor or trainer with expert knowledge to share or pass on to the client.

Coaching is the art of facilitating the unleashing of people's potential to reach meaningful, measurable goals. Coaching is oriented toward concrete impact and results; it is about helping the client, individual or team to articulate and achieve their dreams and goals. The focus is on both current and future goals, including developing a compelling vision for the future.

Becoming a Life and Business Coach is a journey towards self-discovery and personal fulfillment. My biggest challenge has been to trust myself that *I am* an empowering coach; the most important lesson, to listen to my clients so that I can guide and empower them through strongly focused questions and unquestionable support. In the words of Whitworth et al, I simply need to be ready to "dance the moment."

Kathleen O'Grady

The Administrative Duckling

I HAVE OFTEN FELT LIKE A FLY ON THE WALL or an invisible spy into the tumultuous world of leadership. I've witnessed the good, the bad and the ugly of leadership from multiple angles and vantage points. How? Well, for roughly the past decade I have served as executive assistant to several high powered men and women in the hedge fund, financial investment, luxury real estate, non profit and global contract research industries. I have discovered that leadership encompasses so much more than just management of resources ranging from office supplies to human beings.

As a result of my inescapable immersion, I have come to a conclusion: leadership is not simply the result of educational credentials, titles or achieving flawless budget projections. Rather, leadership is grasping visions that span beyond self, pursuing missions despite adversity and recognising that external validation can only get you so far. Leadership resides within us all. It is the cultivation and mastery of our individual authenticity in such a way that inspires others to follow, change, or take a stand for something.

Throughout this chapter, I refer to Hans Christian Anderson's fairy tale, *The Ugly Duckling*, published in 1844, to illustrate how I came to know myself as an Authentic Leadership Coach.

My Hatching

"At last the large egg broke, and a young one crept forth crying, "Peep, peep."

I was born in suburban New York to a first generation Irish immigrant and a hardworking housewife on the first of May 1979. My older sister had two and a half years on me and, for the longest time, I was convinced she was my competition. So much so that I barely graduated from high school, insisting that I would never be able to get higher grades than her, so why even try

31

To her credit, it was my sister who helped me get out of my own way. She introduced me to my first therapist, Valerie. Valerie challenged all of the self limiting labels I had placed on myself and opened my eyes to the magic of self-awareness. This was a major turning point in my personal and professional progress, but only the very beginning of my journey.

Today, at the ripe age of thirty I sometimes feel as though I have amassed great wisdom in my life. But at other times I am reminded just how much I have yet to learn. Like the time I agreed to pick up a dead bird from the taxidermist (on a brisk, windy day in Connecticut) and bring it to the post office to be shipped to Japan. My boss at that time, the CEO of a thriving hedge fund, allowed a client to shoot the beautiful creature on his property during a recent visit and wished to send it to him as a token of his gratitude. Just two years before I had seen a similar bird during a field trip with my ornithology class. Don't get me wrong, I am by no means a wildlife activist (the fact that I am telling this story while referencing *The Ugly Duckling* is sheer coincidence).In a way I found my boss' gesture to his client to be a kind one. Still, the act of safely securing a stuffed bird with a seatbelt, to preserve its feathers in transit, made me question for the first time the types of things I was willing to do for an income.

Despite my ability to see the comedy in most of these events (and there were many), I spent many years of my career feeling displaced, inferior and stifled. I realised I was not alone in my suffering, it was all around me.

Entering The Corporate Nest

"Come, now, use your legs, and
let me see how well you can behave."

I had expected to graduate from college, move back in with my parents, find the ideal job, meet the man of my dreams and live happily ever after. Instead, during my senior year at the University of Massachusetts, I ended a four year, long distance relationship, watched the twin towers dissolve, learned that my parents were selling our home to relocate to North Carolina and scrambled to find a job.

A Coach's Story

In the summer of 2002, I landed in Stamford, Connecticut, where luxury condominiums and apartment rentals were all the rage, as shell-shocked residents of Manhattan retreated to greener pastures. A scenic 45- to 60-minute train ride to Grand Central Station made Fairfield County, Connecticut, fertile ground for refugees of 9/11.

Living in one of these brand new luxury apartments (at a significant employee discount) that it was my job to lease, I got an early taste of prestige. As I sat on my balcony overlooking the pool and sipping a glass of wine after work, I was quite pleased with myself. I naively thought I fitted right in with all of my neighbours, who were paying almost double what I was for the same space. I did my best to furnish and decorate my new home with the few IKEA pieces I had left over from college, complimented by what I could afford on my meager salary. I have and always will be something of a minimalist, but I wasn't fooling anyone with my pseudo-luxury apartment.

In less than a year the building was almost full and my leasing bonuses became few and far between. It was time to find another job and I soon landed a position as executive assistant to a vice president at an investment company in Westchester, NY. My salary had climbed forty percent overnight and I was convinced it was only a matter of time before I could afford the lifestyle I thought I wanted. My unintentional entry into the world of executive administration would prove to be a crucial stepping stone on my personal and professional journey. At first I thought, this is just temporary; I can always find something more satisfying once I get my foot in the door. Temporary, of course, turned into years.

Something about corporate leadership has always interested me. I began my years of supporting executives in a wide variety of industries with a broad curiosity of who did what for the company and why. I studied the organisational structures, the various abbreviations and acronyms, and slowly became aware of how a company's culture can be both a wishful ideology and a myth. The touted mission and vision statements never seem to align with reality. My mild curiosity turned into sheer fascination, which resulted in years of priceless leadership observation.

Everywhere I looked, managers were spewing the same empty jargon to one another in what seemed to me a conspicuous attempt for attention. It was as if the company's processes and systems had replaced reason and logic. Once I started to see through much of the smoke and mirrors that surrounded me, I came to recognise the fundamental Achilles heel of corporations: emotional insecurity, which I experienced as a lack of authenticity. Before I could attempt to put this realisation to good use, though, I had to come to terms with my own insecurities.

Years Of Perceived Banishment

"Can you lay eggs?" she asked. "No." "Then have the goodness to hold your tongue." "Can you raise your back, or purr, or throw out sparks?" said the tom cat. "No." "Then you have no right to express an opinion when sensible people are speaking."

My father used to regularly quote the proverbs that "children should be seen and not heard" and "children should only speak when spoken to". However, he would only say these things when he was playfully rebutting something my sister or I had boldly remarked over dinner. Since my dad worked for NBC News, our family ritual consisted of watching the nightly news on the portable TV which sat at the far end of our kitchen table. As we dined we would each offer our commentary on anything from the socio-political implications of current events to the anchor's choice of tie. As I matured I became increasingly vocal with my ideas and views. My dad soon took to calling me "the mouth",. There were times when I got sent to my room or punished for having used profanities or for telling one of my parents to "shut up", but for the most part I had the luxury of freely exhibiting and voicing my authenticity.

The rules of engagement for an executive assistant are quite similar to those of childhood proverbs. My "tell it like I see it" nature required immediate toning down in order to stay employed. While the organisations I worked for over the years varied in terms of industry, size and culture, a common thread was the way in which leaders interacted with and utilised their administrators.

The modern day executive administrator (or assistant) is a far cry from the secretaries and office clerks of years past. Rather than simply handling my leader's calendar, travel and file structure, I was intimately involved in the day-to-day functions of the business. I would venture to say that, at times, I was considered an operational extension of the person I was supporting. For the most part, I had the same level of awareness of corporate information and functionality, the same expectation of quality service and communication, the same level of responsibility and accountability for approvals and urgent requests, *and* the same level of stress placed on me.

Managing my boss's emotions was an unspoken part of my role. Even if I knew there were urgent matters requiring his attention, I couldn't just knock on the door and walk in asking for documents to be signed or phone calls to be returned; I would first need to assess the stress level I would encounter. based this on the many variables at play: day of the week, time of day, number of meetings on the calendar, number of looming deadlines, etc. I later learned that what I was doing was calling upon my EQ, or emotional intelligence.

The more emails I was copied on and meetings I attended, the more familiar I became with the business systems, processes, politics and strategies. I knew I had a relevant point of view to contribute, one that was both unique and objective. Only, my contribution was seldom invited. Even though I could vividly see where inefficiencies could be improved and where the company could save money and time, no one would listen.

A new approach was needed. I had to figure out the best way to suggest something, without making it seem like it was my idea. It was during this time that I called upon the art of powerful questioning and direct communication. It was like dancing the tango of egos. But, my subtle attempts paid off and I eventually became more closely engaged with my leaders. We even got to a point where I was asked to provide my input or perspective on various matters. Could it be that my value to the organisation was becoming more apparent? I was all of a sudden energised, ready to pull up my sleeves and get down to business.

Unfortunately I soon discovered that my contributions were only appreciated when no one else was around. I also began noticing my ideas being offered in meetings, but with no attribution to me. The intensive level of the work I was given continued to grow, but my salary remained the same. I knew I was not alone in this and vented to others I trusted in the organisation. The response was unanimous: "That's <insert name of organization> for you!" It was apparent to me then that the collective consciousness of each company was one of gradual assimilation and silent contempt.

The veil had been lifted. I then understood that by and large people would rather compromise their convictions and values than take a stand. Even those in positions of power lacked the confidence and courage to go against the grain. If they did challenge an idea it was because they thought that would score them points with their leader, but as soon as their counter-idea was questioned, they caved. "Is this leadership?" I asked myself. My answer would come later, from an unexpected source.

Finding My Flock

*"'I believe I must go out into the
world again,' said the duckling."*

As the overwhelming sense of stagnation began to take its toll on me, I sought various outlets for my frustration. Alcohol was not the answer. Going for a drink or two after a hard day at the office seems all too common these days, yet, it is only a pain-dulling approach. Instead, in an attempt to balance the emptiness I felt at work with something more fulfilling, I started painting again, the first time since high school. Before long I had adorned all of the walls in my house with my own tension-spawned artwork. It was clear my creative energy needed an outlet, a full time, permanent one.

I listened as leadership teams discussed executive coaching in conjunction with their annual performance review process. On one hand, they discussed hiring external coaches to work with "high potentials" or "emerging leaders", as well as the staff they deemed a "problem" or a "remedial case". At one point, my own boss began to work with a coach, and I wondered which category his coaching fell into.

One day, my boss's coach came to see him and, as soon as they entered his office and closed the door, I was immediately overcome by tension. I could not figure out where it was coming from. I had what seemed like an intuitive compulsion to research the coaching field.

I often considered becoming a psychotherapist or counsellor, but I knew I would not enjoy seeing people in crisis or turmoil on a regular basis. Coaching, as I learned from my investigation, was more about helping driven people achieve their goals. My focus quickly shifted from "What is coaching?" to "How can I become a coach?"

I discovered there was a business coaching certificate program offered at the local state university. Signing up for the program was one of the easiest decisions I have made in my life, which is how I knew it was the right one. I was not afraid of how it would affect my full time job and I did not question the hefty financial investment. I just couldn't wait to get started. In the six months before the course began, I memorised the International Coach Federation's Code of Ethics. My vision was clear. I was ready.

There were about fifteen of us in the training program including the two instructors, who were husband and wife. The format of the course was that we met for two, full, eight hour days once a month for ten months. On the first day, I was overcome by excitement and nerves. I imagined the looks on everyone's faces when I introduced myself and what I did for a living. A majority of the other participants had extensive backgrounds in management, human resources or organisational development. I had none of that. But I would soon discover later that my experience was just as relevant, if not more so. My many years of forced silence, stifled ideas and fly-on-the-wall leadership observation would now pay off.

Arranged in triads, we took turns practicing the coaching model. One at a time we would each get to be the coach, the client and the observer. This process was transformational. Through a combination of active listening, powerful questioning and paying attention to how my presence impacted the other soon-to-be-coaches, I was invigorated with a sense of meaning I had never experienced before. We weren't simply role playing, this was the real deal... and I loved every moment of it.

Returning to work after each of the coach training weekends was particularly difficult. It was like returning to the scene of a crime – all I could see were the remnants of caution tape and the outline of where I was last found. This may sound a bit dramatic, but the more I realised my authentic self though coaching, the more I felt as though the previous years of my career had been stolen from me. I shuddered for the others who were still unaware of the power of their authenticity and felt compelled to be a catalyst for change.

I composed a one page memo to the Vice President of the Human Resources Department, succinctly outlining the need for an internal coaching program that would be accessible to staff at all levels of the organisation. I arranged a meeting with her to discuss the memo and get her feedback. She essentially laughed me out of her office, having attempted to humor me at first. By the end of the discussion she practically patted me on my head and told me to run along.

This did not stop me. Since starting at the top was a dead end, I decided to try and gain traction at the grassroots level. Over the course of approximately two years I did everything I could to find a willing executive to champion my internal coaching effort. Almost everyone I spoke to agreed it was a great idea, and sorely needed, but the collective consciousness was too strong to overcome. The conversations typically ended with, the person saying, "That will be hard to do here," and "Good luck with that."

I realised I was wasting my time and energy and decided to shift my focus to building my external coaching practice. Luckily, the coach training program I was attending offered guidance on how to establish a coaching business. The logistical aspects of starting a company are fairly straightforward. Choosing your niche and how you intend to brand and market your services is the tricky part. I didn't want to chose a coaching speciality based solely on its income potential; nor did I want to assume I should coach a certain group merely because I had belonged to that group myself at one time.

As part of the ten month training, we were asked to break into three smaller groups to do a research paper and presentation. As luck would have it, my project abstract was one of the three chosen. The project was intended to formulate how a coach should go about translating their authentic self into a viable brand strategy. In other words, we wanted to create a roadmap for developing one's business from the inside out.

In the process of writing the paper, I realised I had inadvertently found my coaching niche. I now work with other small business owners (not simply coaches) and individuals within organisations as an Authentic Leadership Coach. I specialise in helping my clients increase their authentic-self awareness: this goes deeper than basic self awareness, in that we strip away the labels applied by others, the masks we wear for protection, and we are left with the essential authentic qualities of self. The authentic identity is then cultivated and translated into a more intrinsically driven brand strategy; one that can be utilised both as an entrepreneur and as an individual organisational leader.

Flying Untethered

"Even the elder-tree bent down its boughs into the water before him, and the sun shone warm and bright. Then he rustled his feathers, curved his slender neck, and cried joyfully, from the depths of his heart, 'I never dreamed of such happiness as this, while I was an ugly duckling.'"

As I write this chapter and reflect on my coaching journey, I am struck with the same happiness conveyed by *The Ugly Duckling* passage. There is nothing more satisfying than being recognised and celebrated for exhibiting exactly who you are. I chose to juxtapose this fairy tale with my own story because of its simplicity and its universality. We are all sometimes misunderstood and taken for granted, but to allow yourself to go through life permanently feeling as though you do not belong is a tragedy.

Since I became a coach I have been surrounded by some of the most intuitive and caring individuals. I am now able to be my authentic self one hundred percent of the time. Since I am only projecting who I really am (not what I think people want me to be), I am attracting right clients for me. From time to time, a potential client will come along who is looking for an externally driven approach to achieving his or her goals; I now have the confidence to refer them to someone better suited to meet their needs.

This ability to be comfortable with who I am and own my beliefs is extremely liberating. I no longer hold myself back from what I want out of fear. I have become an abundance-minded, asset-based thinker. As I learned earlier in life from my sister, she was only my competition because I perceived her as such. Once I recognised that I was simply projecting my fears of failure onto her, I let go and began to succeed.

Even when things do not go as I intend, I always try to look for the nugget of truth leading me inevitably to where I must go next. That is not to say everything has been and will be pleasant; it means I am prepared to face challenges head on. I believe in the power of awareness of choice: that we all have control over what we do. To believe otherwise is to limit infinite potential. We are not simply the sum of our experiences and accomplishments; we are an endless supply of creativity just looking for opportunities to release our genius.

Through my personal and professional passage to the present I have become grounded and poised for the next stage of my unfolding. Recently I made the conscious choice to leave the security of my corporate income to further pursue my creative passions – coaching, painting, writing, music and travel. I will soon be free to practise these aspects of identity without time constraints and judgment. I wish this boundless freedom for others as well. I am not merely taking this leap of faith for myself; I am doing it for my clients.

To lead by example is to lead authentically. As your authentic self strives to reach its zenith, embrace the hurdles ahead with ambition and anticipation. Follow your internal compass and you will always find the way to your flock. There your beauty will be fully appreciated.

Arvind Devalia

Finding Your Nirvana Through Helping Others

HAVE YOU EVER WONDERED HOW you might make the world a better place? How you can somehow make a difference to the people around you and at the same time have a fabulous life yourself? I have been asking myself this question all of my life. Some time ago, I realised it was up to me, up to all of us, to make it happen.

From my childhood days in Kenya, when I used to give away my pencils to poor African children, to the many weeks I spent helping at a charity school in South India, I felt called to do something for others. Call it destiny or fate, it seems I was born to contribute and make a difference to others – and coaching allows me to do just that.

My family immigrated to England in the seventies. At school, I got into playing badminton and squash and reached quite a high standard. However, I often ended up coaching my opponents about where they were going wrong. Eventually, some of them even beat me, much to my chagrin. But I didn't mind really. I was always the one people confided in and asked for advice. I was seen as the wise one. Little did they know!

It was only years later, when I came across the concept of life coaching, that it became my profession. I finally began to formally apply all those latent skills.

It all began so unexpectedly. I was a hyperactive, driven guy working in the dot com boom of the late nineties. Helping others was the furthest thing from my mind. From the late eighties I had worked in a bank where the prevailing culture was "greed is king" and was well versed in that philosophy.

So where did it all change and how did I go on to become a coach and a bestselling author, with books and a blog that have inspired thousands?

Journey To Nirvana

My journey into coaching began in South India, thanks to the kindness of one man who completely changed my life. It often happens that people show us great kindness and without being aware of the impact they have as a result of their kind deed.

Mr Roy, a driver working for a hotel in Chennai, South India made a huge difference to my life and that of many others by his dedication to duty and sheer perseverance in getting me to my destination.

Many years ago, well before I was on the life path I am now, I visited Nirvana School in Pondicherry for the first time. From Chennai, this is around eighty miles and, on a good day, the journey takes about two hours by road. We flew into Chennai from North India and somehow got caught up in the heaviest rainfall I have ever experienced. Our planned stay at a beach hotel for a few days was curtailed and we decided to return to North India after just a couple of days. I had been told about this remarkable charity, the Nirvana School in Pondicherry, founded by a Gujarati lady from the UK, Mrs Samani. It seemed like a good opportunity to go and visit despite the heavy rain.

We set off early the next morning. Mr Roy, our driver, was a jovial, wiry and diminutive man in splendid white attire befitting a top hotel chauffer. We had already phoned Mrs Samani at the school about our planned visit and she was expecting us for lunch well before midday. She planned to show us the school and some of the local sights around Pondicherry.

Little did we know what adventures awaited us along the eighty mile journey.

Soon after leaving Chennai, the rain got heavier and at times we could hardly see the road in front of us. There was brown, muddy water everywhere and it seemed like the heavens were releasing some pent up fury as the rain lashed down all around us with ferocious streaks of lightening. Yet Mr Roy was completely unflappable and drove along just like it was another day's work for him - which indeed it was. I marveled at his driving confidence and awareness about the road ahead. Or maybe it was foolhardiness.

As we drove along, the water in the road must have been about a foot deep and yet our white Maruti car cut through the pools and lakes rapidly sprouting up all around us. Three hours into our journey, it seemed we could go no further. However, Mr Roy calmly turned off the main highway and soon got us back on track via umpteen short cuts and diversions. This went on for a while and it felt as if we had hardly even left Chennai yet. Maybe Pondicherry was not in our kismet this time round.

At this point, we suggested to Mr Roy that perhaps we should turn back and plan the trip for another day, or stop and take refuge in a temple in one of the picturesque villages. But he simply smiled and assured us he would get us to Nirvana School. He already knew how important it was for us to get to Pondicherry. Looking back now, it was almost as if he had a sense of destiny about that trip.

Over the next three hours, Mr Roy drove us through many more angry walls of rainfall, muddy lakes and sodden villages. It was nature's fury unleashed, and wading through it all was this smiling, white clad man who just kept going and going. His persistence and faith in getting us there was reassuring and awe inspiring.

We eventually arrived in Pondicherry, over six hours after setting out from Chennai. Almost magically, the sun came out as we finally found Nirvana School.

Alas, the heavy rainfall and resulting flooding over the previous twenty four hours had meant very few children were actually attending school that day. We had a very brief tour of the school followed by a hasty lunch as we had to get back on the road to Chennai before it got too dark. I promised Mrs Samani that one day I would visit the school and stay longer than ninety minutes. A few years later I did just that. It really was a predestined visit.

Mr Roy, replenished by a light lunch and an even lighter snooze in the Maruti, assured us the rain was subsiding and the journey back home would be much quicker and smoother. He chose to take a slightly different route back, along a coastal road rather than the main highway which he had conquered in the morning. The scenery in the dusk was incredibly beautiful and reminded me of the many paintings my father had painted years before. This was rural India at its best and I will always remember the images of villagers in the distance returning home with their pots, firewood and pouches on their head.

The journey home back to Chennai was indeed much smoother and quicker as the rain subsided and the night drew in. We arrived back in time for dinner and Mr Roy was buzzing and unflappable till the end. As he said, it was nothing; all in a day's work. We could not thank him enough for taking us to Nirvana school and for what he had done for us, as who knew when we would be able to return to that part of the world again?

We left for Bangalore the next morning and I didn't see Mr Roy again on that visit to Chennai. Yet the impact of his kindness did not simply end with his absence. Nor did it impact only us who visited Nirvana School on that fateful day.

Mr Roy's contribution to my life is even bigger than simply introducing me to Nirvana School. As a result of my time at the school, I was drawn to working more directly with people and first came across the concept of life coaching as a career.

This new vocation took me away from the world of IT and led me to publish four books. I began writing on the internet about topics to "make it happen" in the world and in your life, thereby spreading the ripple effect of Mr Roy's kindness even further.

Roll on a couple of years after that initial trip with Mr Roy. My life situation allowed me to visit India for two months and I was able to fulfill my pledge to Mrs Samani and visit Nirvana School for a much longer period. In fact, I stayed with her in Pondicherry for a month.

My journey from a hyperactive, stressed out, self centered guy suffering all sorts of stress related ailments to a chilled out, laid back, worldly wise man was almost complete during that month.

The month at Nirvana School indeed felt like a month in Nirvana. I became a different person. Working with children and people seemed like my true vocation. I left with a heavy heart, clear that one day I wanted to do more of this type of work of service.

I also knew I would return to Nirvana School many more times. My commitment to the school has become my own way of returning the kindness shown to me by so many others in my life and, of course, Mr Roy.

Experiencing Unconditional Love For The First Time

During that month at Nirvana School there was one particular experience that changed my life and my career forever. I spent that time simply being amongst the school children and the local people. It proved to be a most fulfilling time and ultimately paved the way for a new career in life coaching.

A friend back in London had donated some money to feed sweets to orphans, so I ended up in an orphanage in Pondicherry within a Catholic hospital. We brought large Indian sweets called ladoo and were taken by the sister in charge to visit six orphan kids who were watching TV on what seemed like a massive sofa. They instantly jumped up and gave us their rapt attention. The sister who accompanied us simply handed over the ladoo.

I felt foolish as the kids looked at us with grateful eyes. I was wearing far too many clothes for the steamy weather and I probably looked quite strange to them in my western trainers and sunhat. Soon the ladoos were gone and the sister explained how two of the children were a brother and sister who had been found abandoned outside the hospital main entrance several years earlier. Instinctively, I picked up the little girl and placed her on a chair and began playing with her. She gurgled and her mischievous eyes seemed to twinkle with delight.

At that moment, time seemed to come to a standstill. Nothing else mattered except this little girl. I was lost in her presence. After a few seconds that seemed an eternity, I instinctively looked up. And there, right in front of me, was the Catholic sister, looking back at me with sheer joy and love on her face. Our eyes locked and melted together into an ocean of compassion. The look in the sister's all knowing eyes reassured me it was okay to feel what I was feeling; it was safe and perfectly okay to be openly loving and kind.

In those few moments, I learnt what it meant to be human. I learnt what it felt like to truly show compassion, love and kindness.

That was probably my first experience of unconditional love towards a total stranger. That little, innocent, helpless, orphan girl had captured my heart. As tears streamed from my eyes, I knew then I had found my calling and my path. My journey of contribution and service began in those few amazing moments of bliss, love and joy.

Life was never the same for me again after that. Looking back to that magical day, everything else pales in insignificance. I returned to London and underwent major life changes very quickly.

The rest is history, as they say. I have been involved with Nirvana School for almost ten years now and it has been an immensely fulfilling experience for me. So many people have visited the school as volunteers after being enrolled and have been inspired by my passion for the school. Others have been equally passionate and very generous with their financial support.

In Life, Always Go The Extra Mile, Like Mr Roy

It is not just the children of Nirvana School who benefitted in the long term from Mr Roy's kindness that fateful day. It is indeed the whole community and many other people in my life who have been impacted as a result of my own involvement in the school. It is a classic ripple effect of a single act of kindness affecting so many lives over many years in a positive way.

And whatever happened to kind Mr Roy?

Well, the last time I visited Pondicherry, I stayed in the same hotel in Chennai prior to returning to London. Mr Roy no longer worked there, but somehow the hotel staff traced him for me. Fortunately, he remembered me from many years before and it was really good to see him again.

Mr Roy looked just the same and it was touching how he brought along the letter of thanks we had sent him from England after that life changing trip to Pondicherry. This time around, I made sure I got a photograph of the two of us as a permanent reminder of the man who so unknowingly changed my life and impacted the lives of so many others.

As I always say to everyone, next time you have a chance to show some kindness or go the extra mile, do so without any hesitation. You don't know what impact your actions will have or how many lives you will change for the better. And of course, remember – there are no traffic jams on the extra mile.

Coaching And Writing – Tools Of Empowerment

Two years after my exquisite experience of unconditional love, I came across the concept of life coaching and realised it was just what I had been searching for as a vehicle for helping others. Even finding out about coaching was accidental, as I stumbled across some exhibition booths advertising coaching schools.

Since I began coaching, I have written and published three books as well as writing a newspaper column and running a major blog. I realised that through my coaching I could only reach so many people. But through my books and my blogging, I could change many more lives. My second book, *Get the Life You Love and Live it*, became a real labour of love as I poured my heart and soul into writing it. This book is like a life manual about living a life with purpose, commitment and making a difference to yourself and others in whatever way works for you.

Coaching is indeed a powerful tool for empowering change, and passionate, inspired writing can truly help people find and follow their own passion. Through serving and helping others, you yourself ultimately become more fulfilled, joyous and happy.

I am passionate about people and making a difference to others whilst of course at the same time having a great life myself. I am committed to a life of contribution, connection and celebration. And I am convinced that, ultimately, we all want the same.

My Own Coaching Insights

Often we take the best path needed for our own development. Through coaching others and seeing what holds people back -- and more importantly, what brings them alive -- I have had many of my own insights.

I found my initial training as a coach to be so much fun and insightful. For the first time in my life, training of any sort did not feel like work. It really felt like I had arrived. In the last few years, I have learnt so much about people and human nature: every individual is fascinating when you take time, take a back seat and let people simply "be".

The most profound and powerful learning from coaching has been that it is okay for me and others to let their light shine. We all hold back so much and yet we have so much to offer the world. If only more people could allow their own light to shine and be the best they can be. What a different world we could create!

I have also learnt that our journey through life is to gain greater awareness and ultimately discover there is nothing that needs fixing. Coming from a place of "nothing is wrong" opens up a whole new world that we can create as we wish. At the same time, it is okay to strive to be the best we can.

What I Believe In

Through coaching, I have developed a specific set of beliefs:

1. We can all have abundant, peaceful and happy lives.
2. We are here to make the most of what we have and leave the world a better place than we found it. This includes creating financial abundance for ourselves, living healthy lives and having loving relationships.
3. Everyone has a right to live with dignity and respect.
4. There is no limit to our ingenuity in improving the lives of our fellow human beings – we just need the will and desire to do so.
5. Ultimately, we all want to live peaceful lives of contribution and make a difference to others in some way.
6. We are here for a short time on the earth and it is up to each one of us to create a lasting legacy for those who will follow us.
7. Though we may face challenging (and at times seemingly impossible) odds, we will ultimately prevail and the world will be a better, more just and safer place.

My coaching and my writing are focused on putting these beliefs into practice and helping many more people. What can you do with your life to do the same for others?

Leaving the World a Better Place

I now know that all of us have the same desire and calling to leave the world better. At the same time, we all wish to grow in our own lives and make the most of our time here.

If, through coaching, I can help at least one person live a better, more meaningful life, then I will have succeeded with my own mission.

My ultimate aim is for all of us to lead happy, fulfilling lives whilst we all do the best we can without harming those around us and the environment. At the same time I believe that, by being the best we can, we fulfill our destiny on earth and leave the world a better place.

Surely that is not too much to ask for?

Some Final Words

Remember that your life counts – and make it count.
You are unique – there is no one like you on this planet.
Never has been and never will be.
Do not sell yourself short.
Do not sell the world short.
This is your life – love it, live it.
One life, one chance – grab it.
Get the life you love – and live it.

ARVIND DEVALIA, NIRVANA PUBLISHING 2005

Jane Bromley

Executive Coaching: Learning To Fly, And Then To Soar

Coaching Is Inspirational

IN RECENT TIMES, I HAVE DISCOVERED I have the ability to inspire people to be who they really are – wonderful beings without limit, with the ability to do and be everything they have ever dreamt of.

What is more, I have discovered that by taking the pressure off myself my results soar and my life can be like that of a child – simply going with the flow and having fun. By living this way things click beautifully into place and, for me too, there are no limits. Life is fun and wonderful.

I am getting ahead of myself, though. This knowledge came only recently, so let me go back to the beginning and tell you about my journey and how coaching opened up a totally new and increasingly fun part of my life.

Setting The Scene – Who Am I?

My early years were somewhat unusual - moving to Canada at six weeks old, to Africa aged four and then back to the UK at six. My parents once told me we had visited over thirty countries, but I now think that was an exaggeration. Despite this, because we moved around a lot, I think I grew to love variety – to appreciate different cultures and dramatic countryside, whether it was the dry dust of Kenya, the never ending sandy beaches in South Africa, the mountains of the French Alps or the lush green of many parts of America.

There was nothing to indicate that I was particularly suited to becoming a coach. I do not think I was an especially good listener as a child. I was not any better than anyone else at building rapport. In fact, I was very shy until I got to know someone well. I was also lonely: an only child with successful business people for parents. I went through different phases as I grew up.

Early on, I was full of bounce, cheeky and a real character. As I became a teenager, I was all over the place with no idea who I was or

51

where I was headed. What is more, I had no idea what I would "become". It worried me. Some of my friends knew they would become doctors, veterinarians, mathematicians, teachers, etc. I did not know where to start. I thought I was worse off for not knowing, that I should have worked it out. As I never did homework I always assumed my friends who worked hard to get great results would always be far ahead of me. I remember my surprise in my first job when I noticed I was earning more than my friends in an exciting role.

Looking back, I think that what makes me a good coach now has a lot more to do with the issues I regarded as problems and failures. They allow me to "feel" my clients' pain and understand it in a way another coach might not be able to do.

After a wonderful few years at university, I started working, at times in great jobs I adored, earning good money;, at other times wondering where it had all gone wrong. At Hewlett Packard I was in my element. They allowed me to set precise goals and gave me the space and resources to meet or, if I could, exceed them. I ended up doing more and more with the Senior Management team, leading specific projects with their blessing, support and guidance. In the early days, I learnt quickly that if I presented at a meeting and did not know my topic inside out and back to front, I would be roasted alive. It was excellent training, as I have since had to hold my own with boards of directors of firms of all sizes. What is more, it taught me to think through subjects from all angles; to become an expert at whatever I did.

In 2001, like employees of many Fortune 500 companies, I reached a point where I wanted to spread my wings. I felt like a cog in a huge complex wheel and knew I could have greater impact with more room to manoeuvre. I decided to run my own business – with no idea what a shock that would be. I had been used to phoning anyone and my employer's name would open the door. I now ran a tiny company no one had ever heard of. What is more, I found selling my own services was one hundred times harder than selling someone else's services. The steep learning curve stopped me from enjoying the whole thing for several years. Fortunately, I won some great consultancy projects which I adored, and that kept me sane and well fed.

A Disaster Leads Me To Coaching

I have found that problems which seem like show stoppers often open doors to wonderful experiences. A large project I undertook for a software company was one of these. It started really well. A PLC business, they employed one hundred people and had been doing well, until a year ago. Then sales growth stopped; somewhat worrying the business leaders. The Board had tried to solve the issue by pushing the sales force harder and making changes of all sorts. Then they asked me to help them.

I was in my element. I set about finding out exactly what their existing and prospective customers wanted and what blocks to growth existed. Very soon it became clear where the problems lay. A major project ensued. The business started to alter and things began to pick up. There were big changes and it took a great deal of focus and effort to ensure they were successful. Ten months later the business was looking much better. Many of the barriers to sales had gone and the others were being worked through. The CEO allowed me to run a strategy session with the entire Board to define the future company direction. What is more, he took us all overseas for the three days; a great treat.

I was nervous. It was a big event. I knew my subject very well and was convinced this discussion would set the foundations upon which the business could grow by another ten million pounds over the next few years. Fortunately, the sessions went extraordinarily well. For the first time since I had joined the company, the Directors were showing their mettle, challenging ideas and also showing what they could achieve together. What a success!

Then it all fell apart. To this day I can only guess what was really going on. I believe the CEO, who until then had always dominated the other Directors, became worried he would lose control. He had built up the firm from nothing to a multimillion company and was a millionaire in his own right. Yet he was concerned that, with his Board pulling their full weight, he might be found to be lacking in some way.

We argued (several times) and eventually agreed to part company. I was mortified. I had given the firm everything I had and it felt like my biggest failure. I had flu for six weeks – and found out later I had adrenal stress, from which I took years to recover. The good thing was that I slept, watched films and read books. I did not have energy for anything else, but I had time to sort my thoughts out. I knew little about coaching, yet somewhere deep down I believed that if I had known how to coach, I would have been able to help the CEO and the project would have been a success.

Training As A Corporate Executive Coach

As I started to feel better, I went in search of a good course. I followed my nose as I had no idea what to look for. Fortunately, I signed up for a course where I was trained as a Corporate and Executive Coach by Neil and Vicky Espin, founders of The Corporate and Executive Coaching Organisation. These two wonderful trainers put us through our paces rigorously yet supportively, ensuring we could not get the qualification without meeting their very high standards. The quality and standard of their work oozed from them and, while they were kind to us, it was obvious they would not be happy until they were convinced we had been transformed into top notch coaches.

The Coaching Course

The course was many years ago. I remember loving every moment of it - and the awe I experienced when, for the first time, I attempted to coach someone. I simply, very tentatively, tried out some of the questions and techniques we had just learnt and found miracles happened. My "client", who was, of course, another coaching student, made a major breakthrough in five minutes flat and the obvious delight on her face was a delight to experience.

Years later I was handed a great article, "The Neuroscience of Leadership". It explained research which seemed to indicate that coaching rewired the "fixed programming" in the brain, simultaneously releasing a chemical which makes the client feel wonderful. So that explained it. In those early days, it seemed to be a pure miracle.

As well as various coaching techniques, Neil and Vicky also taught us some elements of Transactional Analysis and other psychological approaches. The three days of this first course were packed full. Then it was time to go home and find some people on which we could practice, for the training was only the beginning.

Getting Coaching Experience

The largest section of the course involved coaching six people for six sessions each, with all the relevant coaching contracts in place. We then needed to write up our "thesis"- describing what we had learnt, the coaching techniques we had used, what had worked well and what had not – with our explanation as to why we thought this was so and what we might do differently as a result. The final document, including the testimonials, was fifty pages long.

There was also a second coaching course called Advanced Coaching. This included in depth sessions on specific coaching areas, such as Stress Coaching.

Actually finding people to coach was the only part I found difficult. I did not know how to go about it and flailed about for months, unsure what to do. It seems crazy now – I was only too happy to challenge senior executives of large and blue chip companies as a consultant. Yet as a new coach, I felt so nervous asking "real business people" if I could coach them.

The coaching itself was uplifting and still miraculous. Apart from my first "client", that is. He was a challenge. It turned out he was not truly interested in coaching but was merely curious. Though he was not happy with his business or life, he was not prepared, at that stage, to make any changes. I later discovered this is one of the challenges of offering to coach someone for free. After three sessions I no longer knew which way to turn. I called Vicki, who explained it was not anything I was doing wrong; a huge relief. She explained that, as my "client" was just not ready to make changes to his life, coaching could not help him at this time. Phew! I thought I had blown it.

Interestingly, something unexpected happened then. Following Vicki's advice, I told my client that the sessions would not continue. Later I discovered that, by doing this, it shook him up so much that he then undertook massive action to turn his life and business around. How wonderful is that?

The other clients went far more smoothly, I am happy to say. At a high level, one client doubled his revenue in six weeks flat. Another created an entire business plan and we watched his performance levels soar. An MD refocused his business with great results. I coached another lady to define and set up her dream business. Yet another client realised he was in the wrong job and so he designed his new career. Seeing the speed with which people could bring about change in their lives and the incredibly high levels of enthusiasm coaching inspired was heady stuff for a new coach.

To Provide Support Or Not

Unfortunately, the large Coaching Training firm I selected promised wonderful support in setting up my coaching business and winning clients, yet much of it was hot air. In fact, what they taught us seemed well above our abilities. I ended up with an incredibly powerful tool to help clients, yet no idea how to reach the business clients who needed my help. Though many people were in the same boat as I, a few found it very easy. I remember, with amazement, a guy on the initial course who stood up and informed us he had already sold twelve thousand pounds' worth of coaching before he had even done the course.

Powerful Coaching Techniques

Looking back, there are certain techniques I learnt during training which have always stood me in good stead for coaching.

Transparency is one of these. When you are taught to coach, you learn certain processes, such as the GROW model[°]. Especially in the early stages, the tendency is to believe that, as a coach, you need to always know the right questions to ask. At the end of each coaching session, I would ask what worked particularly well and what would have worked even better. The answer came back loud and clear from one client: "Please be more transparent". For instance, if I had two possible paths I could take with the coaching, he would prefer me to say, "I can ask you about x or y - which would you prefer?" or even, "What question could I ask you now that would help you most?" By using this transparent approach the coaching brought about even better results and made it easier for me.

[°] The GROW model, created by Sir John Whitmore, is one of the most common coaching models It provides a way to structure coaching sessions:
- GOAL – defining what the client wants to achieve
- REALITY – exploring the current situation
- OPTIONS – investigating ways to attaining the goal
- WILL – Agreeing on a concrete plan of action

Building strong rapport with clients is essential to coaching. One technique I find particularly powerful here is to repeat back what I have heard my client say, either word for word or, on occasion, checking whether what I think I heard "between the lines" was really there. By doing this, I believe my clients feel I understand them extremely well, and this strengthens the all important rapport between us. In addition, hearing me speak their words seems to help them see what really lies within them much more clearly.

A third technique is actually more than a technique. One of the things I most love about coaching is that, by being one hundred percent focused on my client, I forget myself, my limitations and my worries and I am free to help them more as a result. This puts me in a place where I see my client as he/she really is: an incredible, powerful being with no limitations and the ability to be and achieve *anything* he or she desires. It is worth becoming a coach simply to access that place. Interestingly, as the coaching questions continue, it is almost as if the scales fall from my client's eyes and he also begins to see himself as he really is. At this point, my client invariably begins to feel inspired and excited about the future!

Needless to say, I have learnt many other effective coaching techniques since then. To cover them all would take another book.

Setting Up In Business As A Coach

To be honest, when it came to actually winning business, I nearly gave up. I felt so alone and did not really know where to start. I was suddenly aware there were masses of coaches out there, including many who did not seem to have any training or were not coaches at all, but mentors (i.e., they gave advice instead of asking non-directive questions). Additionally, most prospective clients did not really understand what coaching was, let alone the incredible benefits it could bring. I soon realised that if I was to win coaching business I would need to work out my particular forte as a coach.

Yet I had just been trained. Was I not just like all the other coaches who had had similar training? I did not know the answer.

Five years later, it is clear to me how I *should* have done it:

I should have asked one of my coaching friends to coach me on how I would market myself; what made me stand out. I should have asked them to pull out examples of what I had done in business where I had felt Totally successful. From that, they would have quickly picked up what it was about me that made me different. From that, I would have asked them to push me until I had a simple statement which described one thing I offered which was different; the one thing of which I could be proud.

With this "lighthouse statement", I would then have initially delayed, rescinded my dream of coaching the boards of blue chips companies and paid for a small coaching advert in a local magazine just to build my experience and confidence with small businesses nearby.

In addition, I would have offered to coach business people for free. That way, I would have used my skill to help people while I waited for paid work and those people would, without a doubt, have excitedly told others about the superb results they were seeing from coaching.

With these two techniques alone, I am confident the business would have mushroomed.

Of course, now there are other routes. The best I have found so far is Noble Manhattan's *www.getcoachingleads.com*. It is a powerful, automated, incredibly economical way to ramp your coaching business quickly.

The Personal Impact Coaching Has Had On Me

Coaching has irrevocably altered my life in three ways.

As I mentioned earlier, by coaching others I have seen I too am far more than I ever gave myself credit for. Like my clients, my potential is one hundred times greater than I ever imagined. Yet, before I started coaching I had no idea this was the case.

The progress I have made here has been gradual, often without me being aware I was even changing. This is surely the easiest and, arguably, the best way to change.

In order to experience this fully, I believe you need to be coached as well as coach others. Once you have seen the impressive impact coaching has, I cannot imagine anyone would not want to be coached.

My friends have always told me that, whatever issues your client has, he or she unknowingly chose you because you need to resolve the same issues. I have no idea how this can be the case, but it certainly seems to be true. The interesting thing is that by connecting closely with your client you see your own barriers reflected back to you powerfully. For instance, one Managing Director client wanted to focus on creating a plan to generate more revenue. However, it was obvious his office was so disorganised it was draining his energy. During the sessions, the "office" came up over and over again. Eventually we worked it through and he felt so much better. Spookily, (without even being aware of the change in myself) since then, for the first time in my life, my office is clutter free, my desk is clear and I have sifted out all the files I had been keeping "just in case".

For quite a while, I also often seemed to attract people who doubted their very obvious, incredible ability to be successful in their chosen field. It was only a few months ago that I realised I had previously also chosen to think I was less able than I am. I had attracted well over twenty clients with this sort of limiting belief before I suddenly realised the parallel within myself.

There are dozens of similar examples I could give.

While the coaching company with whom I trained disappointed me by reneging on promises, it so happened that when I signed up, they were running a promotion. As a result, they gave me tickets to attend Tony Robbins' *Unleash the Power Within* (UPW) event in London. I had no idea who Tony Robbins was, but they called him the "grandfather of coaching", so I thought I would go along to see what it was all about. I suspected I would not stay - that I would find it all a bit over the top. That four-day event sparked a major change in my life.

Thanks to UPW, I realised I was not living life the way I really wanted to at all. As a result, I made some huge changes in my life. Looking back now, I feel I have changed immensely in the past four or five years. I now know who I am. Back then, I do not think I really did. I now follow my intuition most of the time. Then, I did what I thought I should. I did not know what "spiritual" meant. Now I love the spiritual journey I am on. I have learnt to focus my thoughts so that I enjoy my life immensely. I have accepted myself. I like myself. This was a major breakthrough. As a result, life is wonderful.

So, all in all, coaching has brought about massive change for the better in my life, although I originally chose coaching as an avenue to help others, not myself.

Becoming a Coach Is Just The First Part

Coaching is an incredibly powerful tool, but its full impact only happens when a coach links their skills with the essence of who they are, a unique individual with their own specific gift.

While a newly trained coach will often be totally inspired by the power of this tool, if he or she goes out into the world and proclaims "I am a Life Coach" or "I am a Business Coach", then a major part of the benefit they can provide and enjoy has been missed.

Indeed, as I now understand it, the coaching qualification is just the first step. They then need to package it, to make it their own.

I will give you an example: I recently coached a man who runs his own coaching business. He was struggling to win new business and wanted to know how he could do better in this challenging financial environment. What surprised me was, though he clearly enjoys coaching, I was not hearing a lot of energy in the way he talked about his business. Then we happened to discuss his favourite sport. His energy powered through. It turned out he had always dreamt of linking the two things. In fact, he saw major benefits as, by building strong trust and creating an environment in which clients would find it far easier to gain even better results, the coaching would be even more effective. Yet, he had never dared to progress that side. Within just two hours of the coaching session, he had attracted his first new clients without even having to try.

Be Careful With Whom You Choose To Train

Looking back, in some ways I was incredibly lucky with my choice of coaching training company. In other ways, I was less so.

I was badly informed. I did not really know what to look for, so it was easy to be convinced by cleverly crafted marketing messages and sales techniques.

Since completing my course I have heard of coaching schools where people can qualify without doing any live coaching practice at all. Yet, I remember, even after being shown exactly how to coach, how nervous I was just coaching a fellow student. I soon gained confidence because the course took us step by step through the process until it became second nature. How on earth will the poor people who were not given that opportunity ever be able to turn their investment into a successful business? What is more, our coaching was checked, honed, and then checked again and again until the trainers were sure we were doing it the right way. Then, during the extended practice part of the course, they were careful to ensure we were coaching correctly. Learning to coach properly is a steep learning curve and not easy. If a student does not have access to hands on practice I had, how can they be sure they are coaching well?

I was not so lucky in this area. I was promised a mentor to advise me how to set up my company. I was promised ongoing support. I was told they would help me and that it would be made easy. By the time I got part way into the course it was obvious that, now they had my money, they did not care about keeping their promises.

Looking back, I would have done well to ask existing coaches who they recommended. Still, it seems that not many companies go out of their way to help their students to create successful businesses. Noble Manhattan is the best I have come across. They really seem to care about their coaches, provide good value packages (such as *www.getcoachingleads.com* which I mentioned earlier) and are continually looking for other ways they can help their extended "family".

A Vision For Coaching

Coaches enjoy being with people. I see a picture of the future. In the picture I see strong, growing, communities of coaches spread across the UK and other countries around the world. In my vision these communities become the pulse, the life blood, which helps each and every coach to become phenomenally good at coaching is his or her specific way.

In these groups, the members are able to:

- Continue to hone their coach skills so that coaches can pride themselves on the high quality results across the industry
- Develop successful businesses, easily generating good money and designing the life they want
- Inspire and support each other, becoming a close knit team which allows each member to soar to greater heights than he or she ever felt was possible.
- Find a place where they can belong, with great colleagues with whom they can laugh, cry, and who will be there for them.

As a result of the improving standard of coaching, more and more individuals and businesses look for help from coaching. The industry now only attracts the very best.

Jane Bromley

Glen J. Cooper

Recipe For Personal Growth

Twenty-five years ago, I wrote down these unifying principles
for myself. Here's how they look, probably revised a bit over time,
on the small piece of paper that I carry with me:

1. **Choose To Be A Creative Force**
   a. Assume responsibility for deciding:
      - What is the truth?
      - What are my values?
      - What do I really care about?
   b. Reach out to family & friends.
      - Plan & join family functions.
      - Remember special anniversaries.
      - Always be helpful.
      - Be tolerant.
   c. Plan for financial security.
      - Establish & keep goals & budgets.
      - Work daily action plans.
      - Conserve all resources.

2. **Always Keep Growing**
   a. Continually increase knowledge.
      - Read & study.
      - Choose new experiences.
   b. Maintain physical & mental health.
      - Enjoy being creative.
      - Exercise daily.
      - Eat healthfully.
      - Rest, recreate & pace self.
   c. Broaden bounds of spirituality.
      - Allow love to flow through to others.
      - Hold onto hope; share it with others.
      - Be honest in all dealings.
      - Keep promises.

Sound great, doesn't it? *Wow, how smart am I?*

I wish I could tell you that this is my recipe for material success. It's not. It's my recipe for personal growth. To me, personal growth is *real* success, but there isn't a universal agreement on that concept. Some insist on measuring success only in terms of money, especially in the world of business.

Sometimes personal growth leads to money. More often, I simply enjoy the personal growth I attain as the result of my hard work.

Following my unifying principles *always* leads me to personal growth. Material success is what happens when I work diligently, grow and get lucky. I can always provide the effort that leads me to grow. Luck, however, is not something I can intentionally create. Luck just happens once in awhile.

Where Did I Learn What I Know?

I have been selling and appraising businesses full time for thirty years as a business broker and business appraiser. When I handle larger businesses, people tend to call me a business intermediary. I have lots of credentials and experience. I now have a reputation as "creative but very competent," as one of my competitors put it. I guess that's a compliment which would have been more resounding if I wasn't so damned "creative".

By my estimate, I have had something to do with selling about four hundred businesses. I have talked with several thousand business owners, as well as about ten thousand prospective business buyers. I sometimes handle big deals (businesses selling from two to ten million dollars in sales price). Smaller deals (businesses selling for under one million dollars) is what we do every day.

Since I sold my first business in 1979, I have been continually energised helping business owners. I co-founded what became the largest business intermediary firm in Maine, USA, in 1981, and sold it in May 2010. I am now starting a new company in my original home state of Colorado. My favourite part has always been facilitating, teaching and consulting with the owners of small businesses. Those late night meetings in their office, or at their kitchen table, are deeply rewarding growth experiences.

On the weekends at their closed factories, as we walk the plant floor together, they often stop and tell me things they can't tell their employees and family.

Sometimes it's the pain of a key employee they must let go, or the disappointment of a child who won't participate in the business, or the loneliness of no longer being able to share things with a partner. Sometimes, they know they're burning out fast, failing financially, or literally dying of some recently diagnosed disease.

On happier occasions, I am often in the position of being the only person with whom they can share something exciting. They are often enthralled at their own new discoveries. Sharing those experiences with me is an event for them. "Wait until you see this!" is not an uncommon start to a conversation, often said in a whisper of excitement.

If it's not something sad we are crying about, or something new we are marvelling at, then it's a laughing-until-the-tears-come experience. We share a laugh at the absurdities of small business life. "You can't make this stuff up!" one of us is likely to say to the other.

Now I Call It Coaching

I never called my life's work "coaching", but now I realise it is. Some people have told me how good I am as a Business Coach. If that is so, it is all those past business clients speaking through me, with all they had to give.

It is the joy of my life to pass it on to my new prospects and clients, and to everyone else I meet.

In 2009, I decided to begin calling it "coaching" and to list myself as a coach. Of course, I am now reading all I can on the subject of coaching, not just my own narrow area of business. I am discovering the many new ways I can listen better, facilitating more than teaching or consulting. I love to work with – and for – the really exciting people who run small businesses, or aspire to. I guess that will be my coaching "niche."

But, what I am discovering is something I didn't expect. I am developing a unique way to re-package the lessons I have learned over my lifetime. In doing so, I think I have something very unique to offer.

I see all the problems ahead of us that everyone else sees – economic, environmental, social and political – but I also see the answers.

The answers are all individually-based small steps everyone can take. That's good, because – really – we cannot control anyone else but ourselves. And, even then, controlling ourselves is no sure bet! Right?

Entrepreneurial And Life-Meaning Seizures

One of my favourite business writers and speakers is Michael Gerber, author of *The E-Myth (Revisited)*, a cult classic among small business owners for over two decades now - published originally in its un-revisited form way back in 1986.

What Gerber writes about business can also be applied to our personal struggles for success, in business *and* in life, however we define success.

His major thesis is that most businesses are *not* started and run by "entrepreneurs". That, he says, is the "Entrepreneurial Myth." That's the "E-Myth."

Most businesses, he writes, are started and run by "technicians suffering from an entrepreneurial seizure." The plumber starts a plumbing business, knows how to work "in" the plumbing business, but *does not* know how to work "on" the plumbing business. As a result, the business finally quits growing when the plumber suffers burnout. The business fails.

Learning to work "on" a business and not just "in" it is a key Gerber concept.

The business the plumber invents to give himself a better life now takes the life he has! Sometimes that's figuratively; sometimes literally. Joe the plumber doesn't know it, but he has his own built-in "exit plan". It's not pretty!

In my personal experience as a business broker over all these years, Gerber is right. That's what happens. It is estimated that eighty percent of new businesses in the US fail within the first five years. It's not just plumbers, of course, but everyone. Even eighty percent of business brokers fail.

Most of us, however, are also "technicians suffering from a *"life-meaning* seizure." We "get by" every day, but we don't know the "secret" to success. We search for meaning in many ways, but we rarely take bold steps to actually *give* our lives more meaning.

Using Gerber's terms with a slight twist, we need to learn more than just how to work "in" our lives. We all now need to learn to work "on" our lives. You don't have to be in business to be working "in" something with the desperate need to learn how to work "on" it.

Think about that for a minute.

For most of history, as far as I can tell, humans have worked "in" their lives with little thought of working "on" them. The idea of controlling one's own destiny is a late notion in the long span of human existence.

After at least five thousand years of recorded human civilisation, the very first known document to proclaim even limited human rights was the Magna Carta, signed in 1215. It took five hundred more years for the Declaration of Independence in 1776, making that human rights claim more universal. Then, it was one hundred and eighty eight more years until an effective Civil Rights bill was passed by the US Congress in 1964.

Today, with the ability to engage in worldwide, real time conversations, it seems we are moving much faster. But, by all reasonable accounting, being free to work "on" one's career, business or life in a pro-active way is a surprisingly new idea for our species.

Especially today – because of an unprecedented rate of change in nearly everything – we all *must* learn to work "on" our lives.

Today, the electronic transparency that threatens our privacy, the 24/7 "time suck" that has become our daily experience, and the complete loss of control over even our own communications is causing a life-meaning seizure for most of us, or soon will.

Now, someone reading this may not be having a life-meaning seizure. Those of you who are wealthy and secure, physically fit, mentally sharp and spiritually well-connected, who know how your latest computer works, are managing your social networks well, and who speak at least one other major language besides your native tongue can quit reading this article. You are already on some *rare* "right track." Please contact me immediately, so I can understand how you do it.

But, the rest of us must stay for today's lesson. Okay?

Where Do We Start?

Today, most of us really need to re-invent ourselves, individually and collectively.

We have to re-invent our economy and our society. Many seem to know and accept that part.

What we may not quite yet understand is that, to succeed economically and socially, we need to re-invent ourselves first. Nothing short of a major change will do.

Some of us know that. But, where in the *hell* do we start! And, for many of us, that's just how it feels to be where we are – in *hell*!

"The E-Myth" answer to where a business owner should start – to summarise quickly for those who are not familiar with Gerber – is to re-think the business' primary aim and mission.

The owner must then formulate a "transforming promise" to customers and/or clients in answer to what they need and want, but also to employees about their work and even to investors, vendors and lenders about what they can contribute to that aim and mission. Somehow, that promise must also fulfil the owner's hopes and dreams as well, to give the owner a cause greater than the everyday, a motivating and empowering force that doesn't wear off with time.

Finally, the business must develop systems (like a franchise has systems) to fulfil promises made. The promise, by the way, must be born of a primary aim and mission that comes from a very *big idea*.

You can't motivate yourself or others without having a "big idea."

"What's *your* big Idea?" Gerber asks.

As I write this, I have just been divorced after a three decade relationship and marriage, with five adult children and six grandchildren. I just sold my business brokerage firm in Maine, and am starting a new business in Colorado. My Maine business was (and still is) dominant in its market, but got badly mired down in the most recent economic recession (2007-2009). And, since the summer of 2008, I have watched all my life savings go away. Yes, all!

When our business bookkeeper finished the 2008 year-end work on January 31, 2009, and I saw the final results printed on paper, it hit me like a hard punch to the stomach. I felt like throwing up in the snow bank outside as I walked to my car that night. I knew I had to start all over again.

I find myself, perhaps like many of you, needing to re-invent myself: to work "on" myself again. Re-educate myself again. Train myself in technology again. Get back in physical shape again. Rediscover my faith again. Make money again.

To do that, I need to kick myself in the butt – one more time. Get back on my feet – one more time. Try to be brave – one more time. Try to feel young and energetic – one more time. Try to let myself cry until I get through it. Try *not* to throw myself another pity-party.

My Answer: Working "On" Myself

Gerber's main question is a start for me.

What is my big idea? What do I really want? What do I believe will actually give me that better life? Where do I go from here?

But, as I have considered this question for myself, I have also found some other authors helpful.

In 2008, I hit 245 lbs. I needed a big idea about weight loss.

Marcelle Pick, in her book, *The Core Balance Diet*, has written an excellent book, (particularly chapters 14 and 15, written by co-author Genevieve Morgan). It's not just a diet book; it's about stress management. In fact, that's its secret. Cope well with stress, get core balance and you will want to eat right and exercise naturally.

I have begun to apply her wisdom. I am now 215 lbs and getting thinner. But, I am still having a hard time reducing stress in my life.

Stanford Neuro-Biologist Robert Sapolsky's ideas about stress are enlightening: he talks about six basic ways all mammals cope with stress and what we can learn from them. Look him up on iTunes and download his talks, or read his book, *Why Zebras Don't Get Ulcers*.

I first heard Dr Sapolsky on iTunes about a year ago, and then listened to him again after reading Marcelle's book. Applying Sapolsky's theories about those six ways mammals handle stress in the wild, I actually came up with a "to do" list for myself along the same lines. I apply it every day as I plan my day.

Just as Marcelle's book addresses the need to handle stress better before you can expect to eat right, so I find that handling stress at the beginning of each day mimicking what baboons do (I write that with a smile on my face, so it's okay for you to smile too), actually makes me more productive!

At mid-life, I had also gotten out of shape.

A great book for core body development echoes the message of the Marcelle Pick book above. It's about physical exercise and is called *Core Performance: The Revolutionary Workout Program to Transform Your Body & Your Life.*

I'm just starting to use it in combination with my new core balance diet. It's hard work, but I find that exercise first thing in the morning mitigates my need for a caffeine wake-up. That's a start that actually helps me eat right the rest of the day, and get a good night's sleep the following night as well.

Getting a divorce, I also needed to get used to the idea of being alone more.

I recently read Byron Katie's *Loving What Is*, about the four essential questions she calls "the work". It's an intriguing recipe for healing one's stressful thoughts! It works very well when you combine her wisdom with Sapolsky's, as I have done.

Katie's "work" actually echoes a method I learned back in 2000 from Sandler Sales Institute's training module on "Enhancing Attitudes, Behaviors and Techniques". Katie has done a much more complete job of describing how it works, however, and adds several new ideas.

Doing Katie's "work", I have found a way now to be alone nights and accept it. It's hard after thirty one years of sharing those nights with a wife, but her methods work without the use of silly affirmations. Instead, I question my negative perceptions and turn them around into the "what is" that I can then love.

Life is much less stressful when you realise that where you are is where you are meant to start. Actually, none of us has any choice.

It's not useful to wish it weren't so, or to say, "if I were rich," or "if I were better looking," or "if I were only smarter!"

You can have everything you need, and much of what you want, but you have to start by loving where you are as the place it starts from. Savour it, enjoy it, and experience it as much as you need to be able to move on.

My Foundation Of Faith And Principles

Beyond helpful books, as I explore my own re-invention, is the contribution of my own core religious faith, the original source of my "unifying principles".

As a Christian in the Roman Catholic tradition, I know the foundation of my faith is best summarised in this quotation from Jesus:

"Love your God with all your heart, soul, mind and strength, and love your neighbour as yourself."

Try diagramming that commandment summary, define the nouns, pronouns, verbs, prepositions, and adjectives and see what you come up with.

Here's my version:

I define "love" (when used as a verb) as "to respect, nurture and celebrate". I define my "God" as "the truth, the life and the way", meaning "what I can discern as the truth, living a full life and trying to do things the best way I know how". I define my "neighbour" as "anyone whose life I can reach out and touch". I define "heart, soul, mind and strength" as "my absolute best effort possible".

Mixing and matching all the parts of the various definitions, I can come up with about a hundred and twenty five permutations, like "Nurture the truth with my absolute best effort possible." Or "Respect everyone whose life I can reach out and touch." Or, "Celebrate my life with everyone I can reach out and touch, *and* with myself." Yes, I need to love my God and neighbour, but how clever of Jesus (or his speechwriter) to remind us that we must also respect, nurture and celebrate ourselves!

Ultimately, I come back to my "Unifying Principles." Everything I read and hear and learn is used to check and re-check my personal life goals implied by my principles; in fact, listed right there with them, as you can see in my "Unifying Principles" list.

In my divorce, I am trying to stay focused on my "primary aim" in life. I am failing to keep my promise to stay married, so how do I explain that to myself, my kids and grandkids? Tough question!

That took, and still takes, a great deal of prayer and tears and thought, believe me. I didn't ask for a divorce lightly. It took me several years of serious consideration of the alternatives. For me, it has been one of those times in life when there are no good choices, only a decision from among bad choices.

So, applying the Gerber E-Myth principles in my business and personal life, Pick's "Core Balance Diet," Sapolsky's mammalian wisdom, Verstegen's "Core Performance" workout, Katie's "work", as well as my own core faith and unifying principles, what can I do to re-invent myself? A lot!

Choose To Be A Creative Force

I can choose, again, to be a creative force. In fact, I have some new opportunities to do so. I can question my perceptions, values and what I care about, and then take responsibility again for choosing what counts that will be consistent with who I am and how I'd like to go – and grow – from here.

I can still reach out to my family and friends, plan and join with them whenever possible, remember their important dates, always be helpful, and be tolerant, especially with those family members still condemning me for choosing to divorce. Time will pass. They may never understand why I am doing what I am doing, but someday they'll realise we can be family once again, I'm sure. We can agree to disagree, especially when we can't really know what's in each other's hearts and minds.

I can treat my ex-wife with great respect and kindness. She isn't expecting much, believe me, especially not right now. Anything good I do will surprise her. There is no selfish advantage to me to do anything more than required, which makes anything I can do above what's required that much more satisfying to me. I will act with charity and kindness because it is the right thing to do.

Yes, my kids and grandkids are watching, so it serves my interest with them to do well by their mother. But, I can also do right things they won't ever know about, and that will be the ultimate test of my character as I look at myself in the mirror.

Another test is my need now to really plan for financial security. How much do I need? Where am I now? What's the gap between where I am now and where I want to be? How do I plan to get there?

These are the questions I have reviewed with hundreds of business owners for thirty years. I never felt the need to do it for myself, but it's never too late. I feel the need to do so now. It's actually part of the Business and Personal Coaching that I provide.

Always Keep Growing

In my business and personal life, I want to keep growing. I can start making a living again if I really "get my act together". I will enjoy a much better life when I do.

As important as my commitment to diet and exercise, I am strengthening my coping mechanisms for stress. I am recommitting myself daily to my unifying principles as well as to my primary aim and mission in my business. I am innovating, quantifying and orchestrating changes in my personal and business systems. I have actually started to get eight hours of sleep again once in a while.

New seminars and webinars about social networking and Internet connectivity are now my weekly digital diet,. I even volunteered to teach the subject nationally to business brokers just to force myself to learn it. I made my first presentation on Web 2.0 in Atlanta in June 2009 and my professional trade association's conference.

Finally, I am re-exploring ways to broaden my spirituality and hold on to hope. Where I once saw darkness on the horizon and worried, I now expect the weather to change to sun again soon. It always does.

Nurturing our personal hope is a human coping mechanism for stress, according to Dr. Sapolsky, a well-known atheist. I often smile to think that, in his work, he has helped me to re-explore my faith. That such an outspoken non-believer would serve to re-kindle my internal flame of faith is exactly the mystery I expect from my God. I may not be able to keep all of my promises, but God's mystery is always there keeping the greatest promise of all – that there is hope for a new day tomorrow. It inspires me to keep trying to improve.

Finally, I am really beginning to "love what is," as Katie writes and speaks about. In addition to loving my God and myself, I also realise I am blessed with all that is around me. For every bad thing one can focus upon, there are many good things. For every reality, there are many viewpoints from which to encounter that reality.

The world may be in turmoil, but we are now talking to each other in real time worldwide for the first time in human history. To me, that holds the promise there is hope.

This is not a recipe for material success, however, just successful personal growth. Choosing to be a creative force and working for continued personal growth are the essentials, at least for me.

As a coach, I am uniquely privileged to listen to others, offer what I know and to serve. In such service, I am a creative force which continues to grow.

Glen J. Cooper

Deirdre Dee

In Sickness And In Health: How Coaching Saved A Marriage

DURING THE SUMMER OF 1997, the corporate event company my husband and I owned was doing very well; we had won a lot of business and, following the August Bank Holiday, we were contracted to organise two large Company Fun Days in Devon for three thousand clients each day. But I was worried about my husband Terry. He seemed preoccupied, had a constant headache, and was obsessed with measuring his blood pressure with a small electronic machine. Two weeks before we were due to travel to the West Country to produce the Company Fun Days, he returned to the office after driving a journalist around a complex teambuilding event. I thought "My God, he looks really ill!" His face was flushed, his eyes looked tiny and strained and I suddenly felt overwhelmed by a sense of foreboding.

Later that day, I asked Terry if he wanted to get away for a break earlier than planned, taking our elder daughter with him. Both our daughters seemed to be following in my theatrical footsteps and attended a theatre school full time. Laura was contracted to the Royal Shakespeare Company and, although only nine years old, had a main part in a West End production of *The Herbal Bed*. We would follow once her show leave started. However, Terry decided to wait until we could all go down together. When we left home, it took us hours to get ready and leave, almost as if we knew that when we returned our lives would have changed irrevocably.

We finally arrived in Cornwall and were disappointed with the holiday home we had rented. It was small and pokey and, as Terry somewhat prophetically remarked when we saw our bedroom, it reminded him of a coffin. The next day was Sunday. We went cycling on the Camel Trail and that evening walked down into Padstow for fish and chips. We climbed back up the hill to our cottage only to discover we had no keys! Terry realised they must have fallen out of his pocket in the restaurant. Taking his bike, he whizzed easily back downhill, retrieved the keys, but then had a very steep ride back up to the cottage. He remembers that his head was pounding, and knew that he was pushing himself to the limits, but he rode on nevertheless.

The following morning was August Bank Holiday Monday and, when Terry brought two cups of tea up, I pulled him into bed beside me. He had been so moody and withdrawn recently, and I thought it was my fault. Perhaps he needed some love and attention. Suddenly, he collapsed on top of me, shaking and jerking and, to my horror, I saw blood trickling from his mouth. I was terrified. I thought he was having a heart attack. Clutching a beach towel around me I ran downstairs to get my mobile; the girls, who had been watching children's TV, realised something was wrong and started to cry.

I ran outside but couldn't get a signal. I ran into the road, stabbing the emergency services number 999 wildly on the mobile and finally getting through. I tried to remember the address of the holiday cottage to tell the operator where we were. She said, "Knock on one of the neighbour's doors while you wait for the ambulance." Still clutching the towel around me, I rang the next door bell at an elderly couple's house. They came immediately; I led them upstairs past the cowering kids and fearfully went into our bedroom, expecting Terry to be dead. He wasn't. The shaking and jerking had stopped, but he was breathing in an awful rasping way, and the blood from his mouth looked frightening. Between myself and the elderly couple, we managed to roll him into recovery position, and I tried to talk to him whilst we waited for the ambulance.

When the ambulance arrived, the paramedics put Terry in a chair and carried him down the narrow cottage stairs and into the ambulance. They told me they would radio for the Devon and Cornwall Air Ambulance to take him to Trelisk Hospital in Truro. I watched the ambulance go and turned back into the house where I became violently sick from the shock. Gathering myself together, I dressed, packed a few things for Terry, collected my daughters, thanked the old couple for their kindness and headed for Truro. During the drive, I managed to get in touch with close relatives to alert them. We found Terry in Accident & Emergency. He had recovered his speech, but was in extraordinary pain from an increasingly blinding and unbearably violent headache. We were shown into a small relative's room and seemed to wait there for hours. Finally a young doctor came in, and told me Terry had had a subarachnoid brain haemorrhage. His condition was extremely serious and he had a one in four chance of survival. He believed Terry might stand a chance if they could get him to the neurosurgical ward in Plymouth.

I wanted to see him. A nurse stayed with the girls while I went to the emergency room. Terry was barely conscious. A consultant anaesthetist, busy with myriad lines and drips, told me that Terry's survival depended on emergency surgery. The helicopter was on its way back and, when it arrived, we followed the stretcher out to where it stood, rotors whirring. Terry was accompanied by the anaesthetist, whose skill we relied on to keep him alive during the flight to Plymouth. Moving away as the rotors roared into life, the helicopter lifted my husband into the air for the second time that day. I wondered if that was the last time we would see him alive. I felt that curious sense of detachment, like watching a TV hospital drama. Loading the kids into the car, I started the drive to Plymouth.

The Worst Was Yet To Come

We arrived in Plymouth. I parked the car on the nearest verge to the Emergency Department and ran inside, quickly learning Terry was still alive but had been taken directly to an operating theatre. We found our way to the neurosurgical ward and went to the nurse's station to ask for news. Apparently Terry had had the emergency procedure and was in recovery. While we waited for him to be admitted to the ward, I gave the staff nurse our details and my husband's previous medical history. I cuddled my daughters and talked to them about the fact that Dad was very ill, and that although he was now in the best place, there was a real possibility he might not make it. People kept asking me if I was ok and I said I was fine.

Being a professional organiser I suppose I then switched to auto pilot. I guess this gave me some sense of remaining in control of a potentially tragic situation. By the time Terry's family and my mother and sister arrived late that evening, I had organised accommodation for them, been in touch with our company production manager and handed over total responsibility for the build up and event management of the Family Day. Little did we know that there was another drama about to unfold that would further cause a dramatic change in our plans.

When Terry returned from Recovery, I left the girls in a small office with a nurse and went to see him. His head was bandaged and he looked very calm and peaceful in his complete unconsciousness. He seemed younger. The lines on his face had almost disappeared and he appeared healthy with a slight flush to his skin. Machines surrounded him, bleeping away, monitoring his breathing, his heart rate and his blood pressure.

During that first evening, I spoke to a young doctor about Terry's condition, which was critical. The implication was that, if my husband survived the night and remained stable, he would be given an MRI scan to identify the exact site of the aneurysm. If it was operable, he would undergo an operation to clip the burst blood vessels. We didn't talk about post-operative infection, nor did we talk about the implications of the stroke and brain damage my husband had sustained, nor the fact that he might survive but be blind. The medic's job was simply to keep him alive for the operation.

On Thursday 26th August 1997, Terry went to the operating theatre for the surgery. The procedure consists of opening the skull and, with the aid of a microscope, the aneurysm is located and a metal clip similar to a clothes peg is used to clip the neck of the aneurysm. As a family we faced a long, anxious wait, not knowing whether he would survive the procedure; he was at risk of suffering another stroke or even a cardiac arrest on the operating table.

Eventually, a young American surgeon, looking absolutely shattered and still in green operating gear, came into the visitor's room asking for me. He was extremely polite and addressed me as Ma'am. He explained that the operation had gone well. Suddenly I was in that TV drama again! It happened that the neurosurgical unit at Derriford had some rather rare arrangement with a hospital in the US, where young surgeons swapped places for several months.

We went in to see Terry and I asked a nurse how long it would be before he woke up. She said in an ideal world, a couple of days as he was going to be kept under heavy sedation to avoid unnecessary movement. Most of the family left the following day. The television was full of footage of Princess Diana's fatal car crash in the Pont d'Alma in Paris. I didn't immediately realise the implications her death would have on our corporate Family Fun days until Alan, our production manager, rang and told me that Princess Diana's funeral had been announced for the coming Saturday. This was the first day of our two major events. The clients were already calling our office in a panic. They asked us how much it would cost to cancel everything, or alternatively to roll the two days into one large day on the Sunday. We agreed on the latter. It was yet another issue I had to deal with and added to an already stressful situation.

Disassociation Leads To A Heavy Dose Of Reality

I come from a line of strong women on both sides of my family and we don't give up easily. When I was told that my husband (if he survived) would never walk, talk or feed himself again, I simply didn't believe it. I think the consultant was offering me the chance to allow Terry to slip away, particularly since he had contracted pneumonia following brain surgery. The rest of the family sat glum faced. I felt annoyed and frustrated and didn't want to hear what they were saying or be a part of the negative mourning process. I left the others and went back to Terry and gave him a good talking to, and even though he didn't respond, I knew he understood what I was telling him.

Imagine my delight and vindication when, a couple of weeks later, as the physiotherapists were working to clear his chest, Terry suddenly said, "Ow, that hurt!" However, I was to pay for my NLP-type dissociation from the real world (being dissociated means watching oneself go through the experience, somewhat like watching a movie of it) when the full impact of what had happened suddenly hit me physically, soon after Terry had turned the corner and I could finally relax my vigilance.

Some five weeks after Terry's brain haemorrhage, we were back home and the last of the major contracts had been completed. I decided that physical exercise was what I needed. I went back to my aerobics class, which I had not attended for a couple of months. I'd been under tremendous pressure and people all around me had been saying how strong I was and how well I was coping. But halfway through the class, something strange happened. I felt like I'd been hit on the head; my vision went really weird. I managed to stagger out of the class into a small ante room where I lay on the floor, expecting the feeling to pass, but it didn't. I ended up in Casualty at the same hospital as Terry. I lay in a cubicle and found I couldn't remember telephone numbers. Eventually I told the nurses where my sister worked, which was very near to the hospital, and she came immediately. I felt sick and had the most severe headache I've ever experienced. As the day wore on, I became anxious about Terry and the girls and discharged myself from Casualty. However, as soon as I appeared on my husband's ward, his consultant re-admitted me and swiftly performed the lumbar puncture, which I had refused to have in Casualty.

The following day I had every other test in the book, from blockage of the carotid arteries to echocardiograms. The effects of the lumbar puncture were very painful. The migraine-like headache persisted and analgesics had little or no effect. Lucy was so upset: when my mother told her I was in hospital too, she sat down on our front door step at home, shivering violently and feeling sick. She wouldn't go to school the next day and my mother brought her in to see me. Laura, who was still playing in the West End, took it very stoically, refusing to talk about it. I was in hospital for three nights. During that time I either pulled on a track suit or, if I was in a dressing gown, I told Terry the nurses had let me stay the night in an adjoining room. I don't think he would have noticed either way -- he was just pleased I was there. Finally, having been examined by a neurologist who diagnosed a severe migraine attack induced by exercise, I was discharged. My mother was angry with me. She said, "This is what happens when you think you're Superwoman!"

A few weeks after this, anxious about the emotional effects this entire trauma might be having on Lucy and Laura, I made an appointment with a therapist we knew well; she thought that the girls seemed okay, but suggested that it might be helpful for me to see a therapist. I think that, on an unconscious level, I was angry with myself for not realising before that Terry's personality wasn't suited to the stresses and strains of event production, whereas I blithely went through life with the show biz conviction that "it would be alright on the night!"

Facing The Future Through Coaching

When I brought Terry back after three months in hospital, he could hardly walk. He was weak and had lost a lot of weight. Christmas was very stressful and Terry and I argued so much that eventually the rest of the family left us to it. By April 1998, the strain was really beginning to tell. Terry was becoming increasingly difficult to live with. He insisted everyone around him was nicer, better, more caring than I and tensions were high. In retrospect, it must have been awful for Lucy and Laura; Terry and I were always at each other's throats. I continued to run the business and we still produced major events, but somehow my heart wasn't in it anymore.

In 2000, three years after Terry's illness, I became interested in self development and trained as a life coach. It helped me to be calmer and more philosophical, not only in dealing with Terry's changed personality, but also in every aspect of life. Suddenly I had techniques to use when impossible arguments flared up. I realised how difficult life had been for our daughters during these explosive quarrels.

During my coach training, in all the "buddy" sessions and pro bono work, I came to realise that coaching really suited my personality and character. A friend of mine once said to me that, above all things, he thought I liked helping people. If that's the case, then I am certainly in the right profession. Clients frequently thank me "for all the help and support" I've given them. I really enjoyed writing case studies for my accreditation and it's great practice for the real world of coaching, especially in corporate contracts where you may have two lines of reporting on how the coaching process is progressing. It was also interesting that some of my "buddies" were training with different organisations and had slightly different approaches, but working with the same basic concepts. One of my first pieces of work was reviewing Laura Berman Fortgang's second book, which I chose because she was the first life coach I ever saw in person and because, with similar theatre backgrounds, I felt a close affinity with her. As well as the transatlantic "laser" coaching session with her, which I talk about further on, I'd also completed a two day workshop with her in London the year before. I really liked her positive can do attitude and I believe my coaching style is similar. My clients have described me as "positive and inspirational".

The Building Blocks Of The Future

On a cold February day, sometime after concluding my coach training, I walked along the beach of a small Northern French resort, wrapped up against the bitter wind, my thoughts with my daughters and my husband back in England. I'd come for a break; to "mourn the package" and to stop "spinning my wheels", as

Laura Berman Fortgang had suggested. "Take the good things that remain and use those as building blocks for the future," she had said. But now that I was here, it didn't seem so easy. It was the first time I had been alone for years. When Terry became disabled, I had to cope with the shock and anger that such a traumatic life experience brings with it and the initial estrangement of our daughters from their father, who had returned from hospital a different man from the father they had known and loved, as well as the struggle to keep our event business going. Indisputably, I was now on my own in terms of bringing in the finances, as well as being the rock upon which the family stood.

Realisation dawned. I hated our events business. I couldn't do it anymore. Terry had continually blamed his illness on "my business" and I had taken so much flak from him about it that now I hated it too. All the fight and abundant energy I'd always had seemed to have deserted me. My intuition said, "Wake up! Do something, and do it now!" This is one of my favourite coaching axioms. I told myself, "You have a disabled husband, two girls to finance through university and a large mortgage to pay. You've lost interest in the events business. You're paralysed, caught like a rabbit in the glare of a car's headlights, that prescient moment before death or survival. The ball is in your court. Understand that you *can* change your situation! Stop giving away your power to everyone else, take it back now!"

And that is exactly what I did. We decided to sell the house and relocate; buying somewhere outright so there would be no more pressure of mortgage repayments. I've always been attracted to the concept of lifelong learning and continuous self development.

"The instant we set our intention on what
we could be instead of want we want to avoid,
we embark on a spiritual adventure."

DR WAYNE DYER

I kept this theory in mind when looking for our new house. Right at the start I wrote the following positive description: "It will be near sea or water. Quiet, restful, plants and trees all around us. A haven, a respite, a place where the soul can expand and flow. It will be beautiful and uplifting, pleasing to the eye and ear, inspirational to the spirit. Away from the hustle, a sanctuary, soothing and calming." We put our house on the market and started looking for the house that fitted this description.

This was a time of great change. Lucy went to Australia at the end of her first year at University. She'd changed, grown more independent, become a woman rather than a child. My little birds were flying the nest. When change comes, we need to assimilate it, not fight it. We need to talk about our feelings. Change is good, stimulating and challenging if you embrace it. Go forward to meet it, with no regret, just a passing nostalgia for the good times enjoyed. I wish I had known this earlier as it would have helped in the first years of Terry's illness and long recovery, but I now acknowledge these times as part of life, best remembered with gratitude. They are part of the sum total of who we are now. As soon as you begin to cultivate "an attitude of gratitude", life looks fantastic.

Coming Home

One day in September, we found our new home, River Cottage. It stands in a designated Area of Outstanding Natural Beauty. The cottage ticks virtually every box I visualised when we first started thinking about where we would like to live. A riverside walk owned by the National Trust leads you to the seafront in ten minutes and there are coastal paths at each end of the town, winding up the red cliffs that form the World Heritage Jurassic coastline.

Although I am not one to look back, (something I don't encourage my coaching clients to do), I have occasionally wondered what our life would have been like if Terry had not become ill. We may well have carried on building up the business and eventually sold it and moved on, perhaps to something different. Perhaps something that Terry would have been more comfortable with. I might never have heard about coaching, much less trained as a coach, thereby missing out on the path to lifelong self development. I would have missed the unique relationship and the profound insights that a coaching relationship allows. As for our daughters, now grown up, confident and intelligent young women, (maybe because they have experienced how illness, disability and stress affect the family dynamic), it will give them a unique understanding as they go through life and eventually have families of their own.

Finally, Terry and I have forgiven ourselves and come to respect each other more through our experiences. Our family survived, where many others don't in the same circumstances and I believe that this was largely due to the fact that I discovered self development through coaching. I feel immensely privileged to be a coach and to be able to help people through challenging moments in their lives and in turn to receive back from every client I coach new insights that help me become better at my job. Terry remembers that I was trembling when I took my marriage vows. Perhaps it was because at that moment I understood that I was embarking on the next stage of my life and the nature of what I was promising to do when I said those time honoured words and promised to love and to honour my husband in "sickness and in health".

Karen Skehel

Building A Coaching And Supervision Business – An Innovative Way

What Attracted Me To Coaching

AFTER TWENTY FIVE YEARS IN MARKETING, culminating in my own marketing services business, I was ready for a change. Becoming a mother coincided with me taking some time off. I used some of this time to undertake a counseling training: a course I took, not because I was considering counseling as a career, but primarily to enhance my listening skills. Like so many others, my self esteem was not where I would have liked it to be at that time in my life, so I undertook training in assertiveness skills as a strategy for helping me with self esteem. I took away many skills which would help me going forward.

A close friend suggested we take a course in personal development which evolved into a Diploma in Group Facilitation. We learnt various psychological models which were to stand me in good stead with my coaching practice. Transactional Analysis and other emotional intelligence models were an intrinsic part of the course. I mixed my studies with parenting: first one son and then a second son.

Following the birth of my second son, I moved my focus entirely from the business of marketing to the world of personal development. Using the training with which I had started, I began designing, facilitating and marketing seminars in educational settings and charity environments as well as those that were open to the public. At that time personal development was in its infancy, and attracting participants in sufficient numbers was a real challenge.

A close friend who had become a coach suggested the euro-coach list as a place where I could advertise my programmes. I joined with the intention of finding a few course participants, which I did. At the same time, there were a few new coaches on the scene who wanted "guinea pig" clients. I offered myself to a few of them in sequence. Not long after, it became clear that a career focused entirely on facilitating was not right for me. It was time to go for something different.

I found myself resisting being a coach at this time. Having undertaken so much personal development work over the years, my self awareness levels were high and I knew myself well enough to recognise that what I resist doing is a clue to where I need to go (and even today I offer the feeling of resistance as a clue for clients on where they need to go to). This insight sent me down the pathway of coaching as a profession. I learned some of the rudiments of coaching through listening to some coaching tapes.

My next step was to practise with some fellow coaches. I asked myself whether I needed formal training, or would my extensive travels down the road of personal development suffice? I decided to put my coaching skills to the test by offering my services on a pro bono basis to a few clients. I remember my fear before my first coaching clients telephoned for their first coaching sessions.

I was both delighted and amazed by my abilities to coach. At this point I was working my own methodology and my clients were coming back for more. Not only were they happy with free coaching, but most of them signed up for fee based coaching after their pro bono coaching trial had concluded.

I keep a record of all my client testimonials -- this is my very first testimonial from a fellow coach who was my first client:

"This coaching did change my life. I now totally believe in myself – your encouragement helped me enormously. I think you are brilliant. I am energised and on my way. Thank you very much for unblocking me and empowering me to be the me I always knew I could be."

Isn't it interesting that belief in one another goes both ways? As coaches, we serve our clients well when we believe in them. As well, our clients encourage us to step up ever higher by believing in us and holding us in high esteem. This is something I have experienced repeatedly in my journey as a coach and coaching supervisor.

Following my work with my first few coaching clients, I finally saw my future: I was born to coach. Yet, as someone who strives for excellence, I wanted to take my coaching to the next level. I undertook a foundation course in coaching. My coaching improved. So I followed it up with an advanced coach training course and my coaching improved again. The more training I undertook, the better my coaching became, the better results I facilitated for my clients and the more my confidence grew.

Creative Marketing

Whilst today coaches are encouraged to find a niche, when I first started coaching, niche marketing wasn't widespread. Coaches were either focused on Executive Coaching, Business Coaching or Life Coaching. At that time I didn't niche at all. I offered coaching tailor made to the needs of each client. My clients were a mixture of some business clients and personal clients who wanted to achieve the more popular things such as meeting a partner, losing weight, finding work they loved... Some wanted to achieve some particularly inspiring, very specific things such as "introduce tennis to underprivileged kids", and "make a real difference to a worthwhile cause". I helped many coaches with various areas of their lives as well as providing insights and experience to help them build their businesses, drawing on my twenty five plus years in marketing: it was a world I knew well and enjoyed and I could help them with theirs.

Early on, I adopted the idea that it would be easy to attract clients given my background and learned skills, and my experience bore out my belief.

Although a marketer by trade, I never had a marketing plan as such. Not because I don't support the usefulness of a marketing plan, but because for me it feels rigid and limiting. I have a marketing menu – which I add to constantly. It feels fluid. I take action according to where I am most drawn. Here are some of the things that worked for me early on:

- Exhibiting at a holistic trade show, and following up with everyone I met.
- Attending a course on networking designed for people in the creative industries.
- Bartering: I piggybacked onto a mailing that went to 1000 creatives - seeking out the services of a leaflet designer and PR executive in exchange for coaching services. This brought me additional enquiries and clients.
- Speaking at the "Festival of Holistic Living"

These activities worked for me because the audiences in each case were like-minded people, interested in holistic activities or creatives.

I Chose One Niche... But Another Chose Me

I did begin looking at one niche area as an addition to my core, non niche business.

Relationship Coaching stood out as an obvious area for me to develop alongside my existing business because:

- I was very qualified: I had trained as a counsellor, and had spent years as both a student and facilitator of emotional intelligence programmes.
- It as an easy market to reach.
- Whilst now I live with my life partner, I had been single for seven years following an acrimonious divorce, so I knew personally the challenges faced by singles.
- At that time, I had been more blocked than ninety percent of my clients, had tried many different approaches to healing these blocks to love – so I had plenty of personal experience to bring to this type of coaching.
- The singles market is huge: in the US, more than sixty percent of people are currently unattached and there is a similar story in the UK.
- As far as I could see, at the time, few other coaches were addressing this market (I know I am at my best when I don't feel I am competing).

Because of my marketing background, I tend to think in strategic alliances, as I spent many years putting together strategic alliances for big name brands.

Here are some of the strategic alliances I put together to enhance my relationship coaching business:

- I picked up clients through an alliance with a dating agency
- I took a team of relationship coaches to "Chemistry", an event with 1,500 singles, said to be the most successful singles event ever and the largest event of its kind. I created the

concept of dating challenges, whereby we invited singles to participate in a personalised dating challenge and report on how they got on. We offered on the spot coaching and gave out coaching gift vouchers. I came away with seven coaching clients, six of whom also had businesses, which gave them a second reason to try coaching.

- At "Chemistry" I met the MD of another events company for singles. He invited me to run singles workshops at his events, and the concept "How to get the most out of a singles event" workshop was born. We followed this up with a joint promotion at the National Gallery. At the "evening of romance" we offered more "on the spot" coaching, and ran a free prize draw to win coaching sessions.

Each of these concepts generated clients.

I thrive on change and variety. I am at my best when working in a new coaching area. I love developing a new marketing initiative and making it happen. Innovation in both marketing and coaching is what inspires me and what I feel passionate about. In my experience, "passion is both catching and enrolling". When I am excited about something, things happen. If change, variety and innovation weren't so important to me, then I suspect I would stick with relationships as a niche, but I choose to focus my energies more widely.

Naturally, then, it wasn't long before I found another niche – this time, the niche chose me.

We all have natural gifts and one of mine is the ability to heal. A number of years earlier I had trained in Reiki, which gave me a taste of my ability to heal. With Healing Coaching, I tended to harness the power of the mind and in particular the higher mind, or spiritual mind, to transform health issues. At this time, I attracted many clients who had pressing health issues they wanted to overcome and hadn't been able to through the medical or complementary therapy world.

For example:

I had a client who overcame tendonitis, which meant not only that she no longer suffers from debilitating pain, but also that she could continue her tennis coaching. She went on to start an initiative bringing underprivileged kids off the streets to play. I coached a client to overcome chronic and severe insomnia. I had a client with an immune system breakdown. She suffered from laryngitis, pneumonia, arthritis, more often than not one after the other. Neither conventional medicine nor alternative therapy could make a difference. It was the largely spiritual work we did that took her from being a constantly ill person to a constantly well person. This piece of coaching became a detailed case study which resulted in a four year contract writing for *Natural Health* magazine. I gained many inspiring clients from this alliance. You can read this case study at *www.wow-coaching.co.uk/joannestory.html*

In the healing phase of my coaching work I had a client with secondary bone cancer. The prognosis was grim and yet this client's goal was to be one hundred percent healthy. Before we started working together she was in constant pain and often unable to get up. She had been ill for more than a year. As the coaching progressed, she had no pain. She was able to do Pilates moves she hadn't done for a year. She shrank her tumour herself using visualisation processes that we devised together.

At that time, I considered Healing Coaching one of my niches – yet it is one that I choose not to fully market in a highly proactive way. I let the "law of attraction" take effect. Why would I choose to do this? Because I believe people initially came to me with other goals in mind: to build their businesses, or find a partner. One of the laws of success that I hold dear to as a coach is the law of detachment: have the desire but do not be attached to the outcome.

In this case, they had the desire to be healed but were not expecting their coach to help them heal (after all, it isn't what coaches do). I have no doubt that this thinking facilitated their positive outcomes.

Working with a supervisee today, I am reminded that having high expectations rarely serves us. My supervisee wanted to be an excellent coach all the time, and was beating herself up for two occasions where she felt her performance was below par. My asking her what an excellent coach does led to a comparison with the performance of an award winning gymnast. Whilst mostly they move with grace and flow, there are occasions when they fall off the beam and the same can be said for coaches of excellence. This was a great insight for my supervisee and allowed her to have more realistic expectations of herself.

From Healing To Business

In the early days, Business Coaching accounted for only a smallish percentage of my business. Lady Luck stepped in at a networking event in the form of a woman who introduced me to a source of funding for small businesses. I have always enjoyed the mixture of Business and Personal Coaching under one roof, believing coaching works best this way, but until this time hadn't made this niche my focus. My many years in sales and marketing prior to coaching provided plenty of experience to draw upon, experience that would prove valuable to clients and add to my credentials. I moved more strongly into what I describe as the bread and butter of coaching: Business Related Coaching. I learnt to facilitate results in the areas of Leadership Coaching – time management, managing stress, building confidence – so that I could serve all manner of business clients on their wide ranging business and personal needs. Although I was already quite savvy, Business Coaching training helped me further raise my game.

I created reader offers and partnerships with trade associations. I spoke at industry events, ran workshops and attended trade shows. I followed up by email and by telephone. I did the work myself to start and then engaged the help of an administrative and marketing assistant. All these activities brought me clients. Most of the clients I work with today are SME's; many are in the creative industries or are creative leaders working in award winning businesses across wide ranging sectors: recruitment, architecture, retail, hospitality, the media, marketing services, manufacturing, sports and leisure, AV, the professions and many miscellaneous sectors. They chose me as their coach because I offer transformational coaching that impacts their success in both their business and personal lives.

Today I earn four times an hour more than I was earning from coaching back in 2001. Why is this important, beside the obvious fact that I am earning more money? Partly because I can now earn more while working with fewer clients. Even more importantly, public perception of me as a sought after coach is enhanced. There is no doubt in my mind that coaches who charge less are often perceived as less competent. It's human nature.

Whilst my highest fees are at the higher end of the fee scale, my personal philosophy is to support clients, and particularly my supervision clients, to work with me at fees that stretch them but are appropriate to their financial circumstances. (We'll talk about supervision clients in a moment.) My mission is to make supervision in particular as accessible as possible to as many supervisees as possible who are drawn to work with me. Hence my supervision rates are very affordable for self funding coaches.

I'd coached in many areas. I had undertaken foundation and advanced trainings, helping me with both personal and business clients. My need for change and variety hadn't gone away. What could be next for me?

Supervision – The Next Big Thing

It was some six years after I started coaching before I discovered the value and usefulness of supervision. Supervision in the "helping" professions is an opportunity for the practitioner to explore and reflect on their work and on their development with the help of a qualified supervisor. Although supervision is strongly recommended, if not mandatory, for counsellors, very few coaches I knew were in supervision in 2001. For the first few years of coaching, whenever I had a client challenge I turned to one of my mentors for input. I *was* lucky. I had some great peer mentoring from all around the world. I didn't need supervision, or so I thought. It took until 2007 for me to discover that whilst I didn't necessarily *need* it, supervision was going to be of serious benefit to me and I could have enhanced my practice if I had come to it earlier.

So what changed my mind about introducing supervision into my own practice? I was turned down as an associate by one of the top providers of coaching worldwide. In spite of being highly recommended by one of the HR Directors of Glaxo Smith Kline (a client who found me through my writing for *Natural Health* magazine) and other impressive credentials I possessed, they were not at all impressed that I was coaching without supervision. Peer mentoring didn't count at all. They saw coaching without supervision as downright unprofessional.

Both being professional and being seen as professional was always important to me, so I tried out supervision to see if it was really worthwhile. Very quickly I saw how the multi-dimensional aspect of supervision was not only much more effective for the work I was doing with clients but, at the same time, it was extraordinarily effective for my own personal development.

Today I am converted to the value of supervision, and I wouldn't want to be without it. So much so that, after more than eight years of coaching my clients, I undertook a Diploma in Coaching Supervision in 2008 including:

- Supervising a number of Executive Coaches
- Working in monthly triads
- Working with my own supervisor and tutor
- Writing a case study
- Completing a learning journal

This was another step up the ladder to building my skills through further training.

Not only has supervision helped me enhance my coaching across the board, it has given me some of my most valuable insights which have supported me with my own personal development. One of the reasons supervision is so valuable is that it is designed to serve the supervisee on so many different levels, as well as their clients.

Having a supervisor say something about your professionalism as a coach is mandatory if you want to work with some organisations and can add so much to your own personal and professional development. I have found supervision to be an effective way of taking my own coaching to a deeper level and can be a useful additional option to the more practical mentoring option which, while beneficial in its own way, does not offer the more wide ranging and transformational insights.

Simply put, I love working with coaches as a supervisor, because:

- I have always enjoyed working multi-dimensionally, looking at what's going on from multiple perspectives. Supervision gives me the opportunity to do this (whether I am the supervisee or the supervisor).
- I enjoy the collegiate relationships with supervisees – we are both coaches and bringing our joint expertise and experience to the table.
- The process challenges me to function at my best: it's an unusual combination of fun and transformation.
- Supervisees work on their own personal development whilst addressing the client challenges that arise.

- I call supervision "coaching in Technicolor" as it is a rich, vibrant, insight-facilitating series of conversations that must be experienced in order to be appreciated.

Where I Am Today

Today I am actively involved with informing and educating coaches about the value of supervision, what it is, and how they can benefit. Although many coaches do understand the value and usefulness of supervision, many more do not. My mission is to raise the profile of supervision amongst coaches and coachees. I wanted, therefore, to create a forum for coaching supervisors and make coaching supervision accessible and attractive to all coaches. With this vision in mind, the Association of Coaching Supervisors was born.

A coach's story is never finished. I am finding myself in a very creative phase of my own coach's journey with many concepts in the early stages of their development.

As well as creating the Association of Coaching Supervisors, a Toastmasters style public speaking group for coaches is on the drawing board, and I have invested in learning how to develop a membership site/coaching gym which I can expand into numerous niches.

I also have plans on the drawing board to lead and teach Mindfulness Meditation Groups. Mindfulness is particularly relevant for coaches because being in the present moment whilst coaching is key to effective coaching. Not only that, but the practice of Mindfulness is both extraordinarily simple and extraordinarily effective in enhancing mood, relieving depression and anxiety, reducing stress and increasing wellbeing.

I also plan to offer a dance and movement based therapeutic process to serve the personal needs of clients who could benefit from "healing the blocks to love"; something so important for wounded singles and couples in hollow relationships to restore intimacy. This dance and movement based process is very powerful for facilitating nurturing, healing and love. In fact, this method is so powerful and effective, I cannot *not* offer it to the world. I feel sure that counsellors, alternative therapists, clients going through difficult transitions such as divorce and fellow coaches will be amongst those who will benefit.

Whilst some may recommend focusing on one thing at a time as the pathway to success, the opposite strategy works for me. Let me explain why. Firstly, having several projects on the go at any one time satisfies my need for change and variety. Secondly, it supports the law of detachment (Deepak Chopra's *Seven Spiritual Laws of Success*). A single project can lead to attachment and create unnecessary pressure – What if that project doesn't work out? – whereas multiple projects create a feeling of liberation and multiple possibilities for me. If you resonate with this thinking, you may find the multiple project process works for you too. Don't be afraid to try it. To do it successfully you'll need to collaborate and delegate effectively. We know multiple streams of focus can work. Look at the businesses created by Richard Branson and many of the *Dragon's Den* entrepreneurs. It is only right for certain types of personalities. You'll know if it is effective for you as you monitor the outcomes you create.

The theme of my coaching story is ongoing creativity. My passion is ignited most when I am into new areas, developing new ideas, many of which will see the light of day sooner or later. Some of my ideas are new. Others are repackaged versions of areas I have worked in before. It is being innovative and creative (alongside making a difference) that drives me forward more than anything. If you have a similar personality, you may enjoy following a similar path to success.

Whilst I have always been creative, in 2009 I shifted into a higher gear. The catalyst for this highly creative phase was a new creativity coach/energy worker/supervisor who supported me in my own personal and professional development in a way I have never known before. She had the ability to see a side of me no one before had seen. She invited me to "shine my light" by seeing me as a "very bright light, all beautiful and sparkly". As she read my energy field over the ether, I was moved to tears. Her steadfast belief in me and her ability to see me as an extraordinary being helped me shift my lingering doubts and fears in a way that feels totally sustainable. She helped me connect with my own "amazing-ness" and inspired me to help other coaches to connect with their own amazing qualities. It is from this place that I go out into the world in my work as a creative coach for entrepreneurs and entrepreneurial-style businesses, a creative supervisor for coaches and a creator of holistic solutions of benefit to many.

How Does My Story Help You?

The secret to successful coaching is to easily and effortlessly attract clients that are right for you and to be an extraordinary facilitator of results. My recommendation to you is to open yourself up to this possibility. You *can* attract clients easily and effortlessly. You *are* a great facilitator of results. Be tenacious, and be willing to step outside your comfort zone. Most of all, be authentic. Trust that you will attract an abundance of clients and that you will serve them well – and you will. Feel, see and experience each day of your journey as joyful and fun.

Don't go on this journey alone. Build a support network to assist you along the way. Take on a coaching supervisor who authentically holds a bright light for you: someone who will really support you in your personal development work and in your client work. Choose someone who sees the brilliance and "amazing-ness" in you, as my own supervisor does for me and as I do for my own clients.

I'd like to finish my story by telling you more about the "You Are Amazing" theme I introduced to coaches at the 2009 Euro-coach Conference in my role as Chairman. I told the audience, "Along with the other 'helping' professions, we are amongst the world's biggest catalysts for transformational change." Maybe I am biased. Although we are probably the newest group of "helpers", we are perhaps the most significant and most influential. I say this because we empower many of the word's leaders: captains of industry, leading politicians, and many well know names in the media.

This is how I see it: the more each of us steps into the brilliance of who we are overall and, in particular, as coaches, facilitators of change, or however you wish to refer to yourself, the more we serve the world. The more brilliant you are, and the more you see your own brilliance, the more you will experience extraordinary results in your clients and in their worlds and the more encouraged you will be to step up – to both market yourself and attract clients to you. By doing so, you will impact the lives of others in a meaningful way that ultimately impacts our world.

Malcolm Nicholson

Who Really Has The Best Job?

"Experience; that most brutal of teachers.
But you learn. My God do you learn."

C.S. LEWIS

WHEN I WAS ASKED TO CO-AUTHOR *A Coach's Story*, I began to take stock of my career as a Business and Executive Coach. It came as a bit of a surprise to realise I've been coaching for over ten years now. It made me pause, just for a while. Looking back it occurred to me that almost all the talented and successful leaders I've been fortunate to work with share one thing in common. They believe they have the best job in the world. And I have to agree with them, they do. They have the best job that suits them. Just like me. I have the best job in the world too – the best job in the world that suits *me*. But that doesn't mean I can't improve, any more than those who I have been fortunate to coach. This is what makes my job so exciting: helping others fulfil their potential and, as I have come to discover, it has helped me along that same path too. That's quite a perk and, for me, bigger than any banker's bonus.

Coaching is a business, a vocation and a continuous journey.

For example, I have spoken to and interviewed quite a few well known personalities. I was lucky enough to have a brief conversation with the late J.G. Ballard, the British author. His most acclaimed novel was *Empire of the Sun*, based on his childhood in a Japanese prison camp in China and made into a film by Steven Spielberg. When I said that I felt he'd had an extraordinary life, he replied, "No, *you* have. If you look at your generation and the period of relative peace and prosperity the western world has experienced over the last fifty years, it hasn't occurred before in history, nor is it happening around the world now. So I haven't had a remarkable life, you have." That was a truly profound moment, and gave a great sense of perspective, particularly to my own journey.

Part of my journey has been about delivering excellent coaching in an intuitive and apparently effortless manner. There is a wonderful description of jazz as "music of the moment" which I think also applies to the art of coaching. In his cover notes to the best selling Miles Davis *Kind of Blue* album, pianist Bill Evans describes *"... a Japanese visual art in which the artist is forced to be spontaneous. He must paint on a thin stretched parchment... in such a way that an unnatural or interrupted stroke will destroy the line or break through the parchment... These artists must practise a particular discipline, that of allowing the idea to express itself in communication with their hands in such a direct way that deliberation cannot interfere."*

He also refers to the "severe and unique disciplines" of jazz, which I feel also applies to coaching; that is to say, developing a robust kitbag of tools and techniques, getting them firmly engrained in the subconscious and then intuitively deciding what to use in the moment. This is an important and ongoing learning, and key to delivering excellent coaching.

The Bitter Sweet Music Of Discovery

Born in South Wales, educated at Cardiff University, where I earned a BSc in Occupational Psychology, I have apparently now reached my mid- fifties, much to my surprise. I've always been extremely interested in both rugby and jazz and started playing the trumpet and flugel horn at school. I played in jazz clubs in Cardiff and my brother and I ran our own ten piece band during my early and mid twenties.

Music would have been my first choice career, as our band achieved some notable successes with a record contract signed and pending. However, in my mid-twenties I began getting electric shock-like pains along the side of my face, triggered by vibration around my mouth. I had a condition called Trigeminal Neuralgia, which generally strikes people in their sixties. A consultant asked me to describe the pain. The nearest I could get was, "It's like ten million volts and a red hot knife being stuck in the side of my face." It certainly taught me how to cope with severe pain. For a number of years, I took a strong medication that quietens nerve impulses, consequently spending this time in a semi-dreamlike state whilst attempting to convince the outside world I was razor sharp and capable of holding down a responsible job. After a number of minor operations, I finally had a more major operation: a hole drilled in my skull to move blood vessels on the surface of the brain away from the nerve.

By this time, I had moved location, met my wife and resumed playing rugby, so the urge to take up music again on a professional or semi pro basis had passed me by...

After graduation, I had followed the urgings of my parents to "get a proper job" and started work by day as a Personnel Officer in a manufacturing plant near Cardiff Docks, in an area known as Tiger Bay, a truly diverse but tough neighbourhood (Hayley Mills had starred in a film named after the area in 1959). Now, it doesn't take a great flight of imagination to realise that, for a slightly green graduate, this sort of environment was indeed the School of Hard Knocks. Literally and metaphorically I needed stitches on my forehead after I had to tell a drunken applicant he didn't get the job. On another occasion, I found a brown envelope on my desk stuffed with ten pound notes after I was requested to hire someone's cousin. Returning the money to its source is a story in itself.

My next role was in what I imagined would be slightly more sophisticated surroundings – the regional newspaper head office. In many ways it was, except that I arrived on my first day to industrial action and unwittingly crossed a picket line, which seemed to involve an excessive amount of spitting on behalf of the pickets – entirely in my direction!

From newspapers I moved to the music industry, working with a major record label in London for a number of years. A great fun environment when I started, it had turned ruthless by the time I left. Spells in broadcasting equipment and then IT followed, until I joined Northern Telecom and was recruited into a new UK Channel Sales team. This gave a new lease on life to my career – it seemed like I was being paid to stand up in front of teams of sales people and entertain them. Whilst it wasn't so one dimensional, it was without the assortment of bin-end issues I'd been used to dealing with when in HR. During my first year review, my boss said, "Malcolm, I bet you wish you had done this ten years ago." This was spot on. I was able to travel extensively, initially in the UK and then abroad, and got a pretty good track record of exceeding my targets.

I was promoted several times and had reached Divisional Director in an operating subsidiary, when I realised that future promotions were likely to be office based and political, neither of which played to my strengths.

I started to think about my next move. I was working at that time with an Executive Coach, who asked the classic, "Here's a blank piece of paper. What would you like to be doing?" question. I replied that I'd like to be doing what he was doing; my transition into coaching had begun.

There were several key factors that influenced my decision to go into coaching:

- It provided an opportunity to be in control of my own destiny to a far greater extent than a corporate role.
- My corporate roles involved UK or international travel, long hours and excessive time away from home. Changing family circumstances meant this was becoming intrusive and I didn't want to continue with it.
- Psychometric assessments all show that the need for balance in my life is quite high. Not that I don't work hard – just that other things are important too.
- The coaching product and its outputs felt far more significant to me than providing a particular bit of telephony equipment, the benefits which seemed far more abstract and remote. The ability to actually help someone develop seemed far more appealing.
- It dovetailed into my only regret; that I didn't go into medicine. If I wasn't getting people back up on their feet literally, perhaps I could do it metaphorically. My children sometimes call me The Doctor, as I'll be the one who gives a poor man's assessment of any ailment and do the simple first aid treatment!
- I was also aware from my sports experience that when captain or vice captain I enjoyed getting the best out of people – what I would now refer to as engaging their discretionary effort.

So coaching seemed to tick a number of boxes regarding the way ahead. I realised there was the potential to get a tremendous sense of purpose from such a career. I have felt, occasionally, , that with my interest in contemporary history and desire to do something on a bigger stage, I could have been involved in international politics, but the realisation that I wanted to have an impact in the world came too late to me, so the ability to get individuals past a stuck state and see them fulfill their potential and flourish, seemed a good way forward.

Bagpipes, Memories And Experience

Transitioning into coaching was a steep learning curve. This involved both experiential and book-based learning; I was constantly reading coaching related material, spiced up with some formal training during my first couple of years.

I continued to work with my coach during the early period, but soon realised there were differences in our approaches, so I tended to plough my own furrow independently.

The reliance on experiential learning did give me some interesting moments. For example, I had specifically booked a hotel suite to do some relaxation and visualisation work with an individual. When I arrived, I noticed a number of people in kilts – not unusual in say, Edinburgh, but slightly out of the norm in Hampton, Middlesex. I asked the receptionist what was happening and she announced proudly, "We're hosting the British Bagpipe Championship this weekend!" The session was punctuated by the discordant drone of nervous pipers warming up whilst pacing the corridors.

In my early years there were numerous occasions when people were "putting the cheque in the post", never to be seen or heard of again. I soon worked out how to stop that. Other memorable experiences include:

- The Breakfast Briefing when delegates were arriving and I couldn't get my holiday photos off the screen.
- Getting dressed in the dark whilst everyone else in the house was asleep and arriving at my early morning presentation to realise I had dressed in non-matching cord trousers and a suit jacket.
- The alpha male client who threatened to punch me.
- The alpha female client who sacked me.
- A dramatic midnight phone call from a team member on a two day offsite team build, who wanted to opt out.
- Explaining to a hotel manager exactly why there were groups of people cooking omelettes on hexi blocks in his immaculate gardens (I hadn't got his prior permission).
- Two clients turning up at the door at the same time.

- Asking some sports academy kids the wrong question so they all reply "I want to be Champion" and recovering that situation.
- What to do with a cheque for £46,000 that arrived un-invoiced, (Don't worry. I sent it back.)

So yes, there were some great experiences during that period, when there wasn't the support infrastructure available that there is now for new coaches. Any coach starting their business today will doubtless experience similar events and for those who don't have a great deal of business experience, I would recommend working with an organisation or coach with business acumen who can steer you through business critical situations.

I think it's fair to say that qualifying *per se* didn't have a direct impact on me or create a major step change,

I was still playing rugby, albeit a somewhat slower but still competitive veteran's game and I applied a couple of the techniques I'd learnt in Sports Psychology Coaching. I immediately wished that someone had shown me this stuff when I was growing up – not just for rugby, but all areas of my life. This was a massive learning point for me; it's amazing how a couple of good old pragmatic examples from the real world, where my muscles were giving me immediate feedback, opened my eyes to the real possibilities of coaching.

What followed was a massive shift, not just as I bought into the potential power of coaching at a coach's level, but also at a personal level. I started everything For my recently married wife, starting a new home in a new house, this must have been a most bewildering time; I'm eternally grateful to Elaine for coping with me.

The Business And Art Of Coaching

As Norman Schwartzkopf said, "You can't help someone up a hill without getting closer to the top yourself."

The pressures which accompany running your own coaching business are different to those of delivering coaching. The three areas essential to a successful coaching business are administration, new business development and delivery.

Let's look at it from a business perspective to start with.

Business results can revolve around the things you *don't* do as much as the things you do. For example, my administration is second to none; third or fourth maybe. So I have help with my administration to enable me to play to my strengths. Also, the need to focus on running your business professionally is crucial. I'm lucky enough to have a good friend who is a corporate director who, for the princely fee of a glass or two of wine, gives me half an hour every month to review a set of (rudimentary) accounts and activity logs. I work on the basis that every business client I work with is either on, or has, a board, so why shouldn't I if it will add value to my efforts? And I can assure you that the threat of having this favour withdrawn or a withering verbal broadside to commitments unfulfilled is enough to keep me on the straight and narrow.

The major focus is, as for any business, revenue stream. Even now, it's a monthly cycle of building the pipeline, getting revenue and making sure there aren't too many weeks in the month for the salary available. We enjoy a wonderful home, which we set up based on quite a high income requirement (I've always believed there is no reason coaching should be a step down in revenue or hand to mouth), and keeping a five bedroom Edwardian property with half an acre of ground in the outskirts of Greater London is a high revenue requirement. So focusing on business development is crucial.

The upsides to running a coaching business revolve around immediacy (e.g. the ability to implement a policy change instantly) and a complete sense of ownership. Whilst the lows are certainly lower, so are the highs higher, and I experience far more of a deep seated buzz than I would working for someone else's organisation. I'm meeting some great people, including the sports people I've worked with, along the way.

I think it is important to be able to present to potential clients some idea of what they will be getting for their money – after all, it is a financial investment they are making that could be used in many different ways. So I have developed a set of testimonials which include actual or estimated ROI (Return on Investment) figures. This, combined with published figures like the Manchester Group's report, provide a compelling case for those potential clients new to coaching.

Now let's look at the coaching element.

Experiential learning and the odd grey hair do have advantages, as I am nowadays rarely overawed by coaching situations.

I do get tremendous satisfaction from enabling clients to achieve genuinely life changing coaching outcomes – and I am determined to keep developing my skills to be able to intrigue and delight clients for years to come. I continue to work with the other member of my board, my new coach, to make sure I'm on top of my game. He keeps reminding me to be inspirational to clients and that boldness is a greatly underrated approach.

I am highly focused on the need to do a good job which, whilst a strength, can become a weakness when I take too much responsibility in a coaching session or programme, or I become too empathetic and extend the coaching beyond the budgeted amount. Everything has a perceived value.

Whilst W.C. Fields said "Never work with children or animals," I do employ a coaching approach with our children, especially to help them develop a bit more independence of thought. Our eldest, Sam, famously once said to me, "Never mind all that! Tell me what you want me to do!"

So how has it affected me, the core, the individual?

Coaching tends to permeate your thinking and approach to many, many things. A couple of years ago while on holiday in Cornwall, I got pains in my chest after jogging. I eventually went to the local Accident and Emergency Hospital. The consultant said that I may have torn an artery from the heart and then promptly left. After cursing my bad luck, the phrase, "Play the cards you're dealt" popped into my head. So I sat next to myself in the hospital bed and 'we' went through a range of questions and answers and formulated various options going forward, depending on the prognosis. It gave me an insight as to how much coaching had permeated my thinking.

I find that some of the most consistently useful tools for myself are visualisation, both tactical and long term (: focusing on controlling the controllables and seeing from both another and a broader perspective. I was extremely impressed by Tommy Hilfiger when I interviewed him for a magazine, as he described goals and obstacles in such a clear and visual manner.

Coaching as a lifestyle has enabled me to be more available to my family, to watch them grow up. As I write this, Sam is having his first driving lesson, which inevitably focuses me on another learning point from coaching (and Zen): enjoying the here and now in a transitory world.

When I am working from the office, I go for an early morning jog with our springer spaniel, then always do my best to walk our youngest two, Bill and Beattie, to school - something I thoroughly enjoy. The physical exercise out in fields or parkland, followed by the happiness of the children's conversations, is a perfect start to the day for me. Put a price on that if you dare.

Work, no matter what it is, provides us with a number of different things: financial reward, a way of life and a lifestyle, a social environment and status; it can also provide learning, growth and a sense of achievement. However, it also provides an identity and the job of coaching is no exception. It is intriguing watching people's reactions at social gatherings. In the earlier years, when I had just started, and coaching was far less known as a profession, the reaction was often an intrigued, "What is that then?" whereas nowadays it's, "Oh I've got a friend who does that." Whichever response I get always makes me respond with intense pride in my chosen profession, and the impact it is having on people.

But that doesn't stop me having the odd twinge of envy, like when I spoke to a client who, spurred by our coaching, had left his corporate life and was building dams in India for water supply for the poor. Back to my not having solved the Middle East crisis, I guess.

A Remarkable Life

"Regrets, I've had a few," as the song goes. But very few indeed.

As I have mentioned, moving into coaching coincided with some big personal changes – and that timing made coaching a big part of me. Overall, I am focused on delivering results, planning for the future whilst enjoying the moment, wherever it is, and certainly those moments involving our family.

As well as travelling to South Africa, Turkey and many places in Europe, I have been lucky to go to India to coach, and the impact of that country on anyone seeing it has to be huge, broadening your understanding of the human condition.

Like most businesses, the recession caused a few months of tough times. 2009 has also coincided with parental health scares and the suicide of a good friend. It is, of course, impossible to militate against such external factors; however, the new perspective I've gained has enabled me to deal with them in different ways than I might have in the past.

I was brought up in post WW2 Britain. If the war was a defining period for those who went through it, it was certainly a defining period for those who came after it as well. My father had extensive frontline experience, including volunteering for bomb disposal. Almost certainly these days, he would have been treated for Post Traumatic Stress Disorder. Consequently, it was not always easy living with – or even living up to – people who were genuine heroes. Applying some coaching techniques and reflection time has helped me to reconcile some aspects of this.

I am aware that most of the people I work with are financially privileged, even though there are many profound problems they may be dealing with. Coaching and fulfilling individual potential with my client population made me aware of the growing gap between "haves" and "have nots", both in the UK and abroad. It has led to me seek out charitable work with ex-service people.

Has coaching made me perfect? Certainly not! I'm rubbish at relaxing, always taking on too much, physically and emotionally, which adds to the pressures I put on myself. Consequently, I must force myself to build in the reflective time I know that I need. And then, there's the usual set of worries and pinch points that make up being a human being. How I react to these now is completely different than before. I am certainly blessed in my life to have Elaine as a lovely wife and a great friend who makes me laugh and has contributed significantly to the home environment along with Sam, Bill and Bea who are just great fun to be around. A local community church had a treasure hunt a couple of years ago. The first we knew of it was when we had kids knocking at our door. The clue had included the words "Iit is at the Happy House" – which was referring to our home.

So, that's one coach's story: how I got to coaching and what impact it has had.

Whatever happens, I'm still going to be agreeing violently with clients for years to come if they have the temerity to say they have the best job in the world.

Nicola Bird

One Coach's Perspective

I FEEL A LITTLE YOUNG TO BE GIVING YOU THE STORY of my life and journey as a coach so far. I'm only thirty seven and only wannabe celebrities tell their life stories before they're seventy, don't they? Simply writing this chapter, though, is a great way for me to gain some perspective on how far I've come. As well, I hope to share with you some mindset shifts to help you grow a successful coaching business and help you avoid the same mistakes I experienced.

Before the word "coaching" appeared on my horizon, I'd had a varied and interesting life: I started a degree in economics, was bored senseless by something that didn't seem to impact on me at all (how small your world is when you're twenty), picked up a friend's psychology textbook and found myself totally immersed in what makes the human being tick. This, I suppose, was the start of my journey – it took me another thirteen years to officially become a coach.

I completed a BSc in Psychology followed by an MSc in Occupational Psychology and then spent some time working with adults with learning difficulties and as an Assistant Psychologist, gaining a far deeper understanding of how many people in this world struggle with things you and I just cannot begin to imagine; and how effective small concrete steps can be once larger goals are decided upon.

I spent eighteen months travelling the world, thought about training as a Clinical Psychologist or a Counsellor, and five years working at PricewaterhouseCoopers. I got married, had a baby, and spent a year working as a business manager for the NHS. I had another baby in 2005 then...stopped.

And thought.

What was it I really wanted to do?

My best mate and I got together for a brainstorming session. "Let's think, Nic, what are you really, really good at, and what do you really like doing?" We came up with "Being bossy". It's true, there's no hiding it, and those of you who know me well know that I am (in a nice way, of course) bossy. Comes from being the eldest of three, I suppose.

So, what career can you have where "being bossy" is an asset? We could only think of two options: teaching and life coaching (knowing nothing about either). It didn't take me long to discount the teaching route; after all, I spent all day with small children and I wasn't about to pay someone else to look after my children so I could spend my time with other people's small children. I decided to find out more about this thing called life coaching.

I went onto Amazon, googled, "life coaching" and up popped The *Life Coaching Handbook* by Curly Martin. I read it, devoured it even, realised it was nothing at all to do with being bossy but still had my first real "aha" moment: this is what I've always wanted to do, but I never knew what it was called.

This wasn't clinical psychology;: it wasn't working with people who found it difficult to function in everyday life. This wasn't counselling: it was action-oriented and about taking control, which fits totally with my values. Within a week I was signed up onto Noble Manhattan's Life Coaching Diploma.

This is where the story really starts.

I flew through my coach training in five months. I twisted my husband's arm and persuaded him to pay for the course and for two days a week of childcare because, of course, I told him what I had read: coaching is a booming industry, you can earn up to £1,000 a day, people are crying out for coaches. So I worked my a*se off to get through my training to start earning all that available coaching money people had just lying around, with the goal of paying my husband back.

I must digress a moment to tell you a story about my training course, just so you can see how far I've come. During the training course, as well as all the essays, coaching hours, mentor coaching calls and thesis we had to complete, we also went on a residential weekend. This was such a great opportunity and a real boost to my training and I met friends there I still have to this day.

But I remember the exercise where actors came in and played the roles of clients so we could have our first real go at coaching a real person. And I spent the rest of the afternoon in tears. I just couldn't do it. I'd ask a question, the client would answer and I'd panic so much about having the next question to ask that I'd go blank and freeze up and then cry. Every single time.

I'd put so much effort, money and hard work into this course, and when it came to the practice I just couldn't do it. In the end, Gerard O'Donovan, the CEO of Noble Manhattan, took me off to one side and gave me some wise words. He also told me he wasn't going to fail me. I can't to this day remember what those wise words were but, as soon as I got home, I called everyone I knew and filled my diary with as many pro bono sessions as possible to get back on the horse and practice like crazy. And it worked.

Why do I share this with you? Well some of you may be going through your training right now, or thinking about doing so, and I just want you to know that it's not all easy. There are personal hurdles to overcome, and the best thing you can do is face that fear head on and expose yourself to the one thing you're really afraid of –and get good at it. Then you won't ever have to be scared of it anymore.

And I got a merit in the end, so it was worth the embarrassing crying thing.

One of the other key experiences I had whilst training was when I requested a mentor coach, someone who I could talk to if I was struggling with improving my coaching skills. She told me this fact: ninety percent of coaches who complete their training can't make a living from coaching. I came off the phone from my mentor coach and I was (a) furious with her – how could she tell me such an awful thing when I was in the middle of my training and (b) devastated – what about all that stuff I'd read about the money to be made, the clients to be had?

And then I had a conversation with a great lady, Barbara Dalpra, from Noble Manhattan, who had given me help when I was practicing my coaching hours. When I told her of my total despondency, she said to me: "What makes you think you can't be one of that ten percent?" Another "aha" moment.

From that point on I was determined.

So, alongside the training timetable I had set myself, I created another column in my spreadsheet for how to build my business even while I was doing my training. I set up a website, set myself up as self-employed, had business cards printed and, the day I graduated from my diploma, I launched my coaching business.

I was a generic Life Coach for about two months before I realised I wasn't going to get any clients that way. I read Hannah McNamara's *Niche Marketing for Coaches* and decided I wanted to work with women who had small children, who wanted to make changes to their lives. I picked this group of women because I was one and could totally empathise with the struggles they faced.

I visited the British Library, did some research and found out that UK women with children under the age of five stated their biggest problem was "finding time for themselves when it felt like there were not enough hours in the day." So that became the focus of my coaching efforts.

Now I had to go where these women went. I went to playgroups and got all the mums to do the wheel of life, shouting myself hoarse above the screaming babies. I stood on the street outside a busy "mum's cafe" and handed out fliers. I partnered with a local fitness instructor who had the same client group I wanted to work with. I put postcards and fliers everywhere a mother could turn in the Wandsworth area including through their front doors. Wandsworth has the largest population of under-fives in Europe, so I knew I was in the right place!

I sat at a table on a gym open day with my stack of fliers and – all of a sudden – I had my first real paying client. You never forget your first real client. "Sarah" stayed with me for over a year during 2006 and she called me the other day to tell me that she'd finished that massage course she'd been talking about and that she and her daughter now had a very close relationship, all of which we'd made the first steps towards in our coaching together. There's nothing better than hearing "and I couldn't have done it without you" and, of course, you have to remind the client that they did all the work.

So my clients started to trickle in and become a steady flow; just one or two new ones each month, but enough to keep me busy. I was starting to realise I wasn't going to be sweeping up piles of cash off the floor and having to employ an answering service to fend off all those clients desperate to employ me, but I was pretty happy with the work I was getting.

I had big dreams of approaching large professional services firms and offering coaching to women returning to the workforce, so I called a few of these ladies and sounded them out about the idea.

The overwhelming message I got was that I was just too small, just me on my own. So another barrier went up.

But I see these barriers as challenges. You can do anything you want to if you want it badly enough (except perhaps be an astronaut or fail to age). In fact, I don't let my children say "I can't do it." I make them say "How can I do it?" instead. Try it for a week and see what a difference it makes.

So I found the organisations that *were* big enough to offer these coaching services and that were already doing what I wanted to do. I sent my CV to Managing Maternity (a wonderful group of women who help new mothers return to the workplace feeling confident and competent) and became a coach and trainer working on their behalf in the City, reliving my old corporate life a little and loving it.

What I noticed was that I really enjoyed working with some of my private clients, but other sessions I would dread all week and have that awful "I'm a fraud, they're going to find me out" feeling. I realised that I really dreaded working with the clients who said "My kids have just started school and I don't know what to do with my life" or the "I just want to improve my relationship with my kids" and I really enjoyed the "I've got so many business ideas, I can't get them into order" and "my business is making x and I need it to make y" clients.

What I realised is that choosing a niche with a set of problems you can solve isn't enough. If you want to do your best work, your clients must be the ones you do your best work with, the ones you love working with, the ones whose appointments you really look forward to.

For me that meant action-oriented women with their own small businesses who either

had a business that was doing so well she was beginning to lose control; or the client had hit the wall and realised they must make the business work *right now* because their bank manager (usually their husband) was fed up with her "playing at this business thing".

But I was still attracting the other kind of clients with whom I didn't do my best work. So again, I turned to Gerard (a great sounding board for me, we regularly have a "coffee on the phone" so I can sound out my latest mad idea) who introduced me to the model of having associates in my own business.

Through my coaching networks, I approached four women who then delivered the coaching for those clients with whom I didn't do my best work. These women were far more effective than I could be. In fact, I read a quote from Thomas Leonard the other day where he said, "Identify your weaknesses. And then delegate them." Wise words indeed.

My associate coaches were happy because they could focus on the one thing they loved doing coaching; and I could focus on what I loved doing - structuring and marketing my business and helping other women do the same with theirs. I put my bossy nature to one side for a while and delivered pure, non-directive, non-judgmental coaching and got some good (but not great) results.

This was also the time I came across an online coaching platform that allowed me to coach my clients, in writing, online. This idea really appealed to me, as the clients I was working with were mothers with young children who slept at odd times (the mothers *and* the children) and were often sick or their childcare-giver was sick, causing, quite frankly, chaos to my diary of coaching hours. The idea of an online programme that meant my clients could complete their coaching whenever they chose was a bit of a no-brainer, so I started thinking about how to use this for my clients.

Before I could put this plan into action, however, something else major happened to me.

At this time I was (and still am) a big fan of Hannah McNamara, who offers useful resource tools and tips to help coaches who want to grow their businesses. One day I listened to a call that was to change my approach to my business forever. It was an interview between Hannah and Karen Skidmore, who helps service professionals grow their businesses. In that interview, Karen explained that, although we're always trained to think that the client has all the answers and a coach must be non-directive and non-judgmental at all times, she didn't work like that. She'd given herself permission to use whatever it took to help her clients and give them what they wanted. Sometimes she mentored, sometimes she coached and sometimes she trained her clients. But overall, she just helped them to get where they wanted to be. Another, and probably one of the most important, "aha" moments for me.

I felt a weight lift from my shoulders. I could be bossy with my clients if they wanted me to be! I could share my knowledge with them if I thought it could help. Instead of saying "Where could you go to get that information and who could you ask?2 I realised I could be the person they could go to and ask for information and, actually, I had some of the answers. I felt like Karen had just given me the permission to be truly me and deliver authentically to my clients. For that, Karen, I thank you always!

I realised that becoming an expert in the coaching field meant I must be able to ask informed questions. If I don't understand what an exit strategy is, how can I ask my clients to define theirs for their business? And if I don't know to ask about that, I'm failing my clients as a business coach.

I'll say it again, because I do think it's so important: become an expert in your field and teach your clients as well as coach them. It might also interest you to note that Thomas Leonard, the forefather of professional coaching, was the one who coined the phrase "the clients have all the answers" and even he, some years later, said that he thought that was a mistake: the clients don't always have all the answers.

So I signed up for the Small Business Coaching Diploma at the Coaching Academy and started my next journey towards learning everything I could about coaching small businesses so that I could deliver the best results for my clients. Currently, I'm studying an advanced strategy developed by Andrea J Lee, author of *Multiple Streams of Coaching Income*. Andrea J Lee comes into my story a little later, but at the moment I'm studying some of her advanced strategies and one I'm quite interested in at the moment is "Make the rules, don't follow the rules". At the Coaching Academy, as well as in my original coach training, I was taught never to suggest solutions or be directive in any way, and I'm afraid that's a rule I've decided to break. My clients ask me for solutions, they pay me for solutions and so I do teach first; then coach next. In fact, this was the basis for the first online, small business coaching package that I created.

While we're on the subject, another rule I've decided to break is the one that says 'you should become an accredited coach (see! I'm holding nothing back and you've got me on my soap box now.) I do believe there are a lot of benefits to holding an accreditation, not the least of which is that coaching as a profession becomes more established if there is a way to monitor who is a well trained coach and who isn't. But I have to say I've never been asked if I'm accredited by a client. Filling in log forms of my hours smacks too much of my monthly, hated book keeping and I don't need it to deliver my results to my clients. Whether you choose to go down the accreditation route or not is up to you; all I'm asking is that when you're presented with "rules" you stop and think whether this is a rule you'll follow or not.

Anyway, back to my story: my husband, three children and I decided to emigrate to New Zealand. So in October 2008 we travelled to the other side of the world and planted ourselves on a mountain on the outskirts of Wellington. Coaching in New Zealand is really well established and there are a large number of internal coaches as well as coaching organisations and solo practitioners so, if you're ever thinking of emigrating, it's a good place to go. If you like going out a lot and drinking lots of wine till late at night, don't. We do, and we couldn't, so we came home ten months later.

The biggest lesson this experience taught me, though, is if you want to continue to earn a relatively good living you need to attract clients from outside New Zealand, due to the relative lack of disposable income there compared to the UK or the US. And although coaching is quite well established, there are only four million people in the whole country and only two hundred thousand in Wellington. I wanted my reach to be greater than this. Local networking events just weren't going to get me where I wanted to be, so it was time for me to bite the bullet and really get to grips with building my online profile and mailing list (which in January 2009 consisted of twelve people, and one of them was my mum).

Enter my first coach: Karen Skidmore. Yes, it took me that long to realise I needed a coach of my own and Karen was the difference that *made* the difference to my coaching business. Karen helped me focus on the fact that I wanted to introduce other coaches, as well as trainers and consultants, to the benefits of online coaching and that I could work with others to help them grow their businesses by sharing the journey I was about to take.

She introduced me to wordpress.org so that I could build my website, *www.takeactiongetclients.com*, for zero cost. She also introduced me to the concept of Twitter and running teleclasses as a way to generate sign ups to my mailing list.

At first my response was, "No way! What have I got to say?" coupled with total stage fright. Karen got me thinking instead about interviewing experts in their fields so I didn't need to come up with loads of content and fill sixty minutes of air space on my own. I had just read Sandra de Freitas' excellent book, *Does This Blogsite Make My Wallet Look Fat?* so I decided to email her and ask if she'd do an interview. She said yes. Simple as that.

I was terrified. I remember emailing Karen: "This is all your fault. I'm sitting here shaking, practicing saying "Hello, this is Nicola Bird" and trying to remember how to pronounce Sandra's surname right (which I didn't in the end), with a large glass of water in case I dry up, and a baby nappy to my right in case I need to wee in the middle of the interview." In case you're wondering, I didn't, nor have I ever, needed the nappy, but a good tip, don't you think?

I had forty seven people sign up to that first call, and I found I loved the adrenaline rush and all the positive feedback. I started running one every few weeks and, for awhile, got carried away running three a week but, take it from me, that pace is impossible to keep up.

Now I usually get as many as three hundred people on each call and teach people how to run their own teleclasses. I've added approximately as many as two hundred people a month to my mailing list using teleclasses and that was, as I've said, starting from scratch.

In August 2009, I hit my target of one thousand subscribers and I've just kept going. What to learn from this? Just that there are a million ways to market your business but, if you happen upon one you're good at, and that gets you the results you want, keep doing it. And then think how can you do it bigger, better and get more results (I'm still working on that one).

The other positive thing Karen did was introduce me to Andrea J Lee's book, mentioned earlier, which provided the inspiration for my business as it stands today.

From Andrea, I learned the benefit of creating products and services that allowed you to sell more than your one to one time, and at my website, I provide loads of advice, tips and resources to help other coaches, trainers and consultants do exactly that.

In the meantime, the whole idea of online coaching was growing and growing in my mind and I decided to create my own online coaching platform that would allow coaches to create one key signature coaching programme and attract clients who could access that key content at a variety of price points (fill their whole product funnel if you're a marketing geek like me). So I contacted a team of developers and built JigsawBox.

I use it myself: after reading Andrea's book, I called her and got her to agree to a beta -test of an online coaching programme based on her book, built it and delivered it to a group of coaches. But what I spend most of my time doing now is licensing other coaches, trainers and consultants to use JigsawBox so that they can create their own signature coaching programmes, package up their products and services and use this online platform to get more clients. Now the majority of my coaching and mentoring is done with JigsawBox owners, helping them to create and market their programmes.

So that's where I started and where I've got to so far on my journey. And that's just the start of it. I've got some MASSIVE plans for things to come.

What can I say to you on your journey as a coach? Here are some great rules to follow – it's your choice whether to follow them or not:

1. Get yourself a coach – really. It is the difference that makes the difference if you want to grow a successful business.
2. Think of coaching as one of many tools you can use to help your clients get the results they want. They are paying you for results, not coaching.
3. Don't be scared by the niche thing, but decide who you want to work with for now. If you look again through this chapter, you'll see how my niche has narrowed, changed, flexed and become more specific over the last three years, and I've no doubt it will again.
4. You don't need to spend more money on becoming a better coach to get more clients. Spend more money on becoming more of an expert in your field, and on learning how to market yourself effectively.
5. Find people who've done what you want to do and know more than you do and learn from them.
6. If I can help you on your own journey to become one of that ten percent who makes it in their coaching business, I'd be delighted.

By the way, I will pay my husband back this year: it's taken four years, but hopefully you can get there more quickly than I did.

David Miskimin

The Coach's Journey

LIKE MANY COACHES, I PASSIONATELY BELIEVE in personal development and, for me, that has been influenced through multiple facets of my life.

Some decades back, there was in the UK an exam for near eleven year olds, dauntingly named the 11 plus, which decided what kind of high school children would progress to. I failed mine and my teachers held a lengthy inquest as to how this could have happened. My best friend passed his and, much to our shared dismay, we were parted. I know he will not mind me saying that for several years he struggled near the bottom of his classes, while I was always in the top three places for most of mine. I was already learning that "failure" is subjective; how we interpret the experience is the key. My high school teacher, Mr Comrie, inspired me when he demonstrated, without using the words, that goals and expectations are powerful motivators. My final exam result was precisely as he predicted.

My marriage to Laura has blessed us with two wonderful daughters of whose many achievements we are proud. Currently, we have four fantastic and uniquely different grandchildren too. However, like most parents, I sometimes wish I had accumulated greater knowledge, experience and skills earlier in life so that I could have been even more effective in helping my children fulfill their potential.

Today, through my work in coaching business executives, I can see the common threads between coaching in organisations and parenting. Many leaders and managers lack credibility with colleagues. If you wonder how that's relevant, ask yourself: how credible are you with your children? Some bosses say one thing and do another – staff really hate that, don't they? Has that ever happened in your home? A good manager will want to develop and grow individuals so that their talent and career aspirations are realised. As a result, the manager feels a sense of achievement and the individual experiences great satisfaction. Isn't this what a parent most deeply desires for their child? Is it possible that, by improving your parenting skills you may also become a better manager at work and better equipped to help your children learn valuable work and life skills? Might becoming a better manager help with parenting?

I believe that my life, and therefore my work, is God-inspired. There have been numerous occasions where my faith has been tested and, over the years, several hundred of my coaching clients have enjoyed fabulous results. I too have experienced a sense of achievement and growth by sharing in their hard won personal change. Isn't that about having a purpose? I have found that checking my own responses, particularly what my heart is telling me, is crucial in knowing whether I am aligned with what I am aiming to achieve for others.

I've concluded that clarity of purpose and, as I mentioned earlier, a fixation on personal development, are key qualities a coach must possess to achieve success. This philosophy is even more necessary when working for oneself. Potential clients are making selection decisions based on the perceived credibility and capability offered. Consequently, there is a responsibility for Continuous Professional Development (CPD). I know my clients across the public, private and non government sectors – that's charities, voluntary organisations and the like, (increasingly called the Third Sector) – really value this investment.

Coaching Philosophy: A Work In Progress

I believe that every client is unique. I tend to work with my clients for several months and the sessions are packaged into what is known as a programme. To make this investment really work, every programme assignment is customised to align with my clients' needs. For many years, I have embarked on a programme of continuous personal development and am constantly inspired and gratified by what people can achieve with a little investment in themselves. While my experience is currently based on over 3,600 hours of coaching over a ten-year period, I have increasingly recognised my own continuous needs for learning through practice and reflection. I think of myself as a work-in-progress. I also know about the highs and lows of business, having personally experienced job loss during a severe economic downturn. My coaching is based upon my belief that the more our strengths (talents) are aligned with who we are (authenticity), the easier is it to deliver at higher performance levels, the lower our stress and the greater our wellbeing. It will be easy to imagine how this belief influenced the strapline for my business – "Transforming talent into performance".

My Coaching Journey Begins

I've observed how the professionalisation of coaching has accelerated in recent years. I first came to coaching in 2000 through the Coaching Academy. At that time in the UK, coaching was almost unknown. Now, as my coaching practice enters its tenth year, I can't believe how things have changed.

Prior to coaching, I held senior management positions including Major Account Management and Consultancy within ICL (Fujitsu), Reuters and Nortel. I have worked with board members at some of the largest organisations in the UK and internationally. In addition to one to one and team coaching, activities have included Account and Scenario Planning and enhanced decision making.

I began to realise that a formal, high-level qualification from an industry-recognised body was required. Over several months I searched the market, identifying and contacting several possible providers. I became attracted to the Noble Manhattan Corporate Coaching Diploma. I had experience of the genuine, caring approach of key staff at Noble Manhattan and what I really liked was that this qualification was particularly geared to the needs of the students. Specifically, the programme offered great flexibility in learning and flexibility over the timing for submission of assignments. Being self-employed, I appreciated this operating flexibility. To ensure ownership, the student was expected to produce and maintain a Coaching Development Plan to share with their Mentor Coach in order to gain clarity over the timeframes, anticipated obstacles and likely support required during the programme.

In the modern world most of us are over-committed in our lives. Finding the space and balance to complete a postgraduate level Diploma requires considerable planning, energy and commitment. Thankfully, many of the tutors on the programme also act as Mentor Coaches. Not only are they familiar with the materials, they are also actively engaged in the support processes for the hard pressed students. NMC Head Office provides much additional support, resources and encouragement and study groups are promoted between fellow students.

From a personal perspective, I found my support group invaluable. It's amazing what can be learned; with a wide international student base this included getting to grips with the dynamics of Skype conference calls across international time zones. Bonding definitely occurred as many of the members still exchange emails and Skype calls.

It took me a little longer than the two years I had anticipated for completion of the programme, as I had underestimated its comprehensive and challenging nature. Separately, my own business needed nurturing and development, I was developing my first book, *The Coaching Parent*, and further grandchildren were arriving.

Thankfully the students' resources continued: teleclasses – downloadable as MP3 files; a members' resources area; and numerous electronic templates to assist portfolio gathering. There is a thorough, easy to read handbook and all manuals and materials are of a high quality. As a result I added significantly to my understanding across all topics, including leadership, psychology, teams, and organisational change.

The programme is structured into three blocks. Passing blocks one and two result in a Diploma. Block three, which is optional, leads to an Advanced Diploma. To achieve this level, a comprehensive Extended Study on a coaching topic is required.

The Extended Study was a significant piece of work, with my final report including appendices running to 139 pages. As part of the study I was keen to understand what other coaches were expecting and experiencing when they worked with clients. To support this, I designed a survey which was analysed across 113 respondents.

Upon further filtering, I established that forty nine coach respondents could be identified as mostly delivering coaching to my focus area of Senior Management. Specifically, 73.5% were most frequently coaching Executives/Directors and 87.8% were working with Senior Managers. In this filtered group, some 37.5% had been coaching for over five years, compared with 23.2% in the full group. Of these forty nine, the "Dominant prior career backgrounds" were:

Coach : Dominant prior career backgrounds

Rank from Filtered Coach Subset/All		Subset	All Respondents
1st/1st	Other	22.4%	29.2%
2nd/2nd	Learning and Development	20.4%	23.0%
3rd/4th	Consultancy	14.3%	9.7%
4th/6th	Operations	12.2%	8.0%
5th=/3rd	Psychotherapy/Counselling	10.2%	10.6%
5th=/5th	Human Resources	10.2%	8.8%
7th/7th	Training	4.1%	6.2%
8th/6th	Sales	6.1%	4.4%

What the Coach Expects from Coaching

Few people seem to discuss the coach's own expectations from coaching activity. From discussion with other coaches over the years, I was keen to find out more and in my survey focused on four frequently occurring aspects:

- Anxiety
- The Process
- Enhanced Reputation
- To Make a Difference

ANXIETY

My survey found that many coaches and coachees acknowledge their anxiety at coaching sessions. I have personally found it good to recognise this feeling and develop strategies to deal with it.

I am constantly learning about the tools and the experience of coaching. In particular, the work of Passmore and Marianetti (2008) on Mindfulness assisted me greatly in understanding and working with anxiety. They propose a solution for both the coach and the coachee which offers the opportunity to focus attention on the session and their learning, effectively setting the stage for personal development and self-actualisation.

Building on their work, I often implement a focus activity at the start of a session, of calming and focusing myself and the coachee. In a mere two or three minutes a valuable grounding takes place, preparing the way for a successful session. Such a simple strategy; so much value.

I maintain watchfulness throughout the session to ensure my thoughts do not begin to wander and I can continually bring my focus back to the coachee. I am aware of the need to remain emotionally detached while also staying focused and remaining empathetic.

I conclude that these activities impact positively on anxieties and will become an ever more vital activity for success in coaching.

THE PROCESS

As a coach, my first priority is to serve the coachee. To succeed with an individual coachee and to succeed with an organisation, I ensure wider stakeholder interests are honoured and managed by understanding different expectations and perspectives.

Based on current trends, when operating at the top I predict much less of the unregulated "Wild West of Coaching". It is increasingly the case that Human Resources professionals are much more proactive and want to tie the interests of the individual, the team and the organisation together. Simply put, they want to ensure what the individual achieves in the coaching is of benefit for the organisation. It's about the Return on Investment. What I'm finding is that coachees are becoming more receptive to this aspect, provided confidentiality is honoured. I deduce that this trend will accelerate, not just in larger organisations but across all sizes and sectors, as best practice extends.

ENHANCED REPUTATION

I have learnt from numerous coaching interventions that the desire to enhance my reputation is a positive aspiration. This desire to be a good coach has led me to be more thoroughly prepared for sessions, have heightened attentiveness during sessions and full follow-up afterwards. For me the drive is primarily outcome focused (i.e. service led), not simply a function of my ego.

TO MAKE A DIFFERENCE

I enquired about this topic in my coach survey as, while anecdotally I hear it, I had no evidence as to whether or not it carried any significance. I aspire to make a difference with my coaching, but this is a feature of my attitude of service.

A Coach's Story

I am pleased to report the respondent data shows that "making a difference" is also significant for the vast majority of the subset coaches.

Coach : Importance placed on 'Making a Difference'

Rank from Filtered Coach Subset/All		Subset	All Respondents
1st/1st	Vital	56.3%	51.8%
2nd/2nd	High Importance	35.4%	36.6%
3rd/4th	Average Importance	6.3%	8.0%
4th/4th=	Low Importance	2.1%	1.8%
5th=/4th=	None	0.0%	1.8%

The Dilemmas, Controversies And Contradictions

CONGRUENCE - TO BE OR NOT TO BE?

The findings of Goffee and Jones (2007) on leading clever people have reassured me. They note that making clever people feel independent and special is important, but also that they recognise their interdependence. On numerous occasions the former has helped me develop credibility and earn the right to work with senior clients. Just as importantly, I have facilitated the latter, the foundation for collaborative working. This means I have encouraged those who might be particularly independent thinkers to appreciate more significant successes would come through greater self-awareness and more effective working relationships.

The unfolding of Emotional Intelligence offers us the potential to demonstrate attunement, that state of empathising tacitly in a relationship, so that our clients know we are on their wavelength. When I notice a client beginning to model this state, I recognise that I am being congruent with myself, still retaining the intention to serve my client and recognising we have established and moved beyond rapport. I then know I am beginning to make a positive difference.

I've been concerned about the Goffee and Jones findings that talented people are not appreciative as, once convinced of the coaching benefits, my senior management clients have tended to be generous in their praise, though it doesn't necessarily last long as they integrate and internalise their own learnings. Nonetheless, acknowledgement of my role in their success is usually forthcoming.

However, to be congruent with myself I have concluded that letting go of the outcome, i.e. any need for acknowledgement, is liberating.

TOUCHY FEELY?

As a coach, I constantly endeavour to avoid explanation around coaching language or models, unless it is going to add real value for my client. I want to keep the interaction simple. Nonetheless, I acknowledge the importance of raising a client's awareness of the interplay between the different aspects involved in our human condition and it seems to me now that emotions and feelings *must* be included in this

What I have found is that, while not all clients will relate openly or readily in discussing emotions, Goleman D., Smart, J.K., Lee, G., *et al*, all agree on the importance of emotions (or feelings, depending on context or your point of view). I have found that a more comprehensive approach potentially produces greater benefits than through addressing thoughts and behaviours without exploring feelings.

Is it acceptable to discuss emotions and feelings?

Survey Question	Ranking			
	Coach Subset	All Coaches	Coachee Subset	All Coachees
Yes	97.9%	97.3%	100.0%	100.0%
No	0.0%	0.0%	0.0%	0.0%
Unsure	0.0%	1.8%	0.0%	0.0%
Don't normally discuss	2.1%	0.9%	0.0%	0.0%

I have a cautionary observation. Some of my survey data above seems to suggest coaches and coachees are happy with discussing emotions. If this question were asked of a coachee before coaching, and particularly with an individual with no experience of being coached, then I suspect this may not be the case.

CHANGE AGENCY

I've found that contradiction and ambivalence are normal, particularly at the start of any potential change process. Grant and Greene (2001) believe the same and that ambivalence is inevitable, arguing "we want to change and we don't." (p 58) – so I've learned to expect it from my clients.

What Were My Challenges, Learnings And Successes?

SIGNPOSTING

Orton and others have commented that signposting is about context; individuals want to know why they are doing something and how it fits with other situations. This need is not always openly expressed and it's the responsibility of the coach to manage the amount of signposting. I consider signposts to operate as topic markers, informing the coachee, for example, that the coaching is taking a direction turn, or perhaps deepening the discussion or activity.

I conclude that while sessions can and do succeed without them, signposts generally encourage an easy flow within sessions.

A FINAL NOTE ON ANXIETY

In presenting my findings earlier, I noted there might be a positive correlation between anxiety and the need to deliver. While that hypothesis is based on my own survey, there is supporting evidence elsewhere. Passmore and Marianetti's premise about "mindfulness" is that both parties *ought* to be experiencing some anxiety. If the focus for coach and coachee is on achieving good outcomes and, mostly, enhanced performance, then anxiety should be anticipated, simply because it is the necessary arousal state to rise to a challenge.

I conclude the awareness and presence of anxiety is a beneficial state and worthy of discussion at the start of the coaching.

A Final Note On The Process

While my study was predominantly about the coach's experience, I was fascinated that one respondent in the subset coach survey commented on just whose needs were in question:

"Well done for pulling this together. There are some big assumptions behind some of the questions e.g. the need to challenge, create value - whose 'needs' are these, it feels a bit coach oriented. Quite a few questions are closed which forces an answer, though does make completion easier, though may distort what really happens. Also values, I would like to know if values appear more in certain coaching interventions (skills through to transformational?). I would be interested in the feedback."

For me these are very helpful comments, as I've found my work as a coach to senior management is measured by my results with the coaches; yet, in the human condition, we have needs as well. I am further reflecting on whether these really are needs or desires, and the place they have in this field of work.

In the continuing debate between directive and non-directive coaching, I conclude a number of healthy tensions exist:

- That of the client in expecting the coach to act as a consultant, or advisor
- That of the coach in knowing the greatest success lies in eliciting growth in the client, rather than acting as an advisor

In my experience, it is possible for the coach to meet this need, at the right time and in the right context. This tension may be an area worthy of further research.

The Chartered Institute of Personnel and Development (CIPD) is Europe's largest professional institute for people management and development. A question about motives was posed by Pryor in the CIPD People Management publication *Coaches are hired to help the client get results... As a client am I in this for me or the organisation?*

While I will not address that point here, I recognise from these important questions that, as a coach, I must be vigilant in regard to, "whom am I serving, and what are the best processes to achieve that?"

In Closing

We all have opinions about how we like things to be done and we will not always agree. A comment from the subset coach survey confirms this for me: *"As given in the last question I don't believe this is a valid question, yet the survey insists I give one, that proves the invalidity point I made."*

I have found there are and will remain numerous dilemmas, controversies and contradictions. Even so, in my view success, while becoming more complex to manage due to multiple stakeholder interests and higher expectations, is achievable for both the coachee and coach.

I have shared only a small portion of a much larger work and trust there is sufficient information provided here to pique your interest. If this leads you to enquire further, I would be interested to hear from you. Additional information is available at the end of this book.

The result of my studies was the gaining of a hard earned, highly prized qualification. I am pleased to report that my expected

Corporate Coaching Diploma emerged at a higher level as an Advanced Executive and Corporate Coaching Diploma. It required focus and dedication which, I'll admit, I didn't always have with my busy and varied life.

Was it worth it? You bet! I have a worthwhile qualification, would not have missed a moment and, as a bonus, made some wonderful new friends. I hope that might even include you!

David Miskimin

PaTrisha Todd

Become The Best You Can Be

What A Triumph!

IT IS THROUGH MY VOCATION AS A COSMIC SOUL COACH that I have been able to help thousands of individuals enter the sacred dimension of the metaphysical world; to explore for themselves and discover the secret of clarification and the ease with which they can design their life.

In fundamental nature, Cosmic Soul Coaching aligns your conscious mind with your subconscious. The spirit of your being, your soul, forms an outer connection with your outer world.

A friend was telling me about his recent wins and the quantum leap he had experienced in his lifestyle and economic growth since he'd decided to take responsibility for his life and go that extra mile. He had literally developed the best mindset he had ever had, gone beyond and stretched his goals, boosted his personal power and pulled out all the stops to make the change he needed for a better life. He chose to step up and master his own destiny. Later, he revealed his secret: he had begun to use an extremely powerful coaching model I had given him several years earlier, accelerating his thinking process in every dimension and committing himself to total focus on his goal.

I'm delighted to say he remains in a good place and, for both of us, life is good. That day, when he shared his success with me, the warmth of the Caribbean sun coupled with the lilt and wane of the waves around the boat worked their magic. Gratitude truly was being celebrated. He'd taken action and his dreams had become real.

And oh yes, an attitude of gratitude was pouring out of me as well, compounding my state of thankfulness for being in a position to hear my friend's testimony to positive living, action and purpose. His action confirms that coaching is a safe place for progression.

Mindset is such a powerful tool. It is the essence of life; a guaranteed method for turning daydreams into a reality, with far reaching endeavours manifesting themselves into the pattern of life.

Mindset is the vibrations of the mind that dictate the rhythms of the body, thus producing the desired outcome.

Success in life is available to everyone who seeks and takes decisive action to achieve the desired outcome. I know that's a very bold statement, but I whole-heartedly believe life can be better for those who choose to explore and follow a set of natural principles – the Laws of the Universe.

The Laws Of The Universe

Let me explain a little about what I mean. Certainly, circumstance and environment can be restrictive. However, circumstance can be fashioned and crafted into a change for the better. There is no need for anyone to become a victim of circumstance when the correct mindset is applied. I am not speaking of victimisation or other forms of bullying, but of an understanding that you have a choice to excel and reach your highest potential when you demystify any clouds that may be blocking your vision as well as forming a plan of action to move you forward to goal achievement. A life plan requires a burning desire to reach a greater height even when adversity crosses your path.

It is my intention to share with you the beginnings of how you can live a life designed by... you!

Loving, Living, Prosperity and Abundance are divine, waiting for the holy mind to claim its cosmic soul. Let it call you to the depths of creativity filled with ancient mystery. The divine is ready, calm and proudly waiting for you to claim your cosmic soul.

My thoughts as expressed here have been crafted over a lifetime. I choose to harness my potential for greater and better living. I tap into my storehouse and select how best to express my spirit. I cannot stand in, nor do I choose to drop into, anyone's space of conscious thinking; I do not have the power to change anyone's circumstances or way of living. Each adult has his or her own feminine and masculine identity, comprised of the sum of many character traits and core values. My mission in life is to contribute to others my knowledge and system of Cosmic Soul Coaching for the sake of sharing with people the technique of gaining access to their inner core and belief system; how they can best clarify their goals and formulate a plan of action, a blueprint of the lifestyle they know they truly deserve.

I believe I was placed on this earth to help other human beings express themselves and achieve more, achieve better and achieve correctly as a multidimensional creature.

The beauty of Cosmic Soul Coaching lies in its approach to facilitate easy learning and, ultimately, brings out the best in oneself. Personal outcome is and will always be dependent on personal attitude and intensity of effort.

Let The Journey Begin

Personal development has been a passion of mine for as long as I can remember. It's a skill set system that brings ultimate quality and extraordinary riches. It is my vision to help as many individuals as I can transform their world through the system of Cosmic Soul Coaching.

It was as a young school girl attending an establishment in South London for "sick children" that my dreams began to rise and prepare me for adulthood. During those early years, I was bullied. At the time I didn't know why I was being picked on and made to experience unnecessary levels of confusion about not belonging. I suffered bouts of crying, because all the other children at school were encumbered with a sickness, suffering from various internal organ disabilities. In my case this was a consequence of post-wartime hardship and the lack of knowledge available to my young parents. They had repatriated to the "Mother Land" from the 1950 new official Republic of India after nearly 100 years of British rule. Perhaps my long black hair and olive complexion had something to do with it. Or was it my continual coughing and susceptibility to catching a cold? Who knows? Who cares?

What I do know is that I was different, and thankfully so.

My parents taught me to stand up for myself and to keep away from the bullies at school who deliberately made trouble and caused me heartache. I also learned to stay clear of anyone who thought inside of the box.

Building A Foundation

Life has a weird and wonderful way of presenting events as a means of testing and moulding our lives. I didn't know it as a young girl, but life was presenting itself to me in various situations as a way of helping me shape my character and lifestyle. I didn't have a

Life Coach at that time to give me the tools and techniques which are the starting point of productive coaching.

It was my parents, teachers and peers who infiltrated my life and planted seeds of thought, some doubting and many positive, that have over the years been nurtured with on-going learning to make me the woman I am today: a happy soul with a whole lot of living to do; a person who loves to share while building a legacy for the good of mankind.

Gradually I was building my own foundation of self-worth, skills of living life, world status, future achievements, financial resources, physical attributes and consistently underpinning all of those elements on a daily basis. Without awareness, I was using the cosmic principle of energy and universal law to grow and develop my destiny: To Be, To Do and To Have.

Curiosity And The Power Of Knowledge

The emotion of curiosity is a form of natural inquisitiveness. Humans naturally want to find out about new things, to explore, to investigate and assimilate the findings which feed the interest and expansion of awareness of any subject matter.

My curiosity took me to the library where I began reading books on personal development, the conscious and subconscious mind and metaphysics (the philosophy of being and knowing). Slowly, I began to understand that I did have a choice. I chose freedom, a choice that has led me to experience personal growth, abundance and prosperity.

From the myriad books to the teachings of ancient and modern day philosophy, personal development teachers and metaphysicians, I have unlocked my thirst for knowledge and am continually adding to my chamber of comprehension.

Disability – What's That?

Today, as I have always done, I have not allowed my medical condition to hinder me in living my life by design. The complexity of the physical pain and breathing limitations reminds me I am alive. That in itself is a privilege.

I build my immune system by eating the best food available in season, supplementing with the finest quality organic products on the market today and daily activities which keep me as mobile as possible – all vital components to a healthy lifestyle coupled with a very positive mental attitude. Long live coaching!

My 'Why'

Over the years "my why" has changed. As it turns out, this is a good thing. You see, personal development and coaching are vital in respect to achieving the goal. At first it's like joining a game of life with a different set of rules all for the sake of what appears to be survival; yet, the prize is a wonderful treasure chest of jewels and freedom to be the person you truly desire to be.

By playing this particular game, you'll notice all kinds of people entering into your life. You'll come across people whom you realise you do not want to associate with, and those other people who have that magical sparkle about them. You know what I mean: pure attractiveness that you too want to capture so you can live life on purpose.

My why is to be the best that I can be. I do that through on-going study of personal development, coaching skills and metaphysics. Professional development in my niche as a Cosmic Soul Coach is important to me. In turn, it allows me to help others who choose me to mentor them in the skills of Living Life by Design.

Perhaps you would like to try the following coaching exercise to help you discover your why?

First off, determine who you really are by analysing your thinking patterns.

Take your time, find a quite place and, in a very special notebook you will use for this exercise and all your future cosmic soul exercises, write the answer in your Cosmic Soul Journal to the question: Who Am I?

In other words, write your biography. Write your life story from as far back as you can remember to the current time. Include passions that turn up in your daydreams. Write about your own self-development, education and habits of implementing a daily routine of positive thinking and living.

Pay attention to thoughts going on in your mind. Dig into your unconscious brain cells and pay attention to what is flashing through. Leave your ego out of this preparation procedure. The deeper you dig and the more attention you pay to your thoughts, the better descriptive information you will be able to write in answering the question: Who Am I?

However long it takes you to write your biography is irrelevant. The point of the exercise is to clear away energy-draining thoughts of confusion that prevent you from revealing your true self. Enjoy the process of this Cosmic Soul Life Coaching mental exercise. It's a method to enlighten and free your inner core, causing your mind and thought patterns to become clear and pronounced.

When you have written your biography you can begin to analyse your pattern of living. You'll be able to identify your strengths and in which situations they come into play. Your weaknesses will also spring off the page in front of you, thereby alerting you to avoid situations that encourage a display of weakness. Re-read your biography; switch on to the insights that pop into your mind. Make an effort to change your mind set for the better. Only you know what your limitations and limits could possibly be. If you are currently working with a coach, share this information and ask him or her to coach you towards the outcome you desire.

Who Is Part Of My World?

I am the reason for Be–Do–Have. Knowing myself and acknowledging my capabilities helps me to exercise my passion of helping others unlock their mind power and reach their true potential. Part of my coaching remit is to facilitate clients to know themselves; after all, if you don't know and understand what and how your personal makeup can instigate a change for the better, you won't move forward and turn your daydreams into reality.

My clients are part of my world – it is because of my clients I have been able to continue to develop, share and contribute to the world that I live in. In my commercial coaching and mentoring practice I have the advantage of working with high calibre clients from around the world. I work closely with entrepreneurs (including Life Coaches), self-made millionaires, TV and film stars and politicians. These people share with me their fears, dreams and aspirations. I offer them the tools to remodel their lifestyle to one of their choosing; dispersing emotional behaviour which no longer serves them, deploying cutting edge thinking to create the outcome they desire and deserve. I enjoy my work and value the high level of commitment these individuals show when exploring the coaching arena.

I can sum up coaching as a journey for what life is all about, what the human soul is all about, that can begin at any point, for we are the sum total of all of our experiences. Each day brings with it a new dawn, ready to enjoy and explore. Coaching is a monumental tool that gets results.

My family is part of my world. My children are my reason for doing. They continue to play a major role in my life and have contributed to this incredible journey of coaching. Together we have reaped the benefits.

The children have, through the years, contributed to keeping my mind active instead of passive. In a wonderful way, they have added to my personal growth and coached me from their own perspective in a tender and loving way. Of course, any coach worth their salt has their own coach. I do. In fact, I am mentored by two separate professional coaches: my Business Coach and a Personal Life Coach.

My parents are part of my world. My darling mother departed this planet in March 2007 after an operation expected to enhance her life. With much pride, I can say her spirit lives on inside of me, emanating daily in all that I do. It was she who taught me to remove the concept of worry from my life and it is my eighty-one year old father who reminds me of her love, her grace and her positive mental attitude.

Systematically, my upbringing with loving, caring and positively minded parents has had a life changing effect on my life, taking away feelings of frustration I had all those years ago when I first realised I was ill and might not live past the age of eleven. The doctors predicted that if I lived to that age I would need a major lung operation. Thankfully, I surpassed all of their expectations. No operation was needed and I will soon celebrate my sixtieth birthday. Other life experiences, such as juvenile bullying, consistent prejudice, life as a single parent raising three children, nearly losing our family home, feeling trapped professionally... life coaching has focused my efforts on finding out who I am and where I want to be, but essentially it has given me my "why": why I would want to make changes and seek better and bigger goals. It's also quite clearly given me the ability to make available Cosmic Soul Coaching.

With certainty, the Circle of Life is a life enhancing tool that has given me a deep insight into measuring where I am at any given moment. The Circle of Life is a basic pie chart, with a cosmic meaning! I use this tool as a yard stick for personal transition. By drawing on the tool, I am able to support my values and balance my state of mind.

This pictorial framework representation is ideal for those who prefer a visual modality for gaining a better understanding. In an instant, I can see a clear impression of my current lifestyle, giving me total appreciation of what is and what is not going on in my life.

Over the years I've worked with the tool, I've noticed a pattern emerge of new belief systems. The tool conveys a reinforcement of my true values. My core is stirred every time I use The Circle of Life and, as if by design, I am transported outside of the box to a place of opportunity, offering me heaps of satisfaction in living life by design in its entirety of abundance and prosperity. Do you remember I mentioned earlier that from a very young age my mother instilled in me to "think outside of the box"? As I mentioned, this advice stood me in good stead when the school bullies decided it was my turn to be the centre of their scary mischief.

There have been many possibilities from the fantastic to the dreadful that have turned up quite unexpectedly, unwrapping before my very eyes and causing a release of human spirit. So many times people have said to me, "How lucky you are, PaTrisha-Anne." But, you know, it is not luck or chance. It's all about knowing. I know myself and intuition forces me to keep my pulse alive, my mind in a state of positive attitude and a huge desire to express an attitude of gratitude.

Connecting to my inner core in this way is a significant edification mechanism which brings inner intuition to the forefront, expanding the joy of true happiness and the gift of love.

The pie Circle of Life has seven sections (a very special cosmic number). Each section has a different title signifying a particular area in life: Health & Fitness, Home & Family, Career, Finances, Friends, Leisure and Fun Activities are the main strands that life circles around. Of course, there have been times when I have used the tool to focus on other areas of my life and, thankfully, the system has given up its magic and helped me sort out what needed to be sorted. All in all, an empowering, motivating and uplifting experience.

The Principles Of Cosmic Soul Coaching

Life Coaching or Cosmic Soul Coaching involves streams of coaching; personal development made up of energy, both negative and positive.

The journey of a coach is to utilise the tools and techniques of the trade with a client for a better outcome, whatever that may be, within the realms of life, health, wealth, personal relationships and career.

Many people allow their environment to dictate their mood and levels of energy. The Principle of Energy is an important part of constructive coaching. The journey needs to be a holistic one, encircling all areas with a balance of mind, spirit and body.

Positive energy brings anticipation to the mindset with the expectation of exploring new ideas. A negative energy quashes those ideas, causing a possible opportunity to pass right in front of you and out of reach. Coaching, particularly Cosmic Soul Coaching, prepares the mind to recognise an opportunity when it floats before it.

Vast possibilities are born and new worlds open up. A tremendous vista comes into view from within, bringing excitement and adventure into your daily routine. Of course, as you are the driving force of your unique universe, you'll have a finger on the energy control dial and you'll engineer the velocity at which you want to function.

The outcome will be the desired result of measureable improvement you have designed, with unwavering energy and momentum to take hold of the keys to your success.

Where Does Personal Development Belong In Cosmic Soul Coaching?

My own life coaching experience has been phenomenal. My life has exploded to an unparalleled height. It's proven to be truly cosmic.

Through the years, several coaches have worked with me on my personal development and I, in turn, have coached and mentored clients in the same way.

We've explored those all important questions of What, Why, Who, Where and When, allowing the conscious to cease its struggle of worry and let go that limiting question of How, in order to do what needs to be done for goal achievement and personal satisfaction.

The cosmic attraction factor of Cosmic Soul Coaching has enlightened my soul, providing the impetus and inspiration to boldly coach and mentor others in the craft of achieving so much more by learning to think differently. This style of coaching is the only one of its kind in terms of living and thinking in a different dimension. Not by any means an "airy fairy" way of living, but a profound and empowering technique attracting new possibilities.

Self imposed limitations have disappeared to be replaced with positive thoughts, clear vision and a mindset to make forward moving, realistic changes for permanent transformation.

Nothing happens overnight, but change can happen in an instant when intention and research are put into place with dedicated action. Step by step, a person's attitude can change for the positive, getting stronger and stronger, thus encouraging creative thinking and innovating solution focused action towards goal achievement.

When Will I Recognise My Success?

In reality, you'll know it when you see it. For the purposes of seeing your reality, have a go at this visualisation time line exercise:

- Visualise your life as it is right at this moment.
- Think back to yesterday. Move further back to this time last week, then last month.
- Now trace your time line back to six months ago, a year, five years and so on until you reach the point of not being able to go back any further.
- Once in that place, rest your mind.
- Next begin to move forward in your time line and, as you travel that path, you will force your mind to think forward and forward and forward and so on. This is how you can set the scene for your future. You can daydream what you expect to see in your life. That's right, daydream.

As we let our thoughts dissipate, so too does our environment. We can become a victim of our environment. Are you a positively inclined person, or are you a victim of your environment? You have choices. Do you utilise your options? Do it now and see where your dreams can take you.

Write your findings in your Cosmic Soul Journal; don't forget to date your notes.

What's Next?

In my musings I have attempted to offer a way forward; a pathway I have personally trodden and continue to follow. My target in life is to be the best I can possibly become. That all important Be – Do – Have factor. Most significantly, I have chosen to share such tools and techniques with those like-minded souls who are ready to make a change. Is that you?

The objective of *A Coach's Story*, in my opinion, is to share a unique message of hope, to offer help in the form of contributing my own life coaching journey and personal fulfillment after trial, tribulation and at last peace.

PaTrisha Todd

Gail MacIndoe

Mining for Strengths

Eureka!

PEOPLE ASK ME WHEN I KNEW. I can't remember exactly, but I do remember how I felt afterwards: choked with emotion, excited, my mind buzzing with ideas, energised, yet peaceful. Most importantly, I felt relief, finally finding a profession I intuitively knew was right. I had tried umpteen careers and felt they were never quite right. Until I found coaching.

To me, coaching is a way of being, not something you do. You are a "work in progress" and never stop learning about yourself and others. There is nothing quite so rewarding as seeing my clients come into their own, finding their strengths, being able to use them to the best of their ability and especially feeling strong in the knowledge they are OK the way they are. Coaching my daughters has been a real test of my coaching skills. My personal delight is seeing both of them studying subjects that play to their strengths and about which they are passionate.

My first experience with coaching was in Cape Town in 1997, when I attended my first personal development course. The biggest enlightenment? Discovering I was responsible for how I felt, that I could control my emotions.

It wasn't till 2000, after a difficult experience at work which knocked my confidence, that I decided to change my career. Coaching was breaking through in the UK and coaching schools were opening up. I attended workshops, instinctively feeling this was right for me. Coaching would allow me to bring all my experiences and knowledge to play. I didn't realise then, but I had discovered a strength I wasn't aware of. It took seven more years before realising how fundamental playing to strengths was to my ethos and in developing my niche as a Strengths coach.

My Philosophy Of Coaching

"Treat people as if they were what they ought to be, and
you help them become what they are capable of being."

GOETHE

My philosophy is strengths-based and appreciative in nature, rather than deficit-focused. It has its foundations in positive psychology. The coachee has the solution. Strengths should be identified, harnessed, developed and leveraged. A strength is a combination of talent, skills, knowledge and enjoyment/passion. The two key elements are talent and enjoyment/passion as, without them, it can be an upwards battle; but with them skills and knowledge are more easily gained. Weaknesses are not ignored but rather are managed, preferably using one of their strengths. The coaching agenda is always driven by the coachee, not the coach. It is challenging, and exploration comes from a place of curiosity, not judgment.

Ilkley Moor To Beirut

In my strengths work with clients, we look at their formative years, teasing out natural talents and values and discovering what made them who they are today. With that in mind, here is a tour around my early years.

Born in Scotland to Scottish parents, I soon moved to Ilkley Moor in Yorkshire. Not for long. My father's partner ran off, leaving debts. We lost everything. When I was five, my father was offered a job in Beirut, Lebanon. That was to be my home for the next fifteen years. I was an average student and did not give much thought to a future career, although being a lawyer looked good. Reading Law was only possible at the French University, so I decided on Psychology which I could study in English.

My years in Lebanon were happy. Blessed with a Mediterranean climate, cosmopolitan Beirut had it all: great beaches, ski resorts, restaurants, shops, nightlife and hospitable people. I grew up speaking French, Italian and Arabic, learning to adapt to different cultures.

My parents were extroverted and sociable. They taught me that determination, hard work and resilience, mixed with a bit of luck, would get me what I wanted. My mother was a gregarious journalist who did volunteer work at Beirut's American hospital. My father was a self made man who often said, "Watch the pennies, and the pounds will look after themselves." As an only child I was spoilt. Our comfortable, expatriate lifestyle, and being "big fish in a small pond", taught me to be confident in any milieu.

I could not attend my second year at university because civil war had broken out. My parents sent me to London for a short holiday until things "calmed down". They didn't. I took a Christmas job at Harrods, a rude awakening. Beirut was war torn, so my parents decided I should continue studying in Europe. London was not for me; I didn't fit in. Though I looked British, I felt and acted differently. I didn't have a posh English accent and hadn't been to boarding school. They sent me to an American University in Strasbourg, though I escaped whenever possible to Italy, which felt more akin to Beirut.

War was still waging in Lebanon when I finished university. I'd hoped to move to Paris, but salaries were minimal so I joined my parents in Dubai. My first job as secretary to a bad-tempered Italian was in a portacabin in the middle of nowhere, now thriving Jebel Ali. On to Sharjah, where I took whatever jobs I could get in sales promotions. Through another connection, I got my first PR and Sales Executive job for a hotel in Sharjah. I disliked selling, especially cold calling, as I took rejection personally.

Eventually, I got a job in an advertising agency. I loved it and learned I had a flair for taking a good, brief understanding of the client's needs and delivering what we had promised. I enjoyed, managing big brand accounts, like Procter & Gamble, Braun, Rowntree Macintosh, Singapore Airlines and British Airways. I felt as though I was finally hitting my stride. But it was not yet to be.

Global Gypsy

I met Alan, an engineer in the oil business and we married before his transfer to West Africa. En route, we spent four months in a hotel in Madrid, where boredom and loneliness set in. Life in Douala, Cameroon was difficult. Alan was constantly travelling for weeks on end. I had given up a job I loved. It seemed to take ages to make friends. A year later, we were transferred to Port Gentil. I had a live-in husband again, a job, a good social life. I took a job with DHL as Assistant to the Manager.

A year later, Alan was transferred to Bahrain. I loved being back in the Middle East and got a job with my previous employer. My personal life and career took off. An opportunity came up as PR Manager at Inter-Continental hotel. I was responsible for advertising the hotel, hosting a weekly radio show, writing their monthly newsletter, editing their quarterly magazine and turning it into a self-funded publication. Colleagues joked I had given birth to two babies: first, our daughter Chloe; second, the magazine, preparing my first edition hours after giving birth. Entertainment revolved around the Bahrain hotels. My responsibility was to promote events and stars visiting the hotel -- Rowan Atkinson, Russell Harty, Pamela Stephenson -- and organise a French *Vogue* feature on Bahrain. I took a PR course and obtained a marketing degree. Two years later, I joined American Express as the General Manager's Business Assistant, with responsibilities for promoting activities with their service establishments' clients, whilst being groomed to join the marketing team.

My husband was transferred again. We embarked on moves to five countries, putting a halt to my corporate career for fifteen years. From Damascus to Holland, where our second daughter, Stephanie, was born, to Oklahoma... then on to Paris, finishing up in Cape Town. I did occasional administrative work, in between doing PR for an active Theatre Group in the US, and coordinating PR for Givenchy's fund raising show at the US Embassy in Paris (whose ambassador was the infamous Pamela Churchill Harriman). In Cape Town I thought I might like to start my own business and completed a small business management course. A PR company was looking for a general manager and I got the job. The owners were amazing at winning business, but hopeless at finances. Upon reflection, I realise how little I knew about management. I micromanaged experienced staff instead of coaching them. My husband was transferred once again to the UK. I was devastated. But as the fates would have it, I completed a personal development course and was beginning to understand my own responsibility for my emotions... and my destiny.

Cultural Shock

I felt I could do anything, but realising I didn't know enough about business, I embarked on an MBA. I was not academic, hadn't worked in corporate life for years, and knew nothing about working in the UK.

A little knowledge and self belief is an amazing thing.

I worked daily for a month, practising exercises and taking a maths class to sit the entrance exam. I failed. My self belief and gift of the gab got me on the programme, but I almost came unstuck at the first hurtle: statistics. I hired a private tutor and, with determination and resilience, scraped through. The next hurdle was my dissertation. An opportunity arose to write a paper on a defensible pricing policy for a multi-national. It was like pulling teeth. Yet, I was one of the top-graduating students on the course.

However, studying, finding consultancy work and adapting to UK living was a steep learning curve. I was still suffering from cultural shock. I joined a media company and introduced a successful advertising medium in schools, giving me an opportunity to present a paper at a conference. I had attended Toastmasters to hone my presentation skills. Overly ambitious and enthusiastic, I didn't fit in. I was too pushy, not knowing the British way of business. I rubbed some colleagues up the wrong way. I had little self awareness of my style and its impact on others.

Again Alan was offered a transfer. It looked to be my saviour. I handed in my notice, but Alan's UK office would not release him. We were stuck in the UK. I had no job and had lost confidence in my abilities.

What I did know well was how to be a "trailing spouse (the spouse of an expat worker), "a third culture kid" (children who grow up in a country not their own) and what it took to survive expat living.

Personal development courses exploring possible careers helped. With the internet boom and a colleague who understood IT, we designed a website aimed at foreigners moving to the UK. Publishing an article about elocution, I was inundated with requests for lessons. So I charged elocution teachers to sell their services on my website. Next, I contacted companies offering help with their expatriate assignments as I saw the potential of a new consultancy. I studied the experts – Hofstede, Trompenaar and Bennett – and taught myself about cultural shock and the dimensions of cross cultural management, building on my experience of living and working in thirteen countries.

I teamed up with another previous expat, Joanne Parfitt, an amazing networker, journalist and editor of *Women Abroad*. I wrote for her magazine, we ran workshops, I was contributing author to her book, *Career In Your Suitcase*, for women on the move, and she introduced me to conferences at which I subsequently spoke.

Barry Tomalin, an expert on cultural training, author of numerous books for a cross cultural agency called Cultural Shock, helped me develop my learning and secured some of my initial work.

As I worked through my cultural shock, I became more interested in using my MBA skills, providing marketing, branding and small business training.

Cutting My Teeth

Coaching was becoming the new profession. I attended workshops given by various schools, feeling instinctively this was the profession for me. I'd returned to my psychological roots.

I attended a brilliant Tony Robbins course. He was passionate, an authentic teacher who gave his all without doing a heavy sell. Interested in NLP without the jargon? Read his book *Unlimited Power*.

I am grateful to coach and solicitor Dianna Keel. A fount of coaching knowledge, she was instrumental in helping me on my coaching path. Marianne Craig, MCC, my current supervisor, is a great sounding board and helps me think through issues.

Whilst I dithered about which coaching course to take, Dianna supplied books to read, teleclasses to listen to. The first course I completed was Newcastle College's Diploma in Business Performance Coaching, which taught me goal setting and how to change limiting beliefs to positive ones. Then followed a Neuro Linguistic Programming (NLP) practitioner course, with Tad James, creator of Time Line Therapy. To gain experience in the corporate market I posted an advert on a coaching website, offering to coach three corporate executives for free, pretending I had a grant. To qualify, they committed to three months of weekly telecall sessions.

Whilst NLP training had provided excellent tools, I realised I would benefit from learning the fundamentals of coaching, as highlighted by the International Coaching Federation (ICF). I decided Corporate Coach U International (CCUI) suited my needs and completed their ICF accredited training which focused on the corporate market.

CCUI believes that "To be the best coach you can be, you must first be the best person you can be." Their Professional Foundations Programme comprised self knowledge, personal presence, professional excellence, personal organisation and extreme self care – outlining what coaches should strive for and providing useful tools to use with clients.

Dianna encouraged me to learn about behavioural styles and values to help me understand my clients faster and in more depth. Over the years, I have became certified in numerous psychometrics and team assessments, including Myers Briggs Inventory (MBTI I & Step II) and Emotional Intelligence Inventory (ECI), which have proved invaluable in both managing my own EQ and helping my clients to become self aware and better able to flex their communication styles.

During my first two years of coaching, I coached anything that moved: my kids, husband, friends. Most coaches did. Half the battle was explaining what coaching was. Ten years on and over ninety percent of organisations now use coaching. (Check Additional Resources section for CIPD Research on this topic.) Getting fee-paying coachees was difficult. Rates were minimal and small businesses were unlikely to bring in revenue, although some did fund sessions to tap into my marketing expertise. My talk at the London Coaching Group attracted one of their largest audiences. Coaches were desperate to find ways to get business. I gave workshops on marketing and goal setting to Chambers of Commerce, BNI and Business Breakfast Groups, hoping to get coaching business. Running workshops and training were my main source of income. I developed a mentoring programme for the Fredericks Foundation and ran courses to help employed people return to work.

Earning My Stripes

One of the few cold calls I made was to KBR, a leading global engineering and construction group supporting the energy industry. They decided to test me out, delivering their own workshops in Aberdeen. This lasted six months. They offered me a job as Learning

& Development Consultant. It was an opportunity to understand corporate clients' needs, learn and deliver their management and leadership programmes in the UK, USA and Azerbaijan, be trained in a number of key psychometrics and coach senior managers. I designed two-day courses for HR and business managers on coaching skills, which I delivered in the UK and the USA. The HR course was aimed at training participants how to be internal coaches. The manager's course taught coaching as a management style. Every month, we received videos and facilitator notes of live broadcast interviews with management gurus like Daniel Goleman, Warren Bennis and Ken Blanchard. Management was invited to screenings. It was a chance for KBR's employees to keep up with the latest management thinking, to network with other parts of the business and for me to "recruit" new coachees. I worked for their sister company MWKL, coaching senior leaders, introducing a Future Learners programme which included mentoring.

In 2005, I joined Aviva (formerly known as Norwich Union), the UK's largest insurance group. Unlike KBR, Aviva outsourced their leadership development, an opportunity to learn from the best consultants and coaches. I managed our pool of external coaches and built a network of preferred suppliers while delivering coaching myself.

I used our existing coaches, their client network and Aviva's membership with the Corporate Leadership Council (CLC) to help me learn more. Debriefing directors on their 360° feedback usually resulted in being asked to coach them on their development needs.

In 2005, only a few organisations introduced assessment centres to source a cadre of coaches for their preferred supplier list. One was Unilever. Some excellent coaches didn't get through the process. In addition to looking for the coaching competencies and experience, organisations want to see whether the coach fits their culture and comes across as credible with their stakeholders. Aviva had a small coaching budget so it wasn't money well spent to run an assessment centre. Instead, I designed our own coach criteria and process to assess coaches. One of the best handbooks was CLC's *Maximising Returns on Professional Executive Coaching*. My strength was the ability to source the right external coach for my clients.

Creating opportunities for myself at Aviva was encouraged. There was a need to develop our rising talent and help Senior Directors develop their coaching skills. As there was a real appetite for mentoring, I was able to effectively kill two birds with one stone by developing a mentoring programme which both up-skilled leaders with coaching skills and developed the next tier of management: Heads of Department. I had previously designed mentoring programmes but wanted to raise the bar. I took a mentoring programme coordinator's programme to ensure I was up to speed on the latest techniques. I recruited the Prince's Trust's Mentor Programme's designer and one of my first mentor coaches, Tom Bird (co-author of *Brilliant Selling*) to help me. Together, we developed a training programme attended by mentors and mentees, achieving every objective we set. I won an internal award for the programme.

I came across Strengthscope in 2007, a tool for assessing strengths. Seeing its potential, I offered to run a pilot for one of Aviva's directors if he agreed to allow me to test out the strengths approach and have it measured by an external assessor.

Strengthscope uses everyday business language. Its founders, James Brook and Paul Brewerton of the Strength Partnership, provided me with support. The strengths approach tied in with Aviva's ethos of enhancing performance excellence, growth and employee engagement. I successfully coached five Department Heads, helping them to improve their performance by focusing on developing their strengths. Results were published in *Coaching at Work* magazine. The return on investment (ROI) of the programme showed an ROI ratio greater than 14.1. One coachee saved Aviva approximately £100,000 in consultancy fees. Another created a sales initiative with potential to earn an extra £250,000 in revenue.

Aviva introduced what was, at that time, the state-of-the-art talent management system. I was one of the development team members, responsible for rolling out parts of it at Head Office. I also completed my Masters NLP Practitioner and trained as a mediator with the Mid-Surrey Mediation Services.

The Coaching Process

The initial stage involved a chemistry session, to ensure I was the right coach for the individual, building a relationship, establishing the coaching agreement and developing trust. The coaching code of ethics was provided with an overview of my background and credentials. We discussed our roles, responsibilities, deliverables, the process stages and boundaries of confidentiality. Also logistics, such as number of sessions, timescales, monitoring progress, evaluation, fees and stakeholders. If working with an organisation for the first time, I requested details of the company's vision, strategy, competency model and how the coaching fits into their learning and development strategy.

In the first coaching session, we set the context and initial goals. A coaching template was completed where they specify their SMART (specific, measurable, achievable, realistic and time bound) objectives (maximum 3), how their behaviour will change, the impact this change will have on themselves and others, and how coaching success will be measured. I recommended a three-way with their line manager to agree on mutual objectives. It is advisable to know who the stakeholders are and determine their expectations.

Some form of psychometric (MBTI, ECI) and/or 360° feedback was recommended and is useful for creating greater self awareness. Other tools, like keeping a Strengths Diary and completing a Strengths tool, help tease out natural talents and passions. Weaknesses were not ignored but rather managed, using a strength.

We reviewed progress at further sessions, discussed strategies and issues, exploring ways to overcome any problems. Between sessions, the coachee completed homework. I included short calls or emails.

Managing the ending of the coaching is important, drawing up a plan for moving forward and evaluation. We discussed what the coachee had learnt, the impact of the change and where possible, measured the return of the coaching programme.

Finding My Niche

Aviva went through a reorganisation in 2007. I took redundancy. This allowed me to spend time with my mother, who was dying from cancer. Three months later, I started up as a self-employed coach and leadership development consultant. Over the past two years, three coaching companies have provided me with associate work, working with global corporations in financial services, banking, legal and defence industries. Eighty percent of my time is spent providing one to one coaching and the rest developing high performing teams and delivering the occasional workshop. Until recently, I haven't had to sell myself.

In 2008, I was nominated as Mentor of the Year in Women of the Future Awards and made the short list. Being a finalist meant invitations to join the Ambassadors Programme and The Inspirational Women's Network in partnership with Lloyds TSB. Through the amazing networker, Pinky Lilani OBE, creator of the network and founder of the Asian Women of Achievement Awards and Women of the Future Awards, I have met numerous leading UK businesswomen. Networks are crucial for coaches. Ultimately, people buy people.

My latest development has included becoming an Appreciative Inquiry Practitioner, taking courses in positive motivation and the science of happiness. I am now an accredited AC coach and one of their coaches working with the charity The Kids Company, supporting vulnerable young people. I have a number of barter arrangements offering coaching in return for business services. Best of all, I completed a Stand Up Comedy course, delivering two gigs in London and, most recently, took a TV presenter course.

Six months ago I got off the fence and stated publicly, "I am a Strengths Coach". I feel so passionately about the subject, having had firsthand experience and also having seen my coachees wasting time fixing their weaknesses, rather than accepting who they are and working at being the best they can be. Since going solo, I have introduced the strengths approach to a number of leading organisations. I am currently piloting with a defence industry client, coaching one of their top talents using the strengths approach. We intend using it as a case study to illustrate how to leverage the strengths of top talent.

My vision is to encourage more people and organisations to start using their strengths and have a number of exciting strengths projects in the pipeline, so watch this space.

Have you played to your strengths today?

Gail's Top Tips

- Love what you do
- Identify your strengths – where do you do things with ease and passion?
- Hone your strengths – refine and learn new approaches
- Increase time spent using your strengths, top performers use their strengths over seventy five percent of their time

- Keep learning
- Go for accreditation, the industry is tightening up
- Find support, a mentor and/or a coach supervisor
- Trust your clients - the person who has the problem has the solution
- Listen, listen, listen
- Be positive, it's contagious

Bee Milbourn

"Viva la Revolution!"

"What you do today is important because you are exchanging a day of your life for it."

"PULL YOURSELF TOGETHER!" "Sort yourself out!" These were common answers to life's daily problems before the life coaching phenomenon. There were no services to suit many of life's dilemmas. If you had a career issue or needed motivation, who was there to turn to? You wouldn't bother a counsellor or doctor with such issues. Your problems weren't emotional; they were practical.

You might seek some professional career advice, generally limited to "What are you good at? Here's how you get a job in that field." No one wanted to know your secret desires or passions or what would fulfil you or help you deal with difficult workplace relationships. You could talk to friends or relatives, but then you'd receive in return their agenda for what they thought was good advice for you.

But to whom would you turn when you could see the results of your own self-sabotage but didn't know how to fix it? Who would ask you the questions that inspired you to find out what would really work for *you* and *your* life? Certainly no one I knew. People would just tell me what *they* thought I should do, based on kindness and well meant intentions; based on who they thought I was (which was often very askew to who *I* thought I was).

It was the year 2000 and I had a full-time job with the local council. Having trained in neuro-linguistics, I was also a part-time NLP coach. I began to realise that, although I could help people overcome negative thinking or stuck beliefs with NLP, it seemed I wasn't truly serving them; somehow I wasn't good at taking people forward with their new knowledge into their brighter future.

Then a Life Coaching advertisement dropped on my doormat. I found out what it was all about and added it to my arsenal. Hey presto! I had the full deck at last.

So what was it about coaching that improved all my other skills; that helped me to be a better friend, mother, partner and colleague? To answer these questions, I'll have to take you back in time.

Struggle

I wasn't a confident child. I was a pretty idiotic and mixed up teenager. I married, divorced, married again and had two beautiful children. The years rolled by and any fears, worries or anxieties I had were handled by talking to friends and receiving copious amounts of sympathy and love. My fears over my own inadequacy stayed fuzzily in the background of my mind. I never really thought much about my thinking; just got on with life because that's what you did. The only ambitions I had for myself were dismissed immediately by my lack of confidence in my ability to do anything worthwhile. I put myself down, assuming I was just lazy or stupid.

Like many people, change was thrust upon me when my world came tumbling down in 1993. My husband and I divorced, leaving me with our two early-teen children. We had to sell our home and move somewhere smaller and I was a physical, financial and emotional wreck trying to pretend to the children that I was a safe island in a stormy sea. Whether or not I succeeded, only they could answer now.

I was angry, frustrated, hurt, resentful and knew I needed help to cope emotionally. Over the next few years I saw a couple of counsellors and didn't find the experience all that helpful. They seemed to want me to talk about what was wrong instead of how to get it right. I read dozens of self-help books which gave me a message loud and clear: "I am responsible". Blame doesn't help. Blaming myself or my husband wouldn't change a thing except my health, which would deteriorate if I kept that up. Looking back at what had already happened and at what I could not change wouldn't help. Grief for what I'd lost must cease before I moved on. My sanity required me to live in the present, make the best I could of it and look to the future with hope. My financial situation required me to find the skills and the confidence to get back into the workplace. My friendships required me to stop complaining! My love-life required me to understand myself better before I could find the right guy. My children needed me to be strong. If only I'd had some great coaching through that time, I'm sure I'd have straightened out my life so much faster.

Over these few years, my library of motivational and inspirational books grew and I grew with it, leading me to become a Master and Trainer of Neuro-Linguistic Programming. My confidence and inner peace had grown. My understanding of others and therefore, my relationships was improving rapidly and I had fully grasped the need to take responsibility for everything in my life – even when it would have been so much easier to blame someone else. Yet I still didn't know how to shape my future or even what shape I wanted it to be.

Epiphany

So back to that serendipitous day in 2000 when the life coaching leaflet arrived in the mail. What the heck was life coaching all about? I didn't know but it just *felt* right. So I began my research. I was doing a good job as an NLP coach but I knew something was missing. What was it? Coaching claimed to help people move forward in two important ways:

1. Overcoming self-imposed obstacles one isn't aware of
2. Overcoming external factors one knows well but hasn't overcome

This sounded like the key to unlocking the part of my being that knew I had more to give, but didn't know how.

And so began my training and the "aha" moment that explained the difference that made the difference. Questions: it was all about asking questions;. powerful questions; often unusually phrased questions – leading my clients on a journey of self-discovery, transformation and inner strength. I wanted some of that!

Judgments

My very first experience with coaching occurred only days into my training. I had been asked to coach another student. He was a golfer and wanted to improve his game. I went into a mini panic, thinking "I know nothing about golf!" But I began asking him questions about his goals and resources, what had prevented him from achieving his ambition previously and, most importantly on this occasion, his motivation for improvement.

He wanted to be "as good a golfer as my wife, as she's moving up the league ahead of me."

"Aha!" went my unruly brain as I made an immediate judgment about him not wanting the little woman to be "better" than he was.

I told my judgmental side to switch off and got on with the job of careful questioning.

Boy, is this job humbling. The real story was that he loved his wife very much, but as she got so much better than he did they were seeing less and less of each other as they had to play in different groups. That was something neither of them wanted.

After more coaching questions, we elicited his fears and blocks, worked through them together and he diarised – on the spot – how he was going to improve, with whom and when. He was beaming and grateful by the end and I was dumbfounded. How could I ever have helped someone with such a problem before today? I didn't have a clue about the subject matter. Even if one of my closest friends had had that problem, I would have sympathised, sure, but with this new skill I felt the thrill of helping someone change their life in a way that was perfect for him, just by asking a few questions.

I may not know anything about golf, tennis, cycling, skiing or most othersports, but I've been delighted to help several sportsmen and women who've upped their game through these powerful questioning and listening techniques. Oh, yes. I haven't mentioned the listening techniques yet, have I?

Listening

What is it about the listening that's so different?

Coaches are trained to listen "beyond the words" to hear the nuances and agendas lying behind the verbal content; to watch gestures; to pay attention to metaphors, expressions, changes in tonality and even eye movements. We're trained to hear the "blocks" or underlying beliefs and values and then to support, challenge and feed back on all of that, rather than necessarily on the content.

One client, talking about his home life, said he felt he was "pegged down like Gulliver." We explored what that looked like to him; what it felt like; what each rope or peg represented and what he was saying to himself in his mind-talk.

These types of questions take a person deeper into the subconscious. If we had only dealt with what was in his conscious mind, he would have given me a list of what was not working for him. But we wouldn't have found out the deeper fears and the meanings he had attached to each issue. When you understand yourself better, you have a far greater chance of change. We often go through life verbalising our problems to ourselves or anyone else who will listen, but never really understanding what changes in thinking or behavior on *our* part could make a huge difference to our anxiety levels and improve our relationship with ourselves and others. It can even change the behaviours of those around us because it's a fact that, once we change, those around us must change in some way to adapt to the new circumstances.

Workplace tensions are a common example. A client comes to me because he's the boss and can't seem to communicate with his staff. Or I may be helping a staff member who's resentful or angry at management. Once life coaching works its magic, the client changes and, amazingly, the situation changes too. We affect one another by our actions so when my client goes into work with a new set of actions… well, you know the rest. I didn't tell them what to do. I simply asked questions and listened and they did the work themselves. That is the beauty of coaching. It opens you up to new possibilities.

I remember one young man who felt extremely self-conscious at work. He had been moved from a small office into a huge zone full of workers busily working away behind low-level screens. As his desk was at the far end of all this activity, he became increasingly embarrassed with every step, feeling everyone was looking at him.

We began the coaching process and one of my questions was, "When do you feel really confident? Any context will do." His answer: "When I'm playing football." It turned out he was a keen sportsman and enjoyed skate-boarding, karate and several other sports.

It's so interesting when we watch our client transform from the frowning, anxious person discussing a problem to the beaming, open, confident person who is, only two minutes later, discussing some part of their lives that they love. We can use this.

I helped him fantasise; to visualise himself playing a fantastic game of football and then, keeping all those wonderful confident feelings, to imagine he's dribbling the ball through the double doors of the office and up to his desk. We went through this process with other fun ideas and, in no time at all, the fears and anxieties just seemed to disappear.

How does that happen? Well, his brain had a pattern for anxiety about the office and we just replaced it with a new pattern that involved emotion, excitement, confidence and, above all, fun. His subconscious couldn't hold both patterns at the same time and we made sure the new one was more desirable than the old one. Abracadabra! The subconscious got the message and he never suffered the same way again.

Listening also involves watching. A coach needs to listen with her eyes. How often have I seen a client agree with me wholeheartedly, whilst shaking her head? Talk about being confident at the same time as frowning, or balling their fists whilst saying how relaxed they feel. You may have noticed a friend saying something nice about someone whilst rolling her eyes in a derogatory fashion. Every picture tells a story. It's the coach's job to watch, listen and learn.

Stumbling Blocks

Clients often want to make some minor or major shift in their work, love-life, behaviours, habits or performance. Naturally, the client tells me what she can't do, why she can't do it, why it's been so difficult and what she believes is getting in her way. As a coach, I rarely discuss the "problem" at any great length, because I'm more interested in solutions. But the "excuses" presented by the client – which of course the client calls "reasons" – are often the stumbling blocks to success. There are a number of common excuses, such as "I'm not the right type of person – I was born this way"; "I'm too old/young/fat/ugly/uneducated..."; "I lack motivation/confidence /energy"; "There's not enough time"; "My family/friends will think I'm nuts/try to stop me"; and so on.

What good would it be for me to say, "That's not true, of course you can do it!" That would be a normal reaction as a friend intending to boost morale and motivation, but these people have heard it all before and they just don't believe it. My job here is not to simply salve bruised egos. My job is to help the client find out if her thoughts are true; if her thoughts move her forward or backwards; whether her beliefs are protecting her from failure or success or some other perceived loss. There are many ways of breaking down negative habit barriers, but that doesn't always lead where the client said she wanted to go.

Failure?

I had been running a workshop called "Manage Your Thoughts: Manage Your Life." A large lady in a wheelchair approached me afterwards. She asked if I could help her to slim down and, in the course of our conversation, I asked her what she would gain by being slimmer. She said she would be able to get out of the wheelchair. This seemed such a powerful motivator and yet she had not taken the necessary action. So I asked her what she would lose by being slim and being able to get out of the wheelchair. A long succession of reasons followed, among which were, "I'll be in a lot more pain," "I'll be alone more often as people won't think I need so much help," "I'll be left to do things I still won't be able to do," "The social services will expect me to go out to work and they'll take away my benefits," "I'd love to be back in the world of work," "It was fun but I couldn't hack it now." There were fifteen reasons / excuses why this lady had decided to stay where she was. Please don't judge her harshly; she was genuinely very poorly.

Is it failure to help a client realise that what they say they want is not what they really want? I asked what it was that had kept her in this miserable loop of "I want to but I can't" for so long and her answer was "Everyone expects me to lose weight and to want to get out of my chair." It wasn't *her* wish or desire at all and it's not up to me, as her coach, to decide what's best for her. In her mind, staying in the wheelchair was what she really wanted and slimming and getting out of the chair was everyone else's wish. In fact, one or two of her relatives were positively vile to her. Maybe they knew that "she didn't have a leg to stand on"; they probably thought that shaming her would motivate her to do what they thought she needed to do (stand on her own two feet?) -- although some people have a subconscious need to put others down in order to feel better about themselves.

So we spent a few moments working on an exercise that would help her mentally deflect the "poison arrows" and help her be comfortable about her own needs and goals, rather than permanently uncomfortable trying to achieve someone else's. She did look enormously relieved at having at last given herself permission, for once, to be just who she was.

Self-Coaching

During this transformational time in my career a few personal changes occurred. First, I found a passion for something that I followed through on at last. Secondly, I felt I was becoming a pretty good coach, which wasn't bad for someone of formerly very low self-esteem. Also, my relationships with my family members improved, especially with my children, and that was enormously important to me. It wasn't that we didn't have pretty good relationships anyway, but they improved subtly and profoundly once I started using my new knowledge that a question is always preferable to a statement.

I had learned early on in my NLP training that I could become over-evangelistic and drive everyone crazy, so I kept it really subtle. I simply became more interested in what they had to say and began asking questions when they told me about their lives, instead of just congratulating or commenting or sympathising (though sympathising is just the ticket sometimes). This was such an invaluable step for me. No judgments. No criticisms. No agenda. Just finding out who my family members really were, what they really cared about, and what mattered in their lives. I let my own need for attention go and gave them more attention instead. Miracles can occur daily with this new skill.

My Dad's never been one for a long chat. He's certainly never shared his feelings with me nor I with him, so it came as a huge bonus the day we were at our annual family party – fifty-two members of the clan from all over the world – and my jumping jack father (he has a reputation of not being able to sit still for two minutes at a time) happened to come and sit next to me. I asked him a question about his lodge activities. He answered, but I could hear some doubt in his voice. I asked another question and there followed a seventeen minute conversation about his concerns. I was overwhelmed with gratitude for this wonderful gift and maybe we could have talked before in that way if only I had let go of my need to be heard earlier.

I was always considered to be a good listener before my new skills and it's true that I did listen to friends and family members, but what I had now gained was a depth in my listening, a change in my vocalising, that helped me feel more valuable and, in turn, helped my confidence to blossom.

I did try self-coaching to help me understand where I really wanted to go and who I wanted to be, but if we are hiding from ourselves, then we don't notice the blockages when we question ourselves either. So I would advise anyone to work with a trusted outsider rather than trying the DIY approach. However, not all coaches are alike. When I first dipped my toe in the coaching pool it was bitten by a crab! My coach was of the "pull yourself together and get on with it" style, which wasn't what I needed. My next attempt was with a coach who took what I said as fact without investigating whether it fitted with my core beliefs and values (something all good coaches would automatically do, providing it's relevant to your needs.) If you're looking for a coach, try out more than one and don't be afraid to keep looking until you find one with the style that suits you.

Style

I wonder what you thought when you first heard of a Life Coach". Was it someone who would tell you what you *should* be doing or someone who would ask you questions that would make you squirm?

Soft and gentle, hard as nails, spiritual, motivational, inspirational – what did you expect? Had you experienced professional Coaching or Business Coaching at work? Did you think of Sports Coaching or maybe just a large bus that would take you on a weekend break to some mountain retreat?

Coaching comes in many guises. There are coaches who help people understand how best to dress and behave in court; coaches who specialise in financial or career progression; lifestyle coaches; Internet marketing coaches; sales coaches; psychic coaches... probably by now a coach for any niche or problem you could name. Some coaches work with visualisation, whilst others rely on more analytical techniques. Some have a ormula they follow with each client, whilst others work off the cuff at every session. Some state a minimum time for their coaching programme, whilst others will work on your more immediate problems and that may just be for one or two sessions.

Mentors are often mistaken for coaches, but a mentor is like a teacher – there to tell you how to proceed, whereas a life coach will help you to decide for yourself how to proceed. Well, that's my take on the two terms. Perhaps this can help you decide which coach might be best for you.

Journey

As for me, I'm still on my coaching journey, both personally and professionally, and it's the most exciting bus trip imaginable. I am blessed to join in each client's journey for the period they work with me. Whether it's their career, their home life or their inner journey, it's a privilege and honour to do this job and I thank my lucky stars for that leaflet dropping on my mat. I could talk for hours on synchronicity, but now is not the time.

All I'll say is "Viva la revolution!"

Steve Roche

Living the Life You Choose

In The Beginning

LIFE COACHING FIRST IMPINGED ON MY CONSCIOUSNESS in the early 1990s. As with many people, the term "coaching" previously had meaning for me only in the context of a sports coach. So the concept of personal or "Life" coaching was a new and exciting one, even if I had little idea at that stage what it was.

As soon as I began to understand, I had an "I want to do that" reaction. It attracted me as a way to combine my skills, experience and values to do something that would be enjoyable and challenging, and make a valuable contribution.

I'd been interested in personal development for several years, had experienced some therapy and counselling, read a lot of self-help books and participated in a few courses. So although the language and ideas made sense, it felt as if there was something a bit different about coaching that I couldn't yet put my finger on.

I started to research a bit, looking for life coaches in my area (there were none) and then in the UK (there were a few). The concept and the approach had, of course, come from America, so the early trainings, materials and initiatives were mainly American. I joined the recently formed British email forum, which still runs today and is now called the Eurocoachlist.

At the time, I was working for a leading national company with a good reputation for innovating and for investing in people development and training. A small group of us who had become interested in the subject of coaching enlisted the support of this company to create a Coaching Network (which also runs to this day).

Gradually changing my career from a technical basis in IT to a people focused role in training and consultancy, I carried on learning NLP and developing a range of other personal development skills. Meanwhile I was experimenting with receiving coaching and trying it out for myself.

Living Life On Purpose

It became clear that my skills and interests were a close match with coaching, and I began to see it as something I wanted to do for a living one day. Eventually, the opportunity arose to accept voluntary redundancy and with it a tough decision. The economic climate had changed, forcing cutbacks in the company. My job had changed too and I was no longer enjoying it much. Like so many people, I was just doing it for the money.

I faced the question: how long could I go on doing something that my heart was not in? I found the courage to take a chance and move into the unknown. Early in my new self-employed life, I undertook another formal training in order to become qualified as an NLP Certified Coach.

Coach training was a remarkable experience which taught me a huge amount. Perhaps the biggest thing I gained was a sense of purpose, as I discovered that, after many years of following a career with no real sense of direction, I had a way to find out what mattered to me and really satisfied my values.

Ever since then, I've had the great satisfaction of helping many other people find out what they really want to do, or indeed to discover they do actually have a choice, and don't have to put up with whatever life throws at them. It has become my passion to help people live their lives on purpose and in accordance with their values, so that they can explore their potential and learn to express themselves in a fulfilling way – to live the life they choose rather than the one that's there by default.

The Challenge Of Change

Over the years I have realised that many people live a life they don't really like or enjoy. They are engaged in work they find unsatisfying, they stay in relationships that make them unhappy, they live in places where they don't want to be, or put up with longstanding problems rather than confront and deal with them.

I've learned that change is something most people find quite difficult or intimidating – which means that most of us will make quite an effort to avoid change. This is true even when there are clear benefits for us in making such changes. It is often easier to stay with the comfortable and the familiar, even when it's not what we really want, than to take a leap of faith by stepping into the unknown.

One of the main reasons is that change inevitably involves loss. That's obvious in some cases, but not so many people realise that *all* change – even a change that appears to be wholly positive – involves a loss of some kind. Suppose, for example, that you are moving to a new house. Even though you are really looking forward to it and excited about all the wonderful things it will bring, you will still be losing the old familiar environment and that will have an effect on you, however much you want to go. Similarly, getting out of a relationship that does not sustain you would seem to be a pretty positive move. But almost nothing is completely negative, which means there will inevitably be some things about the relationship that you will miss.

These feelings of loss and regret, of missing things and people and places, are common and quite strong. We have all had the experience of only realising how good something was once we don't have it any more. Like the "grass is greener" syndrome, it seems to be part of human life. It only becomes a problem if we allow ourselves to be ruled by the fear that we won't be able to deal with it. The sad thing is that many people stay in situations they did not choose – and do not enjoy -- for most or even all of their lives, trapped by the energy-sapping fear of change and loss.

It appeared that coaching offered a way to help ease people through such transitions. I felt it would surely be an immensely worthwhile thing to do – and I wanted to find out how that would work. One of the first things I discovered from my own experience is that it's helpful to recognise these things in advance; then, you can plan for how to deal with the feelings rather than being taken by surprise. I also learned that it's good to learn from your own experience!

Becoming A Good Coach

Sir John Whitmore is a highly respected thinker in leadership and organisational change, and author of *Coaching for Performance*. When asked about the key to becoming a great coach, he responded that the most important thing was to continue working on oneself. That has certainly been my experience; the more I've learned about my own patterns, limitations, unhelpful behaviours and beliefs, and about what helps and how change works for me,- the better equipped I am to help others.

I learned that, to be a good coach, you must become an extremely good listener, as well as a highly skilled questioner. I discovered that both skills are much more complex and more difficult to achieve than people generally think.

A book that had a big impact on my thinking was Nancy Kline's *Time to Think*. It is a wonderful explanation of just what it takes to be a really effective listener, and of the transformational power of good listening. It also offers a fascinating approach to removing our limiting assumptions and thus freeing our minds to think afresh. Only a question can do this, and not just any old question. An "incisive question" accurately identifies the limiting assumption and replaces it with exactly the right freeing one. The key to formulating such a question is to listen with precision.

Suppose for example that you want to take action but are stuck. Ask yourself: "What am I assuming here that is stopping me?" Listen to the answer, which might be: "I am assuming that I don't deserve success here." Then ask the question that removes the assumption: "If I knew that I do deserve success here, what would I do right now?"

Another intriguing idea is the question that cuts through denial, which Nancy Kline calls the "Amy question". It recognises that we usually go about a year before we are forced to see what had been right in our face from the beginning. The Amy question is: "What do you already know that you are going to find out in a year?" It requires you to supply and face your *own* information. It's a great question to ask at the beginning of a relationship, enterprise or change.

Points Of View

Another essential skill for the coach is to be able to change viewpoint. You must develop the ability to put aside your own view of the world and step into the other person's shoes for a time. Only by seeing things from *their* point of view can you make sense of what they do and say – because everything that people do, however daft it may seem to us, makes sense to them in the light of what they believe, think and perceive to be true at the time.

NLP taught me that everyone has their own personal model of the world, a model that is right and makes sense for them, even if it seems absurd or untenable to others. Being able to respect other viewpoints is essential to building rapport and gaining trust. It also implies that all behaviour is meaningful, even if we cannot immediately see or understand the meaning.

It is extremely helpful to assume, or presuppose, that people will always do the best they can, given the resources they have available at the time. If you provide better resources, they will automatically make better choices. That is the challenge for the coach.

NLP offers a powerful technique for working directly with other viewpoints, in which the client physically moves between different positions in order to see, hear and feel what the interaction is like from the other person's perspective, as well as from that of a neutral observer. This exercise can have profound effects in terms of new understanding, which can rapidly lead to new behaviours and the removal of conflict, even where it has been present for many years.

What Do You Want?

One of the most perplexing aspects of change and growth turns out to be the problem of knowing what you actually want. This surprised me, as I'd always imagined that to know what you want was the easy part. The hard bit was making it happen.

Once I'd learned about "Towards" and "Away From" motivation, (also from NLP), I began to notice how many people are motivated to move *away from* things they don't want, rather than *towards* the things they do want. Indeed, a common opening statement for my clients is: "I don't know what I want, I just know I don't want this!" And that is, of course, a perfectly valid starting point.

"What do you want?" is one of the greatest and most helpful of questions. Try it, especially when you are next with someone who is unhappy, complaining or moaning about their lot. Instead of sympathising and colluding with them, or arguing and trying to shake them out of it, try saying something like, "OK, so that's what you *don't* want - what *do* you want?" Often the question will stop them in their tracks and force them to think. It's a big shift, potentially changing their orientation Towards something new, rather than Away From something very familiar.

And note that it's so much more powerful because it's just a "harmless" question. You are not telling them anything at all. It may very well be the first time they will really consider the answer. It may be such unfamiliar thinking that they just stop and say "I don't know..." But that doesn't matter, because if the question has landed, has hit its target and been accepted at the unconscious level, it has done its work. Some part of that person is now working on a brand new problem: what do I actually want?

That exemplifies the power of a skillfully judged and delivered question – it looks innocuous and unobjectionable, but it can have a huge impact.

The Wrong Forest

In the early stages of working with someone, it is immensely valuable to spend time exploring the problem area so as to really understand the current situation before running after quick solutions. Otherwise, there is a danger of hurrying off in an unhelpful direction.

A team of forestry workers were performing too slowly and called in a time and efficiency specialist to help increase productivity. As they were working flat out, one worker kept climbing a tree and shouting something. The specialist was frustrated and tried to get the man down. At last the team stopped for long enough to hear what he was shouting: "wrong forest!"

The point, of course, is that it doesn't matter how hard you work if you are focused on the wrong task. You will simply do the wrong things more efficiently. But so often when we fail to get the results we want we just do the same things again, except we try harder. That's why it is essential to ensure that the problem the client presents is actually the best one for them to address.

It is an easy mistake to make. I remember once working with a female client who was unhappy with her job and brought along a list of new career options, which we immediately started working on. I got really enthusiastic about the plans and enjoyed the process, but it fairly soon became apparent that the actions we agreed on each week were not working, as every time I asked her about progress, she had not done anything.

After a while it emerged that these were in reality things her husband wanted her to do, and were not part of her vision at all. The real work in fact was to address the nature of her relationship with him. If I had explored the problem area a bit more deeply at first and come to understand that, we could have saved a fair bit of time and effort. This is typical of the useful lessons that a coach learns along the way.

Client Resources

As a coach, I believe it is especially useful to work from the basic premise that the client has the answers they need inside themselves or, if not, that they have the resources to find them. That means my job is to help them reveal what they do actually know at some level, or discover something new about themselves. Sometimes there's a stage before that when they don't realise what it is they don't know. It is hugely rewarding when you witness somebody having an "I didn't know I could do that!" moment.

I believe a defining quality of a coach is the capacity to believe in the client – in their ability, their potential, their desire to learn and willingness to explore and grow. The lack of that capacity rules out many potential coaches who find themselves quite unable to refrain from giving advice, or are certain that they have the answers to other people's problems.

Having said this, there is sometimes a reason to be more directive. Occasionally a client really does need to hear you say "Yes, I agree that's the best course of action for you at this stage," or "Why don't you try this..." rather than asking yet another question. The standard therapeutic ploy of "So what do *you* think?" can be clichéd and unhelpful if it's merely a formulaic response.

And what most clients frequently need, sometimes above all else, is lots of encouragement and support. If you never did anything other than listen quietly and respectfully and tell people they are doing really well, you could still be a useful coach.

It is helpful to show people how to connect with their inner wisdom, to build their own resourcefulness and learn to trust themselves rather than looking to someone else to tell them what to do. Of course it can be hard to sit and listen quietly when you feel like you know exactly what this person needs to see or understand or change in order to move on. But things that we work out for ourselves, that come from our own sense of inner knowing, are worth a great deal more than things other people tell us.

Most people resist being told what to do and prefer to follow their own truths and their own beliefs, their own intuition or hunch about what's right – and that's healthy. It's just that many of us don't know what we believe, don't know how to listen to our intuition or don't trust it. The latter may be a particular problem for men, for whom society discourages exploitation of qualities such as "feminine" intuition.

Inherited Beliefs

That kind of stereotyping of male and female qualities is often unhelpful, as it restricts people's ideas about what is appropriate or acceptable for them. Unfortunately, this is true of so much that lurks in the collective unconscious and passes for received wisdom.

The familiar proverbs and sayings we all repeat to each other can be damaging and limiting. People may not deliberately sign up for these things or be consciously aware of them, but they have a pernicious influence nonetheless, because we all know them and they are instilled in our minds without us noticing, only to pop out unexpectedly.

One example is "You've made your bed and now you must lie in it." This is just not true. A bed can be remade any time you choose. You can pick up your bed and put it somewhere else. You can sleep in somebody else's bed. Or even not sleep in a bed at all.

"We reap what we sow" is another version of the same thing. The thinking behind such aphorisms exposes a miserable attitude; it tells us that once you have made a decision you have to live with the consequences. But why? Why not just make a different decision?

In similar vein, we say "You can't teach an old dog new tricks." In other words, it's impossible to get someone to change the way they do things if they've been doing them that way a long time. That's a profoundly unhelpful belief, often used as an excuse for not changing or even trying to change, as in "It's too late, I'm too old, it's too difficult, it'll take too long, too much effort..."

The truth is that sometimes change is easy and quick, even after many years of doing something one way. Often the hardest part is simply changing the belief – if you can get from "I can't do this" to "I *can* do this" you are more than halfway there.

"Pride comes before a fall" is perhaps a typically English attitude that prizes false modesty and affects to despise all legitimate pleasure in our achievements and talents. We'd do a lot better to replace this kind of proverb with something which conveys that it's good to be proud of what you have done and what you have changed for the better.

It's interesting to reflect on how so many of these old saws came to be negative and doom-laden. Where are all the proverbs that promote ideas like "You can change quickly and easily," "You can start a new life whenever you want to," or "If you don't like what you've got, then choose something different"?

The Coaching Approach

My hope is that the growth of coaching will have some impact on this kind of proverbial wisdom; that the new ideas and approaches championed by working coaches will challenge the conventional and institutionalised view of human nature which can so often come across as downbeat and discouraging.

Life coaching and business coaching have many demonstrable benefits, and have already helped many thousands of individuals to greater success and fulfillment. Perhaps there is an implicit wider brief: that ultimately the coaching approach may address our embedded attitudes about what we are capable of and what it would be helpful to believe.

In time the coaching world might even introduce a whole new set of proverbs. There's one axiom from NLP that may not yet have achieved proverbial status, but that is widely known and much quoted: "If you do what you've always done, you get what you've always got." This more helpful maxim points out that it is absurd to repeat the same action and yet expect a different result. To do so is sometimes described as the definition of insanity - even though it is something that we all do.

Action!

The clear implication of 2If you do what you've always done, you get what you've always got" is that if you want something new in your life, you need to do something different. And that's largely what coaching is about: doing something different, taking some action to create something new.

The emphasis on action is one of the things that distinguishes coaching from therapy or counseling – both more concerned with gaining an understanding of the past, with finding causes and explanations, and expressing suppressed feelings. Healing is then achieved by reliving the damaging experiences with a skilled helper in a safe environment, and integrating the insights gained in the process.

People are more likely to come to coaching from a place of being relatively OK, and being able to function fairly competently in the present. Sometimes it is a particular area of their life with which they have a problem, such as a difficult relationship, or a career challenge. Often there's a personal issue too, such as confusion, frustration, low self-esteem, or lack of confidence.

Confidence is almost certainly the biggest single issue I'm asked to help with. It's something almost everyone would like more of – like talent or charisma, I've never heard anyone complain of having too much of it.

I notice that people have a few misconceptions about confidence. Many believe it is an innate quality rather like intelligence or humour. I believe it's more helpful to regard confidence as a skill, one that can be learned and practised. It's also something that depends on the context. So it's probably not helpful to say "I am (or am not) a confident person" because we are more or less confident depending on where we are, who we are with, and what we are doing.

Because it is a skill, it can be modelled - you can find someone who does it well, find out what they do and then do it yourself. You can even model yourself – applying what you do well in one area of your life to other areas. I tell people that the word can mean to "have faith in yourself". And that is something anyone can learn to do.

Finally

Coaching is a job where you are always learning. You must maintain a belief in a person's capacity to change and in your own capacity to change. The greatest satisfaction is in watching that change unfold as you work with others, throwing off their limitations and as they and you grow in confidence and self-belief. When we discard enough of our limiting beliefs, we are finally free to live to our potential and fulfil our life's purpose.

Tania Adams

African Abundance

ABUNDANCE IS A POPULAR BUZZ WORD TODAY. A Google search on the word reveals a multitude of sites dealing with, *inter alia*, secrets for creating abundance, the law of attraction, definitions of abundance, abundance ecology and even relative abundance! A search for the key word "abundance" on Amazon.com reveals a staggering 319,806 books dealing with the topic. There are training courses on offer, manuals for attracting abundance, instructions for using universal laws to create abundance. Talk shows on the topic abound. Everyone wants abundance. But is it possible for everyone to have it? I say a resounding "Absolutely!"

I am the founder and owner of Abundance Life and Executive Coaching, South Africa. My fundamental belief and the cornerstone of my coaching practice is that abundance is a human birthright, everyone is entitled to the kinds of personal abundance they dream of, whether it be abundance in finances, relationships, creativity, freedom, physically or career. My lifetime commitment and the mission of my coaching business is to define and access every client's unique vision of abundance and open up the path for them to create it for themselves.

From Adversarial To Collaborative
– A Journey From Law To Coaching

How does a lawyer become a coach, or *can* a lawyer be a coach? The two sound contradictory, an oxymoron. How does adversarial become collaborative? It happens when the common thread is people; people with the drive to create an outcome with the support of an objective third party who has a vested interested in co-creating that outcome with their client. It happened to me.

Early in 1999, I had just begun serving a two year period of articles in order to become an attorney. I had been working as a Junior Lecturer at the University of the Witwatersrand, Johannesburg, for three and a half years and had recently returned to South Africa from an extended travel break to the United

Kingdom and my childhood home town in Ireland. I was excited about my new career as an attorney; having taught law for so long, it would be wonderful to finally practice it. My car had been stolen just before my European trip and I was looking forward to saving for a replacement. I had studied law for a number of reasons, the most important of which was that I wanted my own practice, I wanted to be my own boss, and this was the beginning of that dream. It was a huge blow when I was unfairly dismissed a few weeks later because I was pregnant. Suddenly I found myself jobless, without a car and soon to be a single mom.

All was not lost however. I was offered a job to begin the following January as a Credit Manager in the motor industry. I took the job, although it was not what I wanted to do with my life. However, motherhood changes a person, and the following January I started the job with determination and a new goal; if the motor industry was to be my new playground, I would get to the top of the game and become a Dealer Principal. If I couldn't have my own practice and be my own boss, I could at least the boss of a motor dealership. So began an eight-year long journey in the motor industry, a traditionally male dominated industry, where I built my career by continuously asking for more responsibility, and more money, with my eye on the Dealer Principal's office.

Those years were filled with personal and professional challenges, and through the challenges I grew. Not only was I working in a very masculine industry, but I had a legal and accounting background, not sales, which is the traditional place leaders in the motor industry begin. No matter what I proved as a credit manager or dealership accountant, it carried little weight with my superiors, who held the belief that accountants are by nature too restrictive to run a sales oriented business. I was undeterred. I had committed myself to the goal of running a dealership and I would not give up. I also knew I wasn't a stereotypical accountant.

I found that I had a unique strength; I was good at working with people. I had the ability to rally a team, to get them to work with me as well as for me, because they wanted to, not because they had to. No matter what dealership I worked in, or what department I ran, the outcome was always the same: I was the accountant who was good with people. I could get the best out of them. Combining that skill with my knack for process and systems meant my departments ran efficiently and effectively, with motivated loyal staff. I turned myself into an asset and never stopped asking for the opportunity to do more, to be more. My persistence paid off and I moved through the finance departments, into sales and ultimately, into the driving seat of a beautiful flagship dealer!

Three months later, on the eve of moving into a fabulous new home, my Managing Director shared with me that my dealership would be closed owing to restructuring within the group's brand holdings. They were willing to offer me another dealership to run as soon as a post became available. Once again I found myself at a point of decision making, and one thing I was sure of was that, this time, I would choose my path, not simply make the best of one I was given.

My passion for working with people, developing them, growing them, supporting them to excel and be the best of themselves was the determining factor. I began to research careers where I could do that without the constraints of a large company's rules, regulations and corporate politics. Coaching was the obvious choice. It was the perfect career for me to combine my clear, practical view of life and my business experience, with my passion and gift for working with people and my desire to run a business for myself.

Today, I have fulfilled my dream of owning my own practice: I am my own boss, my time is my own, and my destiny is in my hands. It is not a law practice that I own, and instead of supporting my clients to achieve their desired outcomes at the expense of an opposition's loss, I support my clients to achieve their desires in a way that produces only winners. As a Life and Executive coach, I coach clients from pre-teen children to Managing Directors, and, instead of cars, I now put people in the driving seat of their lives. I also have a new big goal: to make abundance a world-wide reality through building a coaching company that effectively enables and empowers people to take control and live the life they desire and deserve, irrespective of the circumstances they may encounter along the way.

The Coach "Being"- A Process Of Metamorphosis

With my legal and process oriented way of thinking, I made sure to research the profession of coaching thoroughly and, although it is not yet regulated as a profession in South Africa, I committed myself to coach only with a formal qualification.

I had some experience with esoteric and self discovery work from courses I attended during my twenties. Over a period of approximately ten years, in an attempt to figure out why my past had been what it was and what I needed to do to create the future I desired, I had tried many things: therapy, kinesiology, energy healings, astrology, metaphysics. Among others, my search took me to a metaphysical course, where I learned about setting one's intent on an outcome, the power of intention and positive thinking, the law of attraction, guided meditations and managing one's own thoughts. So, by the time I began my search for a coaching academy through which to train, I regarded myself as somewhat an old hat at that stuff.

I was extremely particular about my choice of academy through which to study. I already had two university degrees from top universities in South Africa and was looking for a course which carried similar weight, and was accredited in South Africa and internationally. I came across a great school, the first originally South African school to have the International Coach Federation (ICF) Accredited Coach Training Program (ACTP) accreditation for its course work. The Cape Town based academy also ran courses in Johannesburg where lived. I made my decision to train with them. What I liked very much was that their introductory course seemed to be a repeat of much of the self discovery, esoteric, metaphysical work with which I was by now so familiar, and that, I thought, would short-cut my process. Why re-do what I was already so well versed in?

Self assuredly I called to discuss enrolling and informed the academy that I had done lots of courses of that style in the past, and was very *au fait* with self discovery work. I requested (with the expectation of receiving a yes) to be allowed to skip the first module and go right on to the "proper" work. Politely and without judgment I was heard and affirmed. I hadn't yet been exposed to the coach "being" and so I misread the affirmation as an agreement that indeed they could see how expert I was. Just as gently, I was informed I would have to complete the process from the beginning; the first module is an absolute pre-requisite for the rest. Humph!

Therein was my first piece of coach training: lesson one - a coach is never too expert to learn more. That first module opened up parts of me and places in me I didn't even know I didn't know about. There was indeed some repetition in the content of the theory, and a lot more that was new to me by virtue of the way it was presented. I completed that module with a deep understanding of the power of choice. I learned the role of commitment and integrity in the process of creating one's desires and the distinction between the conditioned ego self and the intentionally created self; the person I choose to be. I found I had changed in unexpected ways. I had loosened my grip on things I had held as fixed viewpoints about myself, others and the world at large. I was better able to receive feedback without becoming defensive and wanting to justify. I learned how to access energy sources within myself I didn't even know existed, and to do so at will. I left that module with the beginnings of a coach "being" and had as yet learned almost nothing about the coach "doing".

The course was structured in such a way that it is possible for the learner to work at their own pace. Because of the highly practical focus of the course, in between classroom sessions, learners are required to get into the practice of coaching. Part of the submitted portfolio of evidence for the qualification is proof of coaching sessions received from an appointed academy coach. Lesson two: to be a good coach, one must be coachable.

Furthermore, learners were required to provide evidence of coaching sessions given, both paid and pro-bono, as well as proof of coaching sessions given and observed by one of the senior trainers and by learner peers, including the feedback notes. Thus, the duration of the course is quite dependant on the speed with which the learner can source clients to coach. This is a critical aspect of the course as it builds the skill of enrolling paying coaching clients from the beginning. Lesson three: a great coach is worth nothing without paying clients to coach.

I worked quickly through this part of the qualification requirements; I was in a hurry to have my practice up and running. I attended the remaining classroom modules over a period of six months, while building up my practical coaching hours. The classroom modules each consisted of four consecutive eleven hour days. The work was presented as a powerful blend of how to do coaching; providing the learner with the skills necessary to hold a formal coaching session from opening moments through to the completion of the session goal; and deep self discovery work with the purpose of developing in the learner the coach "being". We were frequently reminded of lesson four: the power of coaching lies not in the theory of coaching or the mechanics of coaching, but in who you are *being* as a coach.

There was no definition given in our texts or workbooks for the coach "being, it was not clearly described by the trainers and yet we were scored on it in our continuous assessments. How would we ever master the coach "being" if we were not told what to *be* or *how to be* it? Over time, as if by magic, a true metamorphosis took place, and each one of us recognised in the others subtle shifts whenever we re-engaged for the next classroom module. The "being" was becoming.

I experienced myself as more consistently positive, even in the face of circumstances no different from those I'd faced before. The small things stayed small, and I didn't sweat them. The big things became the subject of creative actions, not stressful anxious worries; I stopped sweating those too. I learned to receive feedback positively and use it as a tool for growth, even seek it out. I experienced a level of compassion for others I had not previously known. I realised the only expert about anyone's life is the person living it, and I was able to let go of my need to "help" and advise. I came to see how disempowering it can be to give advice rather than to support the other to find the answers they already have, but don't yet see. I acquired the ability to forgive, even forgiving myself, the toughest task of all. I developed the courage to share my heart authentically and to be open to receiving heartfelt sharing from another. I saw the possibility, and knew it to be absolutely true, that one who dares to commit, to risk stepping outside of themselves, is capable of achieving anything they truly desire. The coach "being" became clear and it became a new way of life.

The Gift Of Living As A Coach

Coaching is a way of living for me, as opposed to a career or even a profession. Early in my training, my own coach said to me that the most powerful coach is not the person who has it all figured out in life, but the person who is committed to constantly staying the course of growth and discovery. That stayed with me and has informed my way of being on a daily basis.

I am often asked what I do and, although my title is Coach, I answer the question by saying that I give people back their lives. Inertia is the tendency of an object in motion to remain in motion, or an object at rest to remain at rest, unless acted upon by a force.

Described by Sir Isaac Newton's first law of motion, this timeless natural law applies not only to physical objects, but to lives as well. The oft maligned comfort-zone, where many find themselves, is a colloquial description of the effect of inertia.

The trouble with staying in one place too long is that what was comfortable eventually becomes uncomfortable, numbing and stagnant. When people fail to shift from the path and direction their life is taking, it is not out of laziness or a lack of ambition. When a person appears to repeat the same patterns over and over without successfully changing the results, it is not out of stupidity or ignorance. These situations occur purely because the laws of physics govern us all; inertia will keep us on the same path, repeating the same mistakes, until we are shifted by a force greater than the force of inertia. The required force may come in the form of a great and unexpected upheaval or tragedy: a job loss, a death, an accident. There is a greater force, however, that will act upon the effect of inertia in life: the force of commitment.

Anyone who has tried to take a corner in a car travelling too fast, or pushed a car that has broken down, knows how much energy, focus and persistence it takes to change the direction of an object in motion, or create motion where none exists. As I travel with my clients through their coaching journey, I never fail to be inspired by their courage to fully engage with the process and step outside of themselves in service of their commitment to create a new way of life, a life of abundance. Through the force of their commitment, driven by the power of coaching, my clients take back their lives and create what they really want. When I witness this, I am inspired by the knowledge that nothing in this world is impossible and I am reminded of the words of anthropologist Margaret Mead who said "Never underestimate the power of a few committed people to change the world. Indeed, it is the only thing that ever has."

Working with my clients, I am challenged by the process of coaching each one to look deeply into myself and keep growing as a coach and as a human being. There is not one client I have coached in whom I have not seen a reflection of some part of myself. In the process of coaching my client, I often feel as though I am coaching myself. There are many sessions where I smile to myself, and make a note of something I see reflected back at me. And, when I really need to shift something in my life, I seem to coach on the same topic for two or three consecutive sessions with different clients. Whatever courage and commitment I ask of my clients to grow and change direction, I demand of myself. Coaching then, is a continuous, daily process, my way of life. It is who I am, not what I do.

Coaching For Abundance

Webster's *New World College Dictionary* defines abundance as "a great supply, more than sufficient quantity, great plenty, wealth.". In the *Oxford Dictionary* we read that abundance is "the state or condition of having a copious quantity of something; plentifulness of the good things of life; prosperity." Synonyms for abundance include copiousness, teemingness, luxuriance; lushness, wealth profusion, profuseness, richness; cornucopia, plenty, plentifulness, plenteousness, plenitude; amplitude, bountifulness, bounty.

An initial reading of these definitions would seem to indicate that abundance is completely conditional upon circumstance; that in the absence of wealth there cannot be abundance. And yet, a deeper reading suggests it is not necessarily so. The Oxford definition uses the words "state or condition". Is it possible, then, that abundance is not necessarily a description of material wealth, rather a state of being? As a state of being, is the existence of abundance no longer conditional upon external circumstances? Is it, then, possible to experience abundance irrespective of financial standing?

A further look at the definitions reveals they do not define exactly what should be in plentiful supply to qualify as abundance. The Oxford definition comes closest by saying "plentifulness of the good things of life". Both plenty and good are relative concepts: the good things of life to one are not necessarily the same for another. What a billionaire deems to be plenty differs from that which an impoverished person deems plenty. So, then, what is abundance? Can it be defined? How should it be defined?

Since abundance is, in short, a state of having a plentifulness of the good things in life and therefore a relative concept, I'd like to suggest that abundance can be created by choosing to see the plentifulness of the good things in each one of our own lives; by actively seeking them out, acknowledging them and celebrating them. Abundance is a chosen way of being, not a circumstance. Abundance exists in the absence of anything material, in the absence of everything.

Abundance can be defined and accessed by each individual irrespective of the circumstances, especially since circumstances cannot always be changed. By defining abundance for ourselves, every person can actively create an abundant life. The first step is identifying our own personal "good things" whether they are time, money, relationships, health or love. What good things are already plentiful in your life? The second step to creating an abundant life is to celebrate the abundance, rather than focusing on the lack. In so doing, abundance becomes a chosen way of being, not an external circumstance.

What enormous possibilities exist if abundance really does exist irrespective of circumstance? What are the implications if people and nations adopted an abundance philosophy? Neighbours would no longer haggle over a boundary line; food aid would no longer be stolen and sold; nations with an oversupply would no longer need to hold poorer countries to ransom with crippling loans. An abundance philosophy would open up the possibility that there is indeed enough of everything on this planet for us all to survive, abundantly.

African Abundance

South Africa is a land that has transformed itself and continues to do so. Day after day, week after week, year after year, South African society is remoulding itself, redefining itself. There is no singular definition of "South African" that fits all. We are a nation of differences that belie striking commonalities, evidenced even in the landscapes, which range from lush tropics and snow white beaches to savannah grasslands; from stark deserts to rolling green hills and fertile wine lands. Our skin colours range from black to white and every shade in between; our tribes, cultures and religions are multifarious. And yet, we form a cohesive, strong nation, an African leader, a society that is working towards building a prosperous nation for its entire people.

However, South Africa continues to battle some of the legacies of past inequalities. Historical differences in educational systems have left their mark on sectors of the population. Cultural differences impact communication. Assumptions, labelling and prejudice still exist within communities, not only across racial boundaries, but within them too. A consciousness of scarcity and greed lends itself to corruption and crime. Change has not come as quickly to all areas and sectors as was wanted, creating anger, resentment and mistrust.

Coaching has a powerful role to play in such a landscape. Coaching can support the continued growth of the nation through shifting embedded beliefs, widening opinions, changing perceptions, reducing resistance, instilling accountability, integrity, self reliance. Coaching to create a culture of abundance as a chosen way of being would empower people to take ownership and create their own abundance, rather than expecting abundance to be created by a government. Coaching could mobilise the nation from within itself to accelerate the changes still needed, to bridge the gaps of remaining inequalities, to work together instead of against one another.

As a profession in South Africa, coaching has grown rapidly, especially over the past two years. Coaching is familiar to most people. The government is investing in projects to facilitate coaching for unemployed, underemployed and other disadvantaged groups. Corporates are utilising the power of coaching to empower their staff, develop their leaders and improve productivity. Individuals refusing to live mediocre lives are engaging coaches for support in creating their own destiny. Schools are utilising coaches to support learners through transitional phases, for career choice and life skills development. I have committed my life as a Professional Coach to being part of those processes. My wish and hope is that, as a profession, coaching establishes itself as a vital part of the way South Africans live and create their own abundant lives, their own abundant land.

Judy Barber

Weaving a Coaching Career

Becoming A Coach

I KNEW I WANTED TO BE A COACH THE MOMENT I discovered what a coach was. I was sitting on a wall outside the Rudolf Steiner School where I taught teenagers, chatting with the wife of a colleague. I didn't know Fiona Reed so I asked her what she did – that is apart from being the mother of two very small children. If I could remember exactly what she said, I would tell you, because she said it so well I understood in an *instant* – and I don't think it is always easy describing what coaching is.

It wasn't any old light-bulb moment, nor as dramatic as Saul becoming Paul on the road to Damascus. It was a simple recognition of what I had been doing one way or another for years, only woven into a professional role in its own right. I also realised that precious, subtle "helping conversations", which allow the other to be free to ponder and move forward in their own way, were valued in something now called Coaching.

This happened when I was moving to Wales for family reasons and looking for a new professional direction. I resolved to be a coach there and then, and I hired Fiona almost immediately. I am very glad I did.

Soon I took on pro-bono clients: people I would coach out of the goodness of my heart. Put another way, these were clients who were willing to put themselves in the hands of a beginner. This went on for several months, until one client asked thoughtfully, "Well, when are you going to start charging me then?" I did. We continued and I began taking on other paying clients.

The Threads That Led Me To Coaching

How could I decide to be a coach and begin coaching so quickly just from the experience of being coached and mentored by my own coach?

When I met Fiona, I was ready to start my coaching career because I had professional training and experience in a related profession, teaching, and because I had a strong personal development background.

I have woven all kinds of thread into my coaching.

PROFESSIONAL TRAINING THREAD

I had a great deal of directly relevant professional training in a four year, practical teaching degree including English and Psychology, for the teenage and adult age range. Back then, "coaching" simply meant getting a bit of academic support, maths or tennis for example, any kind of one to one lesson. It often still does. However, a lot of what I learned in my training was exactly what coaches need, including the following list of features. (You may have some previous professional experience to consider in a similar way):

- Goal setting
- Supporting people in reaching goals
- Breaking large tasks into small steps
- Beliefs and values – explored in depth through literature
- Being witness to another's life – that of the student and of lives in literature
- Empathy and sensitivity to moods, tones of voice and body language
- Motivation, encouragement and positivity
- Exploring and encouraging self expression
- Clear communication
- Building confidence

Your education might not have been like that, but I was blessed to be learning as an enthusiastic young woman in an enlightened institution, and I had accepted a meaning of education from its root in the Latin word "educere", meaning to "lead out, to bring out from latent or potential existence." The essence of coaching.

My professional training has since included a post-graduate Drama Therapy certificate and Art Therapy training, both of which have been woven into my workshops.

Through being a parent I discovered the Steiner-Waldorf schools movement and Rudolf Steiner's teachings. These have lead to me teaching every age group in Steiner-Waldorf schools from three to eighteen years, have been a central influence in my personal and professional development and, in an understated way, in my work. In fact, professional development training continues every day of one's working life.

PERSONAL DEVELOPMENT TRAINING THREAD
Perhaps I'm a perpetual student – and perhaps that isn't a bad way to be. I've certainly gone on studying, for the joy of it and to evolve personally and in my profession. Buddhist meditation was important for me early on and I went on many workshops with John Garrie Roshi, ex-circus clown and film, TV and Shakespearean theatre actor from Manchester who taught from the Thai Satipatthana and Japanese Zen traditions. I learned so much from him that is essential to the way I coach, even on professional issues. Human nature is human nature, whether in the boardroom or the living room.

Other pivotal personal development learning came from:

- Barry Long, Australian spiritual teacher with an interesting take on relationships
- Jean Houston, prolific American speaker, workshop leader and writer about spirituality, cross-cultural learnings and Social Artistry
- Isaac Shapiro, South African teacher acutely aware of how people affect each other
- David Ure, Australian coach leading seminars for Landmark Education

There were many others as well. I was drawn to learn from these people for my own development and I was lucky enough to have a career in which I could make direct use of what I learned. In coaching and other "soft skills" work, the distinction between personal and professional can be quite hazy.

Have I learned more from other people and courses or from my own interactions in life?

All my own stops, starts and life experiences are woven in with what I have been taught, and it's all relevant to being a Life Coach. Sometimes, it's directly relevant when there is comparable experience, but comparable experience is not essential. What is more important is being quiet in oneself and ready to accompany the client as they work with their life issues, inspiring confidence and enabling them to discover and trust their inner resources.

SPECIFIC COACH TRAINING THREAD

My first specific training was my own experience of being coached. I'm glad I had that experience first. Initially I could stay in my own process without being too aware of my coach's techniques. That gave me an experience comparable with that of some clients, the ones who love what coaching brings but aren't so bothered about how the coach does what they do.

Sometime after I started coaching, I decided I had better do some formal training, even though no one asked me about my credentials. I was living in the sticks so I decided to go the distance-learning route and signed up for the Newcastle College Performance Coaching programme. It included essays, coaching and receiving feedback. It was a good course, created by excellent coach Angus McLeod.

I did a Fraser Clarke Business Coaching course which was very good too, giving me a helpful understanding of coaching in workplace contexts.

What I didn't learn sufficiently well then was how to set up and run a coaching business. That would have been very helpful. I did short business courses and read widely but, to be honest, I muddled along learning the hard way rather than the lucrative way. A course about the practical aspects of building up and maintaining a coaching business such as the Noble Manhattan Business Building Day programme would have been a better reality check and a worthwhile investment. But at least I didn't go into things for the kind of instant fortune I understand some are led to expect.

Another way I learned more about being a coach was by writing a book about it. In coaching sessions people kept saying, "That's a good question." Something went "click" about my ability to ask good questions, so I decided to collect them together in a book called *Good Question! The Art of Asking Questions to Bring About Positive Change*. It is a helpful, all-purpose collection and includes useful stories and exercises. I receive very good feedback about it. I wrote about how to come up with questions that help the client to significantly develop their thinking in helpful ways, hence the title. I wrote from my perspective and also worked with contributions from twenty eight coaches and speakers, including Gerard O'Donovan. Some are widely known and some busy in particular realms. I gained so much insight into the variety of people and approaches in coaching and what coaches have in common. I can see coaching as a distinct profession and also as a set of approaches, skills and attitudes with wide application in various professions, as well as in home and community life. Coaching feels like a helpful genie - well and truly out of the bottle and into individual and organisational life around the world.

More recently, I have learned NLP (Neuro Linguistic Programming) and Clean Facilitation. These have given me so many good skills and approaches to weave into my coaching.

NLP techniques, in a sense, have taught me more about "navigating" in a coaching conversation, for example, moving between overview and detail, between one perspective and another, and forwards and backwards in time.

Clean Facilitation, the wonderful collection of ways of working developed by psychotherapist David Groves that I use so often in my coaching, enables me to help clients stay in their own experience and search more thoroughly. It's about helping them to explore their "inner landscape" and use their own metaphors in helpful and productive ways.

WORKING LIFE THREAD

From a mixture of inclination, necessity and ingenuity, I have made a living in a variety of ways. To be honest, my CV is so long it's difficult even for me to believe it's all true, but it is. Here are snapshots:

- Aged twenty two, going through fourteen locked doors to teach A level English to adult inmates in Wormwood Scrubs Prison
- Teaching various subjects in College of Further Education to hairdressers, engineers, the deaf and others
- Importing Balinese paintings
- Teaching English in Shiraz, Iran
- Hotel cooking in the Australian Outback
- Drama workshops and role playing in New Zealand
- Magazine writing and editing
- Bed and breakfast business
- Producing *An Inspector Calls* with teenagers in Edinburgh

These days I work as a writer, coach and workshop leader, buzzing about networking and speaking, inventing learning activities, mentoring and coaching. I might be coaching someone who is in a suit at their office, while I am home in jumper and jeans.

I love the work thread in my life, protestant work ethic perhaps. I really live into my work. The joy and purpose of work goes way beyond money, important though that is, of course.

"LIFE" THREADS

John Lennon was spot on when he sang that "Life is what happens when you're busy making other plans," and Life Coaching cannot only be learned from formal training and from courses. Between times, I've been boiling kettles, falling in love, worrying about things, scuffing through leaves, playing with children, reading books and generally having a life.

The four threads in my life are Travel, Food, Relationships and Arts and Craft.

My list of travelled places includes well over thirty countries in Europe, South East Asia, America, Australasia and Africa.

I can see that I have taken too many flights for one person, now that we are belatedly watching our carbon footprints. Some trips have been holidays and stopovers. Some were longer stays. I was born in South Africa and grew up in England. I lived in Iran and Australia and, for a long time, in New Zealand. I now live in Scotland. Lucky me to have experienced so much of life on this fantastically diverse planet. If travel broadens the mind, my mind qualifies as broad. Knowing about culture from experience is invaluable in coaching. When a client in the Philippines told me recently about surviving flooding there, of course it was hard to fathom the experience, but at least I had an inkling from a general understanding of life in different places. When in Kenya last year I gave a workshop for some teachers and parents, because I knew I could and that it would be appreciated. That's something any coach could do as a gift when visiting somewhere where resources are scarce. It was the time when Obama was elected and it was incredible experiencing such a big world change. People in a materially impoverished culture were alight with hope, joy and possibility. So much in the world depends on states of mind. I have a strong sense of the importance of coaching around the world for lifting spirits and bringing about positive societal change.

Food has always been central to my life. I love good food and preparing food is my main art form. Food has become more important professionally in the last couple of years since I trained as a Hippocrates Health Educator at the Hippocrates Health Institute in Florida. This training came in the wake of years cooking and eating traditional food, organics, macrobiotics, world food, sprouted seeds, veggies and simply delicious food of all kinds. I now prepare and eat mainly raw food and have learned how to help people to bring energy, vitality and increased wellbeing into their lives with living plant food. I've got so much to say and do in the realm of wellbeing, on the physiological nutrition side and the psychological emotional side which affect each other so deeply.

Relationships include my own family, several long fruitful primary relationships, parenthood, single parenthood, friendship and a lot of love. Since so much of Life Coaching is about relationships, perhaps this particular biographical thread is the most important.

On the Welsh dresser in my kitchen, there's a little silver cup. The Tickenham WI club gave it to my grandmother because she had won it so often – for jam, tapestry, Somerset willow basketry; you name it, she made it. If I could time travel, my first port of call would be back to her house where I visited her as a child. The silver cup reminds me that this essential part of myself, the arts and crafts thread, takes me back before my time as well as forward. I've even chosen a weaving metaphor for the title of this chapter.

I've done willow baskets too, like my grandmother, and sewing, cake decorating, painting rooms and pictures, making feasts and daily meals, creating recipes, making simple toys with natural materials, improvisation, theatre productions, taking photos for my blog, knitting. I couldn't just be academic.

Arts and crafts activities enable me to live right into my fingers, just as walking enables me to live right through my body, my legs and into my toes. Your hands on activities may be similar, or you may garden or fix things. These kinds of activity are so important in claiming a whole self. They help to counteract our cultural tendencies to live in our heads. What about enjoying the whole mansion instead of camping out in the garret?

I suppose I could separate off these kinds of activity as hobbies, but they have professional relevance for me. I bring art activities such as story-telling and drawing into personal and professional development workshops, particularly into Confidence and Creativity workshops. In fact, all my professional activities and decisions are enlivened and strengthened when I nourish my creativity by taking the time to do artistic and practical things.

Life As A Coach

Coaching has freed me up. Of course, I'm not a totally freed-up being, perfect in every way and living an ideal life. I have had ups and downs since becoming a coach and perhaps life is always a work in progress. I climb one hill and see further ranges of hills ahead.

As with many coaches, I've been up to other things as well: writing, running workshops and having other business interests. It's been a very busy time in life. So much happens with family, relationships and running a household. Though life as a coach has been busy and intertwined with others and with events in life, I have still felt freed-up.

What's that like? I've had to keep my own needs and personal development at the forefront. A coach can't always put others first while encouraging their clients to meet their own needs! I've taken off on some wonderful training sessions. Others might like resting on holiday, but I like getting up to interesting things with interesting people, aka going on workshops. It wasn't great for my bank balance, but at one point I went to Fraser Island off the coast of Queensland in Australia for a couple of weeks to study Social Artistry. It was wonderful and I learned things that have changed how I see life – and I legitimately claimed a paradise holiday in my taxes.

Being freed-up means I devise my own working rhythms and beats. I can be at the gym when it's nearly empty, take a free chunk of weekend for solid writing, take a weekday off to be with a friend, burn midnight oil or tap keys before the larks. I get paid for sitting in nice cafes, having deep and meaningful conversations.

In all, being a coach is about being myself, while bringing out the best in people. Everything in life has brought me to here. The joys and challenges have sharpened my wits and given me empathy for human struggles. How wonderful that is, making good use of my life and enjoying freedom.

Six Insights I Have Learned In Coaching

1. Keep your own life clear, clean, simple, up-to-date and open to change. That's a council of perfection I know, but just to strive to have your life that way keeps a clear space around you so the client can approach and be comfortable working with you.

2. By all means have niches, but be ready to work with all kinds of shifting agendas. Your clients may need to reveal and explore parts of themselves and their lives which don't show up until the coaching relationship is established. You don't have to be the expert at their life – that is their job.

3. It's OK to mix mentoring and hands off coaching – just know what you are doing when and make sure the client knows too. You have experience, which has given you expertise, and you have stories to tell which may be exactly what your clients need at times. My way is to ask first – "May I share something, please?" – and this clarifies where coaching approaches are paused for some appropriate mentoring.

4. Your own development, habits and perhaps spiritual practices are the bedrock of everything you do. Just develop a business and that's all you'll get. In your business and your life, keep humble and keep open to your own life lessons. Then you will be rich in so many ways.

5. Listening really does work. There is the story, told as true, of the tired coach who nodded off in a telephone session while the client was talking things through. A little later, the coach snapped awake again to find the client still talking – and telling the coach it had been the best session ever! Short of the "nodding off approach", actively listening in a relaxed way and being ready to form a helpful response or question is key to everything in coaching.

6. We coaches are an important and essential part of what is changing in the world. As Jean Houston puts it in her contribution to my book, *Good Question!* "Coaching is calling another into their fullness, telling them they have the opportunity to play a role in the greatest transition the world has ever seen." She says it's the optimal time for coaches because "They are the midwives of souls". We may be working with individuals who have to deal with their own professional and personal issues first, but we are "changing the world one person at a time," perhaps faster since each person we coach influences many others.

A Seventh Insight

I have been pondering about number seven for the last few days when out walking in the wooded valley near where I live. Some of my best insights arrive when I am in nature. I often to do my best thinking when in connection with something beyond me, the constantly growing and evolving, interwoven world of plants, animals and people.

I find helpful metaphors while observing things, patterned plant forms, new growth, branching paths. It is a bountiful resource. I treasure metaphors and metaphorical thinking, which is what attracted me to the methods of Clean Facilitation.

Nature is a rich source of insight because no one person exists in isolation. Our connections with each other and with all of nature are crucial to who we are. We are nourished by nature, including by each other's nature.

What happens between coach and client is much more than using a certain progression of skills – even though facility with those skills is very necessary to the coaching process. There are coaching forms such as the GROW model, SMART goals, listening skills and specific questions like, "When will you do that by?" and "On a scale of 1-10, how committed are you to doing that?" These forms and questions help the client to bring their thoughts and feelings from their inner world into action, into specific form in the outer world. Let's imagine these coaching techniques as a skeleton, essential for the life of the creature. The rest of the creature is essential too. I could have used the metaphor of a tree, with hard cellulose cell forms and rising sap, but I'll stick with the creature. Whether badger, squirrel, dog or person, life depends on much more than the skeleton. In the same way, what happens between coach and client involves suppleness of thinking, enabling the client to take their thinking beyond hardened, ossified blocks. The client can explore thoughts and feelings in such a way that when they come up with action plans and develop the strength of will to take action what follows can be much better than anything they could have devised from a stuck state. We even speak of a "mind set". Might that be "set" as in concrete? Perhaps things can feel "set" before the coach gets to work.

In my early days of coaching, I wondered what value I could possibly give just by listening and asking a few sensible questions, some of which people had probably been asking themselves anyway.

What I have grown to understand is that by bringing a mind not only analytical and able to work objectively with coaching skill but also able to think freely and creatively with heart warmth, patience and natural, respectful curiosity, the coach can give invaluable support to a client.

This is the whole person approach, weaving the thinking of the left and the right brain together

In a nutshell, whatever else you do to develop skills for coaching, nourish your natural self. Value simply accompanying your client with your honest interest and attention, just as you would pay attention to what is there as you walk in nature.

A Bonus Insight

When people do things for others, for people they know or in more organised ways, such as through work, clubs or community, what it brings into their lives for themselves may feel like an unexpected gift – a bonus indeed. I've found this to be true time and time again in my own life and, no doubt, you have too. It's the golden thread in my life.

We put time into charity and it brings us heart warmth, connection, purpose and unexpected, perhaps unintended, consequences. We make sacrifices for children, family and friends and in the process change our values, setting priorities in ways that also improve our own lives.

We stretch our comfort zone for others and find it increases the size of our comfort zone. This is important to keep in mind both for our clients and for ourselves. Perhaps acting for the greater good is an essential part of being human.

So I'll end my piece here, thinking about each individual one of us taking our part in life and about us coaches supporting others to be the best we all can be and to make our best contributions to life.

Judy Barber

Catherine Joyce

Coaching Excellence – A Look In The Professional Mirror

The Wake-Up Call

SOME YEARS AGO, WHILE WORKING ON a corporate coaching assignment with a client called Mike, I had an experience that made me take a good look in the mirror of my coaching. As a consequence, I learned one of the most valuable lessons of my entire coaching career.

Mike had been identified by his Director as "having potential", but his recent Performance Development Review suggested there were obstacles in his way. The aim of the coaching was to help Mike develop and adapt his style of approach to become more visible (to senior leaders in his part of the organisation) and more influential across other departments within the business. The secondary aim was that, by removing the obstacles, building and implementing "an influencing strategy", supported by developing the necessary skills, he would achieve the next job level within a period of six to nine months.

To begin, we covered the usual procedures, such as contracting, stakeholder involvement, goal setting and some 360° feedback. The first session went well as we worked together to build rapport, understand the context and explore the issues Mike was facing. They seemed straightforward.

After three coaching sessions, I had an inkling something was amiss – though I'd have been hard pressed to name it in any kind of concrete way. The interaction between us was fine on the surface, yet I noticed as each meeting progressed I seemed to do less coaching and more "teaching", explaining and showing. He reported finding it difficult to gain access or opportunity to "be more visible" to senior managers we identified. There was always some reason why it didn't happen, despite the fact that we had engineered an invitation to several meetings that he wouldn't usually have attended.

In coaching session three I did most of the work, most of the talking; he was like a willing passive receiver of my input. It occurred to me that he was relieved not to be in the driving seat of the meeting. I perceived a number of these tell-tale signs but looking back, it took me a while to put two and two together and, even then, I wasn't sure whether it was just me.

After one of the coaching sessions I noticed I felt exhausted. On reflection, it seemed that, while Mike was intellectually engaged in principle, I wasn't seeing or sensing a real shift in him or his behaviour. He repeatedly returned to coaching with little or no action taken. In one meeting he asked if I could send him a reminder of what he had agreed to take action on. If a client said that to you, how would you interpret it? What would you do or say? At the time, I perceived it as a sign of a disconnect between intent and action – what I hadn't yet understood, was what lay behind it.

Over the next couple of coaching meetings I noticed he increasingly positioned me (unconsciously I believe) in the "expert" role. Looking back now, I see that as a parallel process of what he was experiencing in the organisation. He was being put under pressure to act out of his usual role; to prove himself. The organisation valued people being able to "sound good" and frequently didn't hold people to account for their actions. Being well intentioned, looking good and sounding good was what mattered. In the coaching assignment, as I became more expert, he became less resourceful, less confident in himself.

With each subsequent coaching meeting, Mike returned with reasons why he hadn't been able to implement many of actions he committed to. "I'm so busy I didn't get a chance to do everything," he would say. "I just didn't get a chance to attend the meeting with the Director (a target stakeholder that would be evidence of success in terms of the coaching assignment)," "My manager asked me to take on this other project."

Increasingly, these reasons seemed feeble excuses. He wasn't standing up for himself and prioritising his commitments. I wondered if it was a confidence issue. Could there be something else going on in the environment or the department that I wasn't aware of that was stopping him?

When I challenged him about his lack of following up on his actions, he assured me of his commitment, of his confidence and explained it was "just circumstances" – and when I looked into his eyes they seemed genuine.

In my heart of hearts, I knew something wasn't right. But what it was I couldn't put my finger on. At the same time, I was alternating between questioning how accurate my perceptions were and telling myself my instincts are so often spot on. I wondered silently to myself, "Am I judging this correctly?"; "What am I missing?"; "What is my role in effecting the needed change?"; "What should I do?"

Experienced coaches know it can be easy to convince ourselves it's ok when the client says "it's ok.". Looking back now, I wish I had read a book I came across recently; it would have given me an interesting insight. It's called *Leadership and Self Deception* by The Arbinger Institute and I highly recommend it. It can be satisfying to believe a client when they tell you the coaching is working; the challenge comes when they say it yet you have genuine doubts.

Aware of my responsibility to the organisation as well as to Mike, I decided to speak to the sponsor, who was a fairly remote character, and seek feedback from him. He said Mike had reported the coaching was "invaluable" and was taking opportunities to be "more visible" to several senior managers. Nevertheless, I expressed my thoughts to him, only to be reassured that "if it's working for him, it's working." We agreed to review again after three further coaching sessions and keep in touch in the meantime. Mike achieved his promotion within ten months and, as far as the company was concerned, the coaching was successful. Happily, despite my reservations it wasn't all bad and it was clear that something had shifted with Mike and the coaching had made a difference.

The coaching assignment ended, the sponsor and Mike were very happy, yet *my* dilemma was unresolved. I had a sense of unfinished business, with myself and my practice. This coaching experience was a wake up call for me, revealing a disconnect in my coaching practice that I became determined to resolve. I knew if I was to continue as an Executive Coach, I needed to up my game – to do something differently. And to do that, I needed help.

"Destiny Comes Not Through Chance But Through Choice"

Interestingly, around that time I began working for a small psychology-based charity as Assistant Director. Because of the nature of the work and the clients we were supporting, I was required to attend supervision on a regular basis. The first day I turned up for a session I had no idea what it was all about, what its real purpose was or how it might help.

Over the next few months my experience with supervisor Brett Kahr showed me just how invaluable it was. Soon I understood what supervision was all about and how it could help me in my work within the charity. It didn't take me long to make a parallel connection in relation to my coaching practice. The penny dropped. Looking back to my coaching experience with Mike, I could see I would have benefited from having someone outside the coaching relationship to help me get perspective: on the dynamic between Mike and me, on my coaching approach, on the organisational relationships and system in which I was working. In other words, I knew as soon as I returned to coaching I would find a coach supervisor.

I also learned I wanted to develop more concrete processes for contracting, review and discussion with organisational sponsors that would not breach confidentiality with the coaching client. Having a more rigorous process would enable me to bring potentially challenging material or insight to the organisational table for discussion and consideration – and very importantly, give me the confidence and permission to do so. This was easily remedied and has been invaluable to me ever since.

Looking back to the Mike scenario, I wish I had known better; that I'd been less willing to go with the flow. Unwittingly, I failed to hold my own boundaries with both the client and the sponsor. I fell into the parallel "de-skilled" role of feeling powerless in the face of the organisation and of "happy" clients.

"When The Heart Opens, Learning Begins.... "

One of the potential traps of working as an independent consultant with large organisations is finding a balance between living my value of telling the "truth that needs to be told" (as Hawkins asserts) and maintaining a supportive yet challenging relationship with sponsors in the business on whose goodwill my employment rests. Being skillful enough to facilitate the uncovering of the truths in a way that builds, not destroys, can be a precarious process. Achieving the "happiness" of the coaching client while holding my own integrity has sometimes required a fine balance, and something I haven't always managed. At times, these objectives seem in service of different agendas and, when they are, you know you're in the trap. My "hero" script brings benefits and disadvantages for me as a coach.

During my employment in the charity, we frequently had opportunities to work with numerous, often disparate agendas and issues. Our core purpose was preventive work in supporting the emotional transition of new parents and their infants in the antenatal and post natal (birth to three years) period. It was leading edge work. At times, when tempted to get involved with something different, interesting or stimulating but not really core to what we were doing, The Director, Dr Mel Parr, would refocus us by asking, "Who is this serving?" "Is it aligned with our core purpose?" "Does it contribute towards the emotional development of the parent-infant relationship?"

Mel was, and remains, a powerful role model. She kept her heart open, even in very trying circumstances. Her clarity of purpose was astounding. She taught me that if one holds in mind "who we are ultimately there to serve," one is much more likely to stay on track. If your activities don't stand up to that, you know that following that path will take you away. Of course, it may be that you want to re-scope or alter your core purpose or direction. Making that active choice is about acting consciously. It's about knowing the boundaries and deciding whether or not you want to hold them or decide to change them.

Back in the corporate world, the "scarcity" mindset we get drawn into can invoke conscious and unconscious beliefs and behaviours that don't, in the end, help the organisation, the coachee or the coach. Yet the temptation to unwittingly collude with coachees, sponsors and ourselves can assert itself when we prioritise our need to generate income. One of the responsibilities we have as Executive Coaches is to help our sponsors and coachees set robust goals for more than the feel-good self confidence factor or a high ranking on the "happiness scale".

When I open my heart to working for more than the client is expecting, going beyond everyday expectations and being a learner and a coach throughout the coaching process, I better serve my coachees, the sponsors, the system within which they work. I am able to bring a level of integrity to my work that will never be out of sync with my core purpose.

The Accidental Coach

As a child, I admired several teachers and aspired to help others develop as they had me; but I knew I didn't want to be a teacher in academia. I put it aside and decided to study management and business studies.

Soon after graduating, I was working as a junior manager in a large organisation. I attended a management training course, where tutors, who were both women, coached each participant. I experienced such a benefit from the approach that in that moment I knew what I wanted to be "when I grew up". The scales fell from my eyes when I realised I could find the balance of teaching by becoming a facilitator and growing people through coaching in business. With few, if any, opportunities to find this kind of role in the organisation where I was working, I faced a choice. Stay or go.

Within six months and through pure determination, I joined one of the major oil companies as a Technical Trainer. It was a new role and I soon developed the scope of the role to include interpersonal training targeted at high potential supervisors and junior line managers. Within a few years I was unexpectedly catapulted into a senior line management role with one hundred and twenty staff in seven departments reporting to me. Despite having a management qualification and a couple years of management experience, this was a baptism of fire, not only due to the scale and complexity of the situation, but because of the subculture I inherited. It was command and control in action as I had never experienced before.

"Whatever You Think You Are – You Are Always More Than That"

My management style was to assess competence and experience quickly then delegate. With the exception of one manager who was new to the organisation, they were all more than competent. Within weeks, the teams were destabilised by my approach (one of them said they felt "cast adrift" by the uncertainty of it). I was exasperated and knew something had to change. I began by holding one to one "courageous" conversations (using what has now become my Seven Step Approach) to share and clarify common goals, wants, expectations and needs. Soon, I began to hold cross-functional team conversations, encouraging this group to think for themselves, to support each other, to bring solutions and answers rather than problems and issues for discussion or resolution. Over several months the shift happened, first with one, then with others.

Fast forward three years: we had a magnificent team, confident in their management, engaging of their teams; we had reduced headcount and associated costs by thirty percent; absence levels dropped by sixty percent; we had trained and developed our managers and, best of all, we had identified the organisation's next "talented" generation of managers.

Then one day, out of the blue, I heard there was a vacancy in the Learning and Development Department. Excited beyond belief, I knew this was what I wanted to do. I also knew the powers at play in the organisation were keen to have me stay put. Fortunately, after some persuading, I moved, joining a team of bright, creative, articulate and challenging trainers and facilitators who were intent on supporting the continuing move towards involvement and development of teams and individuals across the organisation.

At that time, the Learning and Development Department was transitioning from an internal provider of training courses to working in the business with managers and teams across the business. The goal was to achieve buy-in and involvement from staff through engagement and development.

Over the next two years I had a fantastic time. With my colleagues I got involved in designing and delivering a number of highly effective change programmes. Two in particular stand out for me – the Women's Development series, which was part of the diversity drive, and the Manager as Coach Programme, which I'll focus on here.

Hundreds of managers were living with a culture change to becoming a decentralised business. This involved both a physical shift of location and a mental shift. They needed the capacity to handle themselves through a period of destabilisation. They needed to manage repercussions in their teams due to the change generated by the transition from a London-based business to having multiple locations. This meant dealing with selection, redundancy, relocation and managing the day job, all at the same time.

Those who attended the Manager as Coach programme knew they must take on a new mindset and develop the underpinning enabling skills. But knowing and doing is not the same thing. The four day Manager as Coach programme was born and with it (indirectly) my future as an Executive Coach.

Catherine Joyce

The programme developed as we did and so did requests for off line support from the Line Managers, who were at the point of putting their learning into action. I used the coaching skills I was teaching to help them develop and use these skills back in the office – we would now say it was an early form of modelling and coaching in action. As I was helping them take a coaching approach, my coaching skills were being honed. Over the next few years, coaching became a central part of my role and my life.

"As we let our own light shine, we unconsciously give other people permission to do the same."

NELSON MANDELA

I had finally reached the stage in my life where I was feeling confident in my abilities to help others develop their own innate talents and abilities. I soon began to see I was relying upon three key elements which supported my entire approach to coaching:

- Understanding myself and developing my skills (brings range/flexibility of processes, structures and approaches to coaching)
- Experience as a Line Manager in business (helps me understand my client's context and brings real cost benefit to my clients)
- Supervision – looking in the mirror (how I continue my journey to becoming the best Executive Coach I can be)

Understanding And Developing Myself

It's a never-ending journey, this *understanding myself* process. I love learning, working with others, designing new processes, through reading and applying my thinking and experiences in new situations. Over the years, my learning journey has taken me into NLP, psychotherapy, hypnotherapy, counseling, reflexology and reiki, time line therapy as well as specific coaching skills development. My practice is to make it my own and integrate it with what I do and how I relate to others. In all these I have learned about myself, improved myself and applied my learning to my work and life. My life long quest is to be the best person, mother, friend and colleague I can be.

Ten years ago, when I was completing the Master Practitioner in NLP, my children were both in junior school. I remember practicing my questioning skills with them about their day at school and watching which way their eyes moved (eye accessing cues), using submodalities to get rid of their tummy aches. With a friend who was at a critical juncture of her career, I used the Cartesian coordinates exercise to help her explore and deepen her insight and ultimately help her chose the direction she followed.

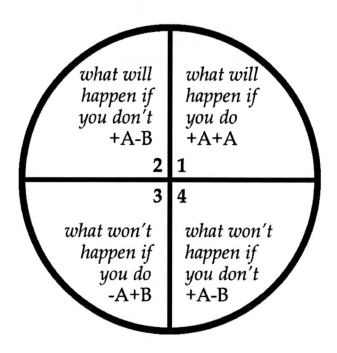

In terms of understanding myself and others, a number of NLP approaches helped me personally and professionally. These included, among others:

- Reframing
- Change personal history
- Meta-programmes
- Language patterns
- Rapport building
- Time line therapy
- Logical levels

These days, I no longer use my hypnotherapy, reflexology and reiki skills with other people. Rather I use them myself to keep me resourceful and balanced, especially in times of crisis or stress. I strongly believe that in order to help others, we have to look after ourselves, just as when the air steward reminds adults to put their own life jackets on before attending to their children's.

Looking back, I can clearly see my journey has been one of discovering who I am; of letting go of old stuff and becoming someone I can be proud of and admire. My drive has been to learn new ways of being and doing and to bring those ways into my corporate work. As an Executive Coach working primarily in with blue chip organisations, my constant questions are those I reflect on after each coaching meeting: "What did I do well that helped my client to shift?", "How was I that helped my client ?", "How can I do this better?", "How can I be better?", "What else could I do that would be even more effective for my client?"

Getting People To Deliver With Executive Coaching

One day I went for lunch with an ex-colleague from my oil industry days who now worked in one of the big brewing companies. As with others at that time, they were down-sizing and de-layering tiers of managers throughout the organisation. As we talked, he described some of the challenges he faced with several technically brilliant and hugely qualified brewers who were, because of changes in the organisation, now having to manage teams of people as well as brew beer. Several were struggling with the transition from having responsibility for technical process delivery to getting their people to deliver.

He suddenly looked at me and said, "You were a manager recently – you know what becoming a manager is all about. Can you come in and, if they're up for it, help them transition?" That simple question led to eight years of work as a mentor, coach and facilitator in the organisation. At the time, mentoring was the preferred term – coaching was largely reserved for the sports industry To date, I have worked with over thirty individuals and acted as a mentor or coach to each of them. This is where my coaching skills and experiences became more deeply crafted

The focus on my mentoring with the Master Brewers built on my management experience through helping them:

- Defining their role as manager: realise that taking on the title of "manager" doesn't automatically generate obedience to management edicts.
- Gaining buy-in and clarifying accountability: helping them realise that "telling" someone to do something doesn't mean it will be done.
- Maximising the potential of the team: playing to the different strengths in the team, rather than seeing differences as an issue.
- Holding the team and individuals accountable: getting employee agreement is not the same as getting their commitment to action.
- Leading by example is the strongest way to build the culture.
- Tapping into people's drivers: getting to know individual team members' motivations help you communicate and influence.

Recently I coached a Senior Auditor named Ralph, who worked in a large organisation. Though a very competent and reliable member of staff, Ralph had been passed over for promotion for the second time recently and was feeling de-motivated and undervalued. An external candidate was given the role. Over the course of the next nine months, the relationship between the two men disintegrated, impacted the wider team, impacted the clients they were working for and undermined the performance of both men. After five years service, Ralph was on the verge of resigning as he couldn't envisage a future with the organisation. I was asked to work with the Senior Auditor and over a period of six months I coached him through a range of issues, problems and goals. It was a challenging assignment and one that eventually expanded to include the new manager.

Later, in reviewing the coaching assignment, John, the Head of Finance, was gracious in his praise for the effect of the coaching. He was appreciative and relieved. I was interested in having something more concrete in terms of evidence of the benefit of the coaching I had carried out with Ralph and asked John if we might calculate the value the coaching had achieved. Sometimes it's hard to prove the value of the benefit of executive coaching. Here's how we went about it.

John started out by saying that had coaching not been initiated he would in all likelihood have exited Ralph from the business due to the damage the breakdown in relationships was causing to customers and the internal team. He calculated that had he not initiated the coaching and resolved the situation, the already spiraling damage would have likely increased inevitably leading to:

- complete breakdown in working relationship between the two auditors
- loss of benefits accrued from effective team-working across the wider audit team
- increased frequency of negative feedback from internal and external stakeholders
- reworking due to errors caused by fractious atmosphere, mistakes and pressure
- greater levels of self-certified absence levels in the team
- loss of revenue due to lower levels of performance
- staff turnover – calculated at loss of three staff who were known to be ready to leave due to stress, disruption and being "caught in the middle"
- loss of the Audit Manager, who would likely have been managed out of the business

I asked John to put a figure on the calculated savings; his answer was over £1.2 million.

Needless to say, the provision of coaching had cost the company a tiny fraction of what it saved the business in time, energy, costs and aggravation. Not only that but the relationship between the two managers was now working satisfactorily, the teams had settled down and positive customer feedback had increased to a much more satisfactory level. We were both astonished at this figure and, incredible though it seemed at first, he commented that while he had been sceptical at first when executive coaching was recommended, he is now a complete convert.

More than a year later, I know from John that the gains have been sustained and that those gains have made a significant difference in the ongoing success of that part of the organisation.

Looking In The Professional Mirror With Super-Vision

Recently I heard someone say "We give the coaching we need to receive." This thought provoking statement is one that deserves some reflection. If indeed it is true, then self awareness and honesty is key. If I believe my client's success in the coaching space is limited by my skills, my awareness and my belief in their capacity to grow and develop then I owe it to myself and my clients to self-develop, so I can be the best. I owe it to myself and my clients to "look in the professional mirror".

Coaches can look in the professional mirror – can "wake up" – through a range of continuous professional development methods. Currently, one of the most effective ways I do this is through coaching supervision. The other way I am developing my competence and confidence is by undertaking coaching supervision training. These are by no means the only or the best ways, they are rather a reflection of where I am on my professional journey at the time of writing.

"Excellence comes from having many choices;
wisdom comes from multiple perspectives."

My coaching supervision space is a time and place to bring the thoughts, fears, projections, hopes, anticipations and challenges about my practice. Here is a place where I can stand back and explore a super-vision of the coaching space, where I discuss and reflect what I am thinking and feeling about what goes for and in me as I work with my client groups and organisations.

If coaching helps managers harness the power of their behaviour in performance, then supervision helps me deepen my understand of how to make a deeper impact in the coaching space; it brings me insight and new perspectives; it challenges my prejudices and assumptions; it encourages me to continue to struggle with the uncertainty or un-knowing and helps me plan how I want to be when I next see that client.

In contrast to coaching, which often focuses on helping the client solve problems or make decisions, supervision is focused on me as the coach: how I am, how I respond to my coaching client, my perception as they react to me, the parallels between what happens in the coaching supervision space between us and what happens in the workplace between the coach, and the environment within which they work.

Coaching often helps people realise they can set goals that enable them to progress, stretch, change and grow their own potential. Supervision is the parallel vehicle, helping coaches progress, stretch and grow – and become the best they can be.

Coaching excellence is for me a journey. It describes what I want to provide for my clients, what I'd like them to experience as they work with me and what I aspire to bring in the provision of that service. Here are a few of the principles I keep in my mind:

- Join, don't judge
- Probe, don't assume
- Stay loose, until rigour counts
- Fight problems, not people
- Act 'as if' the idea works
- Jump to favourable conclusions whenever possible
- Don't justify pessimism as realism; be an optimist with concerns

Going Forward: The Changing Space Of Executive Coaching

Executive coaching as a profession is still in its infancy and, given the potential it can achieve in organisations, we can feel proud of the contributions we are making. As the profession matures we will want to ensure standards are set and maintained; ethics and integrity are taught and maintained; return on investment can be demonstrated and that coaches demonstrate an ongoing commitment to continuous professional development.

People who lived a hundred years ago wanted to improve their lot. Today, we are no different. Few people are content to continue living their life as it is right now – or would choose to if they felt they had that choice. Most people want to have more, want to be different, want to become more than they are in this present moment. We are programmed, as a species, for improvement and growth.

In business and corporate life, the reputation of executive coaching is overcoming the "remedial" stigma and becoming better understood for the business benefits it can bring and the return on investment it can achieve. Increasing numbers of leaders and HR managers now realise that executive coaching regularly improves performance, increases personal and professional effectiveness, greatly increases engagement and impact of senior executives, and all these affect the bottom line.

*"Standing still is the fastest way of moving
backwards in a rapidly changing world."*

Without a doubt, executive coaching is one of the best strategies for developing current and future leaders and a very cost effective one. Without a doubt working as an executive coaching is one of the greatest privileges a person can experience. And that privilege comes with responsibility.

What then are your responsibilities if you want to achieve coaching excellence? If there are words of wisdom I can impart here's what I say:

- Know who your clients are (coachee, sponsor, organisation etc)
- Build on what you know and love
- Coach from your passion
- Learn when to bring your true self into the coaching space and when to leave it at the door
- Be honest with yourself about your strengths and areas to develop
- Coach within your comfort zone and knowledge
- Know what to do if you're moving towards or past your comfort zone
- Be ethical in your practice always
- Lead by example; have your own coach or supervisor
- Keep mindful of the purpose of coaching; keep calibrating; keep flexing
- Stay curious
- Be grateful, every day

*"Beyond living and dreaming, there is
something more important: waking up."*

ANTONIO MACHADO

Catherine Joyce

Annie Kaszina

Coaching: A Chain of Miracles

Getting to Rock Bottom

HOW DO YOU GET TO ROCK BOTTOM? People do it in different ways. For me, it was spending twenty years in an abusive marriage. From the outside, my life did not look like rock bottom: I was married to a successful, middle class professional. We had a beautiful home, nice cars, and one delightful child. I was well groomed, well provided for, had a PhD, a couple of academic books to my name – a thoroughly credible list of accomplishments.

Yet most days, I could barely drag myself out of bed. I didn't drink, smoke, or take drugs, not even the odd anti-depressant. Still, two decades with an emotionally abusive man had sapped my identity, eroded my sense of self worth, and left me paralysed with misery. I was totally drained emotionally; my "love tank" completely emptied by an "emotional vampire"'. Additionally, I was to blame for pretty much everything bad that 'happened' to him and, given that he was a very negative, angry person, a lot of unpleasant things occurred in his life.

What little energy I had, I divided between caring for my child and avoiding "provoking" my husband. Not that this ever worked for long, of course. His sense of power and control came from making me feel small and powerless. Any trivial cause, or trigger, was grist to his mill – a look, a tone of voice, not being attentive enough to his needs, being on the phone when he came through the door, the dog's behaviour: almost anything could serve to provoke an abusive outburst. Like so many people who are emotionally abused, I developed tunnel vision: at a time when I most needed to break free, I could not see beyond the marriage. Staying looked, at the time, like the lesser of all evils.

I'd heard somewhere that when you reach rock bottom, you start to come back up. It doesn't work quite like that in an abusive relationship; rock bottom becomes, as it were, a movable feast. For as long as you *choose* to stay, an abusive partner will always find ways to improve upon destroying you. Like so many other people in that situation, I left only when I knew that staying would have destroyed me completely. It was the vista of another twenty, maybe thirty or more, years of progressive misery *without even the strength to react* that drove me to put an end to my marriage.

Now, I don't delude myself that my abusive marriage is of any great interest to you; it is no longer of great interest to me, either. However, there are hundreds of thousands of women (and men also) who limp forward in relationships just like mine. (In fact, women frequently ask me: "Were you married to *my* husband?")

Abusive relationships impact on society in various ways:

- Leaving an abusive situation is not, per se, sufficient to guarantee healing.
- Survivors of domestic violence (and don't be fooled, emotional abuse *is* a manifestation of domestic violence) may well suffer from Post Traumatic Stress Disorder and fall out of society and the work force for years.
- The children of domestic violence suffer considerably, are usually unsupported, and are, therefore, likely to repeat the pattern of one parent or the other, thereby perpetuating the cycle.
- Nobody (including the victim themselves) likes a victim. Although we may initially feel compassion for someone's suffering, if they don't "pull themselves together" and "sort it out" fairly fast, *we* start to feel uncomfortable. Victimhood connects with some of our own unresolved feelings. Victims end up being alienated from society.
- Because domestic violence survivors are too traumatised and ashamed to be vocal, society overlooks them and fails to utilise their resources to assist the victim in breaking the abusive cycle.

The Slow Burn Of Twenty First Century Miracles

When I ended my marriage, I was an Alexander Technique (AT) teacher. I worked primarily helping people to use their bodies better and overcome physical pain. Teaching the Alexander Technique is a vocation. It's wonderfully rewarding work, and a horrendous business model: to be truly effective it can only ever be delivered one-to-one.

Among the many merits of the AT are that you *have to* walk your talk, quite literally, and the connection between body and mind is absolutely clear. You cannot undo physical tensions without addressing emotional pain also. My clients often talked to me about their emotional pains, their stresses and their worries. The first link in my chain of miracles is the *Daily Mail* - part of my liberation as a single woman was that I could browse the pages of this tabloid without my broadsheet reading partner railing against me.

It was in the pages of the *Mail* that I first discovered the new profession of coaching. Coaching, I realised, offered a way to listen and help people more effectively than I was already doing, and to increase my income. That article led me to Rachel Turner, and John Niland, who led the first Coach U workshop I ever attended. It also led me to Jilly Shaul, my first coach, the Coaches' List (an immensely supportive and informative online coaching community) and Nicola Cairncross. None of them, except possibly Nicola, would be aware of the miracle they helped create, not least because twenty first[t] century miracles can be a slow burn. They tend not to be heralded by thunderclaps, a booming voice from on high, or even a fanfare. These days, miracles may present as risks, challenges, opportunities or just plain hard work. Miracles are no longer thrust upon us, as they were in Biblical times. Rather, I believe we are all responsible for playing a part in creating our own miracles.

Certainly, I was looking for a miracle in those early months after my marriage ended. My favourite song at the time was Mike and the Mechanics, "All I Need Is A Miracle". (Curiously enough, playing that song and singing it obsessively and tunelessly did not seem to change much.) And then, an email from Nicola landed in my Inbox.

She had just created her first year long Money Gym programme, with the offer that the first five people to reply would get the £3,000 programme for free. First I did my best rabbit-caught-in-the-headlights impersonation for what seemed like forever. I was, quite literally, paralysed with fear. (Women who have experienced domestic violence often are.) What if I signed up and I was too late for the free offer? I was – or, at least, I *felt* – far too poor to invest in learning how to become financially free. What if Nicola decided that I was so hopeless and helpless it disqualified me? What if…? And what if I did nothing?

Maybe that last thought was what led me to click *reply.* In the outside world, only a few minutes had passed while I agonised and my reply turned out to be one of the first five, if not *the* first. Only many months later did I find out that I was the only one of the Free Five to have stayed the course: my miracle was, potentially, available to five people, and four just disregarded it.

Working With The Miracle

So, how did that miracle look and feel over that Money Gym year? A lot of the time it felt remarkably akin to terror. That year started with the ever positive, ever resourceful Nicola *not* hearing what I couldn't do. So I stopped telling her, essentially by the end of our first coaching call. (It would have been churlish to keep bleating negatively at someone who had been so generous to me.) Instead, having always had quite an obedient streak running through my naturally anarchic being, I did as my coach suggested: I started to take action in as small a way as I could get away with. The easiest part was reading the books on wealth creation, including *Rich Dad, Poor Dad*; and I duly played Cashflow.

Having survived, even enjoyed, my first game, I took my daughter with me so she could learn what I was learning – the pub where we met to play had excellent chips, still hook enough for my thirteen year old. My daughter ate chips, played Cashflow with a group of adults, who played cooperatively and made a great fuss of her, and the scales fell from her eyes. That Sunday evening, as we walked through drab North London, it really felt as though we had walked together through the Looking Glass. I remember she kept shaking her head and saying: "I can't believe my friends are wasting so much money on 'doodads' when they could use that money to secure their financial freedom." (How my heart sang on the train home!)

One direct result of that evening was that, unlike her peer group, my daughter never, ever suggested that her quality of life depended on having designer trainers, a Louis Vuitton handbag, truckloads of expensive cosmetics, or a walk-in wardrobe full of Miss Sixty clothes.

Nicola wasted no time in driving home her advantage: my next task was finding out about property. A few months later, my trusty Shih Tzu and I found ourselves heading north on a property buying mission. (One thing that nobody told me is that if you want to find out about an area, you only have to walk around it with a dog. Not only will you get a feel for the place swiftly, but the dog is a great ice-breaker. Sharon Shih Tzu initiated conversations with milkmen and other locals that elicited masses of useful information. Over the months she developed her own fan base in one small corner of Lancashire.) My dog's composure in this new situation helped me no end. I was scared witless; I'd never bought one house, let alone several, by myself before, and yet, with Sharon's doughty support, I did it. Nicola, I felt, expected and deserved no less from me.

For most of that year, I felt remarkably like a Weeble. I read the books, played Cashflow, trotted north to buy properties, dealt with endless estate agents, solicitors and tradesmen, and still there was more to do. Each time I thought I might be able to retreat into my fluffy alternative practitioner's persona, mentally put my feet up and sip weak camomile tea, Nicola pointed out something else that I could be doing. The next thing on the list was to get into internet marketing and create another stream of income.

Now, Nicola was not a fan of the "I'll work with anyone who comes to me about anything" style of coaching. She suggested that I niche myself. These days I don't remember quite how I came to metamorphose into a Women's Emotional Abuse Recovery Coach. Maybe I had been foolhardy enough to try to explain some unusually reticent behaviour of mine with reference to my experience, or maybe I had said that I would like to help other abused women, and Nicola was immediately on to me.

Suddenly, I had to build a website, write an e-zine, generate a list, find out about Google Adwords, and do so many other things. Because Nicola never once doubted my potential, I had absolutely no room for failure; not least because she guided me every step along the way. My fluffiness nearly drove my website designer to drink. But somehow it all happened, and the first e-zine got written.

In the years that have passed since then, I have written so many e-zines that I often forget what I have said, until someone reminds me of it, but I still remember writing the very first piece. It was about taking charge of my life by unblocking drains myself. One of the laws of the universe is that women who leave abusive relationships keep finding abusive men popping up in front of them, until finally they clear their victim mentality. Then it changes. As a newly single woman, I'd had very unpleasant experiences with a few extremely aggressive (cowboy) plumbers. By comparison, clambering up a ladder and deploying industrial quantities of caustic soda struck this new e-zine writer as a good bet. I did quite a good job of recreating Vesuvius in my back garden before I achieved success. But that was then; now I have a couple of surprisingly attractive, we treat ourselves well, the world treats us well also.)

Still Nicola was not satisfied. She believes, rightly, in always building on successes. The day came when I moonlighted on my Money Gym commitment and deferred to the outlook of my Alexander Technique guru, Margaret, who often said that every (well) woman needs one day a month in bed to rest and recuperate. With the stresses of my divorce still continuing, that pronouncement sounded more and more attractive. One morning, I lifted my weary head off the pillow and dropped it straight back there. That was all I saw of the morning. I had been doing my "morning pages" (as recommended in Julia Cameron's *The Artist's Way*) for some time by then, and kept a pile of paper and pens by my bed. When I eventually surfaced, in the early afternoon, I grabbed writing materials and dashed off the first chapter of a new book.

Now, I hadn't had the slightest idea that I was going to write a book when I went to bed the previous night. I didn't really know what I was writing when I wrote that first chapter, but the words just flowed through me with simplicity and ease. Within a month I had written *The Woman You Want to Be*, a book that has helped many women heal from the trauma of their abusive relationships. That part of the miracle was pretty easy. The academic writing I had done in the past, by comparison, had been incredibly slow and painful, with each word wrenched from my flesh.

So, now I was a professional property investor, an Emotional Abuse Recovery Coach, the author of a self help book and, in a very small way, an internet marketer. It felt to me as if I had spent the whole year on the type of scary amusement park ride I have always pointedly avoided.

I'd love to be able to say that my transformation was complete, that by the end of my Money Gym year I emerged from that chrysalis, my wings unfolded, soaring skyward. But it wasn't like that at all. I still carried a goodly portion of the abused woman's load of fear and self-loathing.

That was the downside. The upside was that, through the Coaches' List, I could not help but become aware of all the wonderful tools and resources available to me. I signed up for an NLP training course – not for myself so much, but so that I could work with *other people* more effectively. I was still enough of a people-pleaser and fluffy alternative bunny not to think in terms of caring for myself first. Although, by now, I was writing a 100-day e-course for abused women, which began with Lucille Ball's injunction: "Love yourself first and everything else falls into line." But *nobody had given me permission* to love myself first and I still had not got the hang of a proactive approach to life. I was also still brainwashed enough by my yet-to-be ex-husband to be very sceptical about the possibility of personal transformation (despite everything that was going on in my life). I was especially sceptical about the power of language to effect profound personal change.

My first inkling that NLP *might* work came halfway through the training. My daughter's drama teacher and Head of Year had made some damning and inappropriate comments about her emotional state. I needed to go in and persuade them to back off.

Having been a teacher myself, I knew that this was the best outcome I could hope for. I also knew that, in similar circumstances, parents all too often become angry and offensive and, if anything, exacerbate the situation. A meeting with the Head of Year and the Deputy Head was set up. Without a great deal of faith in the outcome (I was still in "it's-always-harder-for-me" victim mode) I tried out my nascent NLP skills. I mirrored the Head of Year's body language, listened to her account of the situation. Then, I simply asked her questions.

Faced with my calm, she became increasingly emotional, and eventually exclaimed: "This is hopeless!" Not a wise thing to say to a new NLP convert. In my most non-threatening tone, I enquired: "Mrs X, what, specifically, is hopeless?" To my amazement, she got up, hot-footed it across the rather large room, and disappeared through the door, not to return. The Deputy Head and I looked at each other in amazement. Then he started to laugh and so did I. Problem solved. No teacher ever visited their inappropriate, personal opinions on my daughter after that.

I learned an unforgettable lesson both about the effectiveness of NLP and about my own personal power: in this new life of mine, with the resources that I was assembling for myself, I only ever needed to feel powerless if *I* chose to abdicate my power. To paraphrase Eleanor Roosevelt, I learnt that nobody can ever make me feel powerless without my consent.

Paying It Forward

One Money Gym year down the line, my divorce was still rumbling painfully on (and I'd discovered that my not-yet-ex-husband had a curious attachment to *our* tea towels, since he repeatedly demanded fifty percent of them, as well as everything else). But so much else had changed: my daughter was becoming financially literate, my dog was a property investor, and I was recreating myself, so that I could be useful in helping other women either avoid or recover swiftly from the hell of an abusive relationship.

The Women's Emotional Abuse Recovery Coach was now working in the virtual world and the real world also.

In the real world, I ran ten-week Accelerated Recovery courses at my local Women's Refuge. They were, in some ways, the most challenging thing I have ever done in my life. The women I worked with were in desperate straits. To escape *yet more* physical violence, some had abandoned their abusive partners, their homes and even their children, only days before, and moved into the refuge. They had, quite literally, nothing. One woman's ex-partner had just come out of prison vowing to kill her, and kept turning up at her home to do just that. Because he had turned informer over an important crime, the police were unwilling to lock him up again. So they were going to move *her* to another part of the country and provide her with a new identity.

These women were traumatised, despairing and initially cynical. Their histories and present situation were impossibly difficult – far, far worse than my own ever had been. I could not change their circumstances. The only thing I had to offer to turn their lives around was twenty hours of my time and the power of the spoken word. For some, English was their second or third language; they spoke it haltingly and their understanding was patchy. The native English speakers all spoke "estuary English" whereas my own accent is unmistakably received pronunciation. The moment I opened my mouth they couldn't miss my middle class, private school background. Mine was not an accent to generate spontaneous rapport.

The work I do with abused women sometimes feels like walking a tightrope: provided I do not look down, do not focus on where they have been, but only on where they want to go, the magic of coaching works. In fact, it works amazingly well. Even – or perhaps *especially* – a client group that has been through so much trauma will move on fast when you show them a light, and an end to their tunnel. They showed extraordinary courage, open mindedness, and focus.

To this day, I remain in awe of how much some people can achieve with surprisingly little input. My ex-husband was a great fan of psychoanalysis. He paid for years and years of it. He became fluent at using psycho-babble and talking, at length, about his dreams. But the process of focusing constantly on his problems only exacerbated them. He became more and more entrenched in his ways. The women that I've worked with don't have that luxury; when faced with a simple sink or swim choice, they largely grab hold of whatever lifebuoy or piece of wood fortune sends their way and use that to create their own rescue.

Of course, not every woman succeeds in putting the trauma of her relationship behind her, but an extraordinary number do. Clients all around the world amaze themselves and me with the speed with which they let go of a relationship they believed they could not live without. Often I receive emails from women whose names I don't even know. They have worked with the information in my e-zine and it has been enough of a catalyst to jolt them out of the trance of despair and powerlessness that characterises any abusive relationship. I frequently joke that I specialise in breaking up people's relationships. In reality, I have been the trigger for getting hundreds upon hundreds of women out of bad relationships. (Let it be said, en passant, that I have also encouraged a number of people, men and women, to stay in functional relationships and develop communication skills that will improve any relationship.)

Why do women fall into – and stay in – an abusive relationship? Only because they do not know any better. Once they grasp the true nature of the skewed world they have lived in, and the impossibility of ever changing an abusive partner, they will not repeat their mistake. The women I work with learn how to recognise an abusive prospective partner at the outset. They will not end up in another abusive relationship: they have learnt too much. They want to present their children with a more inspiring, functional role model. Every time I can educate a woman and help her move away from an abusive relationship, I feel I have done my part to break the age old cycle of abuse, once and for all.

Had I been able to choose my life's journey, I doubt very much I would have chosen the path I have trodden. But more than twenty hollow years of misery are meaningful, even precious, inasmuch as they are helpful to other women.

Practicing What I Teach

Passionate as I am about extricating other women from abusive relationships, that is not the only work I do. I went on to train as a Money Gym coach, and now work around creating financial intelligence, and especially around helping people to clear the limiting beliefs about money that prevent them from achieving financial security and plenty. Working with abused women has proved the most fabulous training for learning to dispel limiting beliefs generally: abused women are, at the start, one of the most negative client groups on the planet. If you can help them move from negative beliefs to positive self worth, the chances are you can help anybody.

And what of me? There have been so many insights, so much spiritual enrichment along the way. It's not surprising that I became a coach; I had a long history of putting other people's needs before my own. But the integrity that underpins coaching does not let me get away with that; I am compelled to practise what I teach. So, I've had to work with the difficult challenge of putting myself first. Life post-divorce has had its challenges, large and small, but it is the most meaningful, joyful life I have ever known. Of course, I have more resources and can call on more skilled support than most in addressing these challenges. With a couple of personal development books to my name, more in the pipeline, and a business book coming out shortly (co-written with the most engaging and witty "ex-corporate soldier" I have ever known), the ex-most private person on the planet has a nasty habit of transposing most of her experience into the written word. That has been relatively easy. Learning to open my heart again, after an abusive relationship, has been more challenging. There, too, I like to think that my experience is useful for other women.

In the final years of my marriage, my then husband talked about retirement, and I would look forward, in terror, to more of the same, to a time when life would shut down completely *because he would be around to control me the whole time.* My future looks very different now. There is so much more I still want to do and create and enjoy, so many ways in which I intend to grow the coaching I already do.

My life, as it is today, would never have been possible without coaching. Coaching is, I believe, an extraordinarily powerful tool for positive transformation. Nicola Cairncross touched my life. I, in turn, have been blessed to touch many, many others also.

Coaching is not complicated. Coaching is not even necessarily difficult (although it requires certain innate qualities and well honed acquired skills to do it really well). But, I believe, there is no more valuable method for adding value to the lives of those who yearn for help.

Annie Kaszina

Biographies

Tania Adams

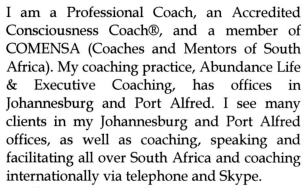

I am a Professional Coach, an Accredited Consciousness Coach®, and a member of COMENSA (Coaches and Mentors of South Africa). My coaching practice, Abundance Life & Executive Coaching, has offices in Johannesburg and Port Alfred. I see many clients in my Johannesburg and Port Alfred offices, as well as coaching, speaking and facilitating all over South Africa and coaching internationally via telephone and Skype.

The success of my coaching and facilitating lies in my insightful, dynamic approach and ability to quickly connect with the essence of my clients and their individual requirements. It is by combining these qualities with my extensive management experience and my steadfast belief in people's abilities to excel, with the correct support, that I am successfully able to assist my clients to meet their objectives. I draw on my experiences of coaching, mentoring and managing staff at many levels to create unique coaching programs which are motivational, inspirational, effective and specifically tailored to meet individual needs. With the power of Consciousness Coaching® the results are sustainable because the client experiences a fundamental shift in core beliefs and thinking patterns that have previously blocked their successes.

I believe everyone is entitled to the kinds of personal abundance they dream of, and I thrive on working with people to achieve this. I promise my coaching clients they will achieve so much more of what they desire with much less effort than they did before.

In addition to individual work, I am passionate about relationships and team dynamics and do a great deal of group coaching in the corporate context, as well as relationship and family coaching for private clients. I have had great success working with entire family units; the families find themselves far more effective, healthier, less critical, more creative and loving towards one another.

At a corporate level, my work includes increasing profitability through improved productivity and a reduction in the hidden costs associated with staff turnover, stress related absenteeism, lack of accountability and poor communication. This is achieved by shifting attitudes towards accountability and integrity, relationships between team members and with the organisation itself. My clients report greater staff motivation, higher output, reduced levels of stress and higher staff retention after participating in my facilitated programs and coaching.

For full details of Youth, Personal and Executive Coaching packages and workshops offered, please contact me via the Abundance & Life Coaching website: www.abundance.org.za
www.twitter.com/TaniaAbundance
taniamadams.blogspot.com
www.facebook.com/pages/Abundance-Coaching-Human-Development/26441108436

Mike Armour

In a career path spanning over 25 years, Mike has held roles as Director of Training and Development and worked in both public and private sector organisations within Australia and New Zealand in both full-time and and contract roles.

Mike's holds Diplomas in Multimedia Design and Training & Development along with Certificate IV qualifications in Training & Assessment and Coaching for Life & Business. Mike is also a licensed user of the Myers Briggs Type Indicator and Hay Group's Emotional Competence Inventory and hopes to commence a Masters Degree in coaching in 2011.

During 2008, Mike's role as an independent contractor ended as a result of the global financial crisis and he was left wondering what to do next. Mike recalls that his daughter prompted the change in direction with a powerful coaching question. She said "What do you really want (to do) Dad?" Returning to his passion for developing people and becoming a full-time coach seemed like the ideal way to answer that question.

In March 2009, Mike trained as a Life and Business Coach undertaking a Certificate IV in Coaching for Life and Business through Success and You Pty Ltd in Sydney and gained a renewed sense of purpose and direction along with a desire to achieve some really big goals in his life such as, learning to create Ceramic Mosaics and even taking a trip into space in the future.

Through the coaching process, Mike's goal is to act as a powerful force for change, helping clients focus on their dreams and goals, and taking action to make these a reality.

Anyone can live an inspired life. The secret is to know your purpose and act with determination.

Mike's company, Optima Coaching (Aust) Pty Ltd, has worked with a variety of life and career coaching clients and is currently expanding into the business coaching market along with a number of colleagues.

Mike lives in Sydney, Australia with my partner Marg, who is currently completing her PhD in Politics and History focusing on international relations. Our two grown children – Katie, aged 27 and Stuart, aged 25 -- have both been involved in the hospitality industry and are currently exploring new career direction.

Mike can be contacted as follows:
Email: mike.armour@optimacoaching.com.au
Phone: +61 400 779913 (outside Australia) or 0400 779913 locally

Judy Barber

Judy has been a Life Coach since 2003.
Amanda Wise of *www.WiseLifecoaching.com* says Judy 'thrives on creativity and has a passion for making a very real difference and contribution. She is a wonderful listener who can draw you into taking action to meet goals.'

John Standaloft of *www.Standingaloft.com* calls her 'a brilliant coach with great insight backed by a wealth of experience which she uses with empathy and caring.'

Marion Ryan of *www.OnlineBusinessGym.com* says 'In the premier league of coaches, Judy is wise, warm and wicked good fun to work with.'

As an enthusiastic coach, workshop leader and presenter, Judy loves bringing out the best in people so they get beyond what was stopping them, develop confidence and creativity and bring their visions into being. Judy also mentors in Workshop Design and Writing Personal Development Books, and, as a trained Hippocrates Health Educator, in the Raw and Living Food lifestyle.

Judy is the author of the classic best-selling coaching book, *Good Question! The Art of Asking Questions to Bring About Positive Change,* for coaches and everyone else. She asks Good Questions to encourage finding inspiration, noticing feelings, developing enthusiasm and motivation, and creating pathways with practical steps.

Judy brings a strong personal development background and experience from a long varied teaching career in FE, Prison and Steiner Schools, and from running businesses. She has travelled the world, lived in the UK, Iran and New Zealand and done all sorts of interesting study and work including Art and Drama Therapy, Meditation, Social Artistry, NLP and the World Cafe. David Grove's 'Clean Facilitation' informs her work in wonderful ways.

Walking in nature and in the city brings her alive. She loves arts activities, good conversations, creating healthy delicious food and being with people who are bent on making the world a better place.

Visit her site for her blog and various interesting and useful recordings and gifts: www.judy-barber.com

Nicola Bird

I am a qualified coach, international speaker and experienced trainer. I am also the creator of the easy-to-use online coaching tool, JigsawBox

In 2009 I grew my database of contacts from 13 to just over 1000 and ran over 40 live teleseminars and webinars. In January 2010 I created over $24,000 in coaching revenues and in September 2010 hit my first six-figure month while building my mailing list to over 4500. I now concentrate my time on teaching more and more coaches how to package up what they do, stop trading time for money, and coach their clients online.

I am also married, with three young children, and love the frantic pace of juggling kids, school runs and London traffic, alongside my business.

Head over to www.JigsawBox.com to join my latest free webinar about how to start selling more than your 1:1 time and experience JigsawBox yourself with our free 14-day free trial.

Jane Bromley

As an internationally renowned Corporate Executive Coach and Senior Business Consultant, for over a decade I have helped businesses develop powerful clarity, overcome barriers and achieve fast-track business growth.

I have a strong reputation for inspiring Boards, CEOs and their senior management teams to achieve outstanding business results. I particularly enjoy coaching roles where Senior Managers and their teams wish to push the boundaries, setting the standards for others to follow. Based in Oxfordshire, in the UK, I work across the UK, Europe and USA, with Fortune 500 and smaller fast-growing organisations. I am fluent in French and Spanish.

A FEW RESULTS

Some of the results I have achieved with my clients include:

- The MD of a coaching firm clarified his business/ marketing strategy to increase revenue by 300%
- A market leader in the academic world increased revenue by 400% in just 2 years
- The Directors of a creative design firm, previously at loggerheads, regained their belief in their business
- A Senior Manager in a major bank, feeling that his boss was limiting his results considerably, realised he could achieve everything he wished
- A Senior Manager of a major pharmaceutical defined the company's vision for turning customers into loyal advocates

WHAT CLIENTS SAY

"You helped me to rediscover the joy and fun in my work. And, in the 6 weeks you were coaching me, I doubled revenue!"
Sales Manager, Business Services

"I found the sessions with Jane to be incredibly inspiring and I believe I gained a great deal of value in the timeframe. I am focused and excited about facing the goals I have set for myself, whereas beforehand I did not believe I could achieve them."
Managing Director, Support Services Firm

Would you like to achieve similar business results? Then simply call me! I look forward to meeting you and learning more about your business: www.growtharrows.com/coaching

Email: jane.bromley@growtharrows.com
Telephone: +44 (0)207 0604 006
LinkedIn: uk.linkedin.com/in/janebromley

Glen Cooper

Being "Coach, President and Owner" of Maine Business Brokers in Portland, Maine was my full-time gig for nearly 30 years. In my spare time, I transformed myself into a business and personal life coach for business owners. I sold my company in May 2010, moved to Colorado, and am just now forming my new business, named after its website, *www.GlenCooperColorado.com.*

On days when I get more than 20% of my to-do list done, I allow myself to claim that I am also an author, speaker, instructor, workshop facilitator, seminar leader and futurist in business growth and innovation, business selling, business valuation, social networking, stress management and personal time management. And, yes, I know it's hypocritical to bill myself as a stress and time management expert when I can't even get my own to-do list done – please be kind.

Helping business owners and professionals cope with all the stress and changes, achieve work/life balance and still build a valuable enterprise is my passion. We all yearn for more time, less stress, greater profits and a better life. This is what I help my clients obtain. I am a deep listener, a facilitator, a cheerleader, an objective viewer, an idea generator, some-time critic and an always-close friend.

I pay lots of dues to professional associations so I can continue to be a Certified Business Intermediary (CBI), a designation awarded by the International Business Brokers Association (IBBA), a Certified Business Appraiser (CBA) and a Business Valuator Accredited for Litigation (BVAL), designations of the Institute of Business Appraisers (IBA). I was also given the honor of being named a Fellow of the IBBA for my many years of service to the association.

In my private life, I have been a lay minister in the Catholic Church and was an adult catechist in the Rite of Christian Initiation of Adults for nearly 20 years. In that capacity, I met weekly with people exploring faith issues in their lives, just as for 30 years I have helped business owners deal with the challenges of selling their businesses.

As this biographical sketch is written, I am going through a painful divorce after a 32-year marriage, and 37-year relationship. I never expected this, but then I must accept it as a re-invention of my life. It has given me a far richer view of the chaos of the times we are all living through. I have found some new answers because I have been forced by circumstances to seek them.

Contact: GlenCooperColorado@gmail.com

More info: www.Linkedin.com/in/glencooper
www.Facebook.com/glen.j.cooper
www.GlenCooperBlog.com
www.GlenCooperColorado.com

Deirdre Dee

I have led a rich and varied life, spanning several different careers all connected with creativity, people and the performing arts. I originally trained at theatre school and went on to perform in many West End musicals, plays, summer seasons and pantomimes. At that point a friend of mine the well known actor and Music Hall aficionado Roy Hudd persuaded me to research, produce and appear in my own one-woman show based on the life of Edwardian Music Hall star, Marie Lloyd. I toured this show throughout the UK and Scandinavia. This gave me a a taste for production and running my own business. I went on to form a medium sized corporate event company which produced creative events for major business clients including Hitachi Data Systems, Procter & Gamble and British Airways. We responded to our clients needs, and introduced many corporate events ranging from promotional tours of Europe to large scale Family Fun Days for several thousand clients at a time.

Following the serious illness and subsequent disability of my husband in 1997, and in an effort to hold my family together and to help come to terms with our changed family dynamic, I became interested in coaching and all forms of self development. I trained and qualified as a Coach with Distinction in 2003 and from then on introduced an element of coaching into team events for our corporate clients. I now coach clients from the creative industries, both face to face and on the telephone. My goal is to help clients discover and develop their unique talents so that they bring their best qualities to every job or project they tackle.

I moved from London to East Devon, England four years ago and continue to work as a coach, facilitator and mentor throughout the West Country although still retaining commissions with past regular clients such as The University for the Arts in London. I have also taken coaching into schools for Enterprise in Action and I lead the Noble Manhattan Coaching Support Group in Exeter, where we have a membership of over 40 practising coaches. I've also written a two woman presentation with a professional actress friend of mine which we are about to launch in the West Country for corporate groups, arts centres and private parties.

I am married to Terence and we have two daughters, Lucy 24, who recently graduated with an MA in Creative Writing from Royal Holloway, University of London and Laura 22, who graduated this year with an English degree from Cambridge University. She is currently awaiting the publishing date for her first book.

Twitter: www.twitter.com/deirdredee
MySpace: www.myspace.com/deirdredeecoaching
FaceBook: www.facebook.com/deirdre.dee1?ref=profile
LinkedIn: www.linkedin.com/pub/deirdre-dee-lint/1/724/15

Arvind Devalia

My coaching journey began in 2002, soon after my visit to Nirvana School.

Since then, I have worked with many companies and professional individuals, such as lawyers. I live in central London and am on a mission to make it happen for myself and others.

Prior to coaching, I had a varied corporate career with Shell, BP and NatWest Bank. I also spent a few years marketing exotic food and that's where my passion for good food and healthy eating started!

During the dot com boom, I was part of an internet start-up which raised millions of pounds of funding, and at one time we were all internet paper millionaires.

I now coach go-getting clients who are already quite successful and happy in their personal and professional life and who now wish to contribute to the world in a bigger way. I am also a published author of two books, *"Get the Life you Love and Live it"* and *"Personal Social Responsibility"*.

All of us have this deep down desire to make the world a better place and leave a lasting legacy for the generations to come. If I can help at least one person live a better, more meaningful life, then I will have succeeded with my mission for my work. At the same time, I believe that by being the best we can, we fulfil our destiny on earth and also leave the world a better place. We all deserve to lead healthy, wealthy and joyous lives with deep meaning and fulfilment – it is time to make it happen for all of us!

A big part of my working life now is spreading my message via my blog and other internet projects. My main online project is my inspirational "Make It Happen Club" at *www.MakeItHappenClub.com* which is for individuals who want to create a great life for themselves and make the world a better place.

Please subscribe to my blog at *www.ArvindDevalia.com/blog* and download your FREE copy of my famous, life-changing e-book, "Make It Happen". You may also wish to subscribe to my "Make It Happen" newsletter, which goes out to thousands of readers around the world every month.

Please feel free to connect with me at
Arvind@ArvindDevalia.com or
Twitter: twitter.com/arvinddevalia
FaceBook: www.facebook.com/arvind1
LinkedIn: uk.linkedin.com/in/arvinddevalia

A Coach's Story

Catherine Joyce
CFCIPD, MAC, M.NLP

"Life shrinks or expands in proportion to one's courage."
ANAÏS NIN

As we enter a new decade, this is a great time to think about what you want to achieve in the next ten years. But a ten year strategy is a tough ask right now. Many of us are at a time or place in life where we are dissatisfied and unsure; we're ready to change, but don't yet know how. Full of uncertainty, as well as potential, we want to be able to look back in years to come with pride and delight at a life well-lived. You know it's time now to create a way forward about which you can be confident and excited.

For individuals and businesses, irrespective of location, The Changing Space offers virtual coaching programmes (online and telephone), seminars, and workshops to help you make the right decisions for you and your business that reflect your values and REAL core aims; that help you act with courage to improve your situation; that help you turn and face the future with confidence.

My warm Irish style, blended with an encouraging, inspirational outlook and an uncanny ability to stretch and challenge others to grow and evolve, fuels my passion to help people understand where they are and where they want to be –.and to create the right decisions to get there.

As a professionally trained coach with fifteen years' experience, my background is both inside and outside the corporate sector. I am regularly asked to work with senior people in a range of industries including IT, construction, manufacturing, media, engineering and retail. I founded The Changing Space and have operated a successful coaching and leadership development business for over ten years in the UK and internationally.

"Changing Perspectives" is a free 30-day e-mail programme -- a worthwhile and thought-provoking journey and the first part of our 2020 Vision Series. It will help you develop greater certainty within yourself about what you truly want, explore how to make the right decisions , and put you on the right path for your business and yourself, despite not always knowing where that path may ultimately lead.

The Changing Space is ever-evolving. Face to face Executive Coaching, leadership development, mentoring and consulting services are also.

To be notified about our new programmes, workbooks, interesting resources, workshops and offers, please go to: www.thechangingspace.com to register online and sign up for our blog: www.thechangingspace.com/blog Email me directly at ask.us@thechangingspace.com

Annie Kaszina

Suppose there were an elegant, economical, all terrain vehicle that would transport you quickly, and in comfort, from the known, the mundane, even the intolerable, to a place of infinite possibilities and unprecedented worth... Would you be willing to step into that vehicle?

Had someone asked me that question at the start of my coaching journey, I would probably have frozen in disbelief, looking for The Catch.

I went into coaching to learn tools to support other people through their difficulties. I never expected to find a way to help other people, and myself, grow in stature until our personal resources dwarfed all the problems and challenges in our path. Yet that is what coaching has enabled me to do for my clients, and myself.

Now, I work with bright, giving, caring people who put themselves last, and don't – yet – have the wonderful, sustaining relationship they long for. My clients are invariably gifted, engaging, delightful, able individuals who don't believe how fantastic they really are, and what a richly rewarding personal life they deserve. It is my pleasure to help them to do just that. Having shed my own heavy load of negativity, I specialize in helping other people replace their paralyzing, negative beliefs about self-worth, relationships and their own abilities, with a more accurate – and heartening - view of who they really are.

For the past seven years, through my writing, seminars, teleclasses and 1-2-1 coaching, I've helped thousands of abused women to ditch their abusive partners' distorted image of them, so they can discover their own magnificence and reclaim their joy. Along the way, I'm happy to say that I've helped end hundreds of bad marriages.

I've also coached many women (and men) to "reverse engineer" the loving, nurturing relationship of their dreams, and transform lacklustre relationships. I teach women how to nurture themselves and claim centre stage in their own world (instead of staying in the wings). Because when they become visible to themselves, and others, they maximize their chances of creating a lasting, fulfilling relationship.

When not working, I love spending time with friends, family, my lovely partner, and my irrepressible Shih Tzu puppy. I especially enjoy holidaying in Italy, my spiritual home.

For more information about abuse recovery coaching, as well as teleclasses, the ebook "The Woman You Want To Be", free resources, and a free twice monthly newsletter, go to www.EmotionalAbuseRecoveryNow.com

For more information about my relationship coaching go to: www.lovelifelessons.com

Contact me at annie@anniekaszina.com or Mob 07712 924124

Julie Kennedy

Hello dear readers, thank you for your interest!

I set up Kennedy Personal Coaching in the summer of 2009 with special emphasis on motivational coaching and coaching for expatriates. I help my clients move their personal and professional lives forward and help expatriates adjust their lives as they move. I coach local clients face to face but do the majority of my coaching over the telephone via skype.

So far I have lived in Great Britain, France, Holland, Austria, Spain, Cameroon, Uganda, Senegal and currently Germany picking up French, Dutch, German and Spanish along the way and accumulating various traditions and cultural elements so we are practically always celebrating something!

Before turning my attention to coaching, I earned a B.A in German, Spanish and Business studies, worked as management consultant, in development, in sales and marketing and as President of a very dynamic association of 250 women where motivational coaching played an important role.

On returning to Europe I realized I could reach out more professionally by doing a serious life-coaching course and getting accredited which was the best decision ever. The skills taught me how to optimise my natural abilities and join an enhancing, professional body.

My high energy comes from regularly spending and recharging my batteries.

I jog in the woods by the lake where we are lucky to live and have recently taken it to the next level by leaving my comfort zone to run half marathons.

I also enjoy step aerobics, cycling and am unstoppable on the dance floor! Travelling and any cultural outing I find hard to say no to and am still fascinated by Berlin and Potsdam.

My husband and I share three children: Kylian aged 13, Dylan aged 11, and Shannon 8 years old.

Coaching for me is more than a profession; it is a way of living. I get tremendous satisfaction from helping my clients move forward, but also ensure that I am also continually moving forward myself both privately and professionally and involve the whole family in the process.

I am a fervent believer in positive thinking and making the most of everything and aspire to enabling others to become their personal best.

**Please contact me at kennedy@kennedy-coaching.com
or visit my website www.kennedy-coaching.com.
I would love to hear from you!**

Gail MacIndoe

My passion is helping people to measurably improve their performance by focusing on what energises and comes naturally to them. Finding and playing to strengths seems such an obvious thing to do and yet we find ourselves repeatedly, in vain, trying to fix our weaknesses which do not result in excellence.

As an executive coach, my clients are directors of multinational corporations in the financial, energy, defence and professional services industries. A common request is to help corporations' top talent improve their personal impact and influence and develop their leadership skills. This requires self awareness and self management and then an understanding of personality types and behavioural styles. Armed with this knowledge, the executive has more behavioural flexibility and is able to communicate more effectively with their stakeholders. Other development areas include strategy - establishing a vision and personal brand, building high performance teams and creating a leadership pipeline.

I have been very fortunate to have lived in over thirteen countries, which has exposed me to different cultures, attitudes and career opportunities. While I studied psychology at university, my career for over fifteen years was in advertising, public relations and marketing. Projects included launching Pringles in Qatar; coordinating French Vogue's feature on Bahrain; hosting a weekly radio show; raising awareness and prevention of teenage pregnancy in Oklahoma, and as general manager of a PR company in Cape Town, fighting adult illiteracy and raising funds for the Red Cross.

In 1998, I completed an MBA in the UK and qualified as an executive coach, initially specialising in cross cultural relationships. I am a Master Practitioner in NLP and Appreciative Inquiry and am certified in several psychometric tools. Prior to setting up my own practice, I was Learning & Development Manager at KBR and then Aviva, the UK's leading financial services company. One of my key roles was delivering executive and team coaching and managing our external pool of coaches.

Previously the International Coach Federation (ICF) chapter host in London, I am a contributing author to "A Career in Your Suitcase", a guidebook for women on the move and am writing a new book on leading with strengths. In 2008, I was a finalist for Mentor of the Year in the Women of the Future Awards.

If you are interested in participating in my strengths programmes, or would like a speaker or workshop facilitator to motivate and inspire your team, check out my website www.macindoe.com and contact me at gail@macindoe.com

Bee Milbourn

SQHP. MNCH(Lic). LNCP. MANLP. LAPHP. DipNMC
Life Coach, NLP Master & Trainer, Clinical Hypnotherapist, SFBT Psychotherapist

For the last seventeen years I have been privileged to help people change those things in their lives which were not working well for them; whether that was to sort out an unwanted behaviour, a negative mindset, a fear or phobia or a problem in the field of relationships, career or health.

My mission is to help people understand we can choose our responses and attitudes -- that's what makes the difference between a fulfilling life and a drab or even dreadful one. I've been so lucky to have learned how to make these changes in my own life and to witness others transform problems they had thought insurmountable with ease and grace.

I'm now developing an online presence so that I can support even more people. Over the next couple of years, I'll be producing many videos, downloads and e-books using the techniques I've developed within life coaching, hypnotherapy, psychotherapy and NLP. These will be listed on my web site *www.TheLifeDesignStudio.com*

One of my other passions is inspiring those over 50 to live well and happily. To think again about any old mind-sets which are getting in the way of a new lease of life. My blog for the over 50s is *www.50PlusLifeDesign.com* – do take a look especially if you feel you're a bit stuck in your ways now that you're in your second half-century!

For some years I've worked at a leading private hospital, running the Stop Smoking Unit and useful information about the side effects of smoking can be found on *www.sideeffectssmoking.net*. You can purchase smoking downloads and e-books on *www.stopsmokingcd.org* and see what former smokers have to say on *www.happytobesmokefree.com*. Links to further information can be found on all these sites.

If you would like to book telephone coaching in the areas of Confidence, Motivation or Performance, please e-mail me on info@thelifedesignstudio.com

David Miskimin

I am an experienced and accredited coach, consultant and trainer working at CEO/Senior Executive level across all sectors in the UK and internationally. This gives me the ability to view issues from many perspectives, to understand my clients' situations, and work with them to clarify purpose, direction and action. I hold an Institute of Learning & Management (ILM) endorsed Advanced Diploma as an Executive and Corporate Coach.

My approach is both structured and adaptive and I am particularly skilled at identifying conflicts between personal and organisational effectiveness. My coaching approach is emergent, believing that while certain presented needs may seem similar, no one method fits all, and at those times when both the client and coach are stuck, different tactics need to be applied. I am highly effective in supporting, challenging, stretching and developing them, so that they become generative in their subsequent growth.

To help younger people begin to realise their talents, I co-authored *The Coaching Parent*.

I live with my wife in Cheshire, Northwest England. We are blessed with two wonderful daughters and, to date, four fabulous grandchildren!

SOME CLIENT COMMENTS
Charity Sector: Assistant Director, The Children's Society
"As a manager in a busy public sector organisation, my initial fear was that coaching would be just another task on my – very long – things to do list.... His ability... has measurably improved my confidence and ability to plan strategically... What helped me to achieve it was David's focus on clarifying my vision and making the right step towards it."
Private Sector: HR Director, NES International
"David Miskimin... impressed with his knowledge and insight, combined with passion for his work...unbiased and non-judgmental approach won the trust and confidence of the Senior Manager, which in turn resulted in the Manager's personal growth and development, which impacted beneficially on the company. I would have no hesitation in recommending David Miskimin to any organisation looking to raise the individual performance of its Directors and Managers."
Public Sector: Senior Manager, NHS North West Strategic Health Authority
"David is empathetic... has a strong ability to reflect back a situation and allow me to realise where my thinking is based on 'factless assumptions'...Working with David has increased my ability to be self-reflective... He challenges but always in a positive way."

Website: www.thedirectorscoach.com
LinkedIn: uk.linkedin.com/in/thedirectorscoach
Ecademy: www.ecademy.com/account.php?id=78248
Twitter: www.twitter.com/dmiskimin
Book: www.amazon.co.uk/dp/1905430094

Malcolm Nicholson

Not all Executive Coaches have been described as "Thought Provoking, Life Changing, Inspirational, Challenging & Perceptive."

That's because not all Executive Coaches are the same.

As owner and Principal Coach for Aspecture since 1999, I have successfully worked with senior business people across the globe, as well as sports professionals, supporting them as they make changes at individual, team or organisational levels, and improving business results through individual performance.

My coaching philosophy is simple. It is to inspire people to recognise their potential; to discover how to remove the roadblocks stopping them from achieving that potential; and maximise momentum to achieving that potential. My approach has a deep behavioural base, and is underpinned by world class research from the behavioural sciences, sports psychology and business theory. I work at two levels:

1. A pragmatic level, allowing people to take something different from each coaching session to impact their performance
2. A transformational level, working on deep seated or underlying causes of certain behaviours

Current ratings from clients include:

- Quality of coaching - 9.5 out of 10
- Rating of coach - 9.8 out of 10
- 98% made positive change as a result of his coaching
- 93% said coaching helped them improve how they dealt with new challenges
- 95% thought the coaching helped them achieve their personal objectives

This approach has been described as 'engaging – yet ruthlessly results oriented'! Combined with 10 years' coaching experience at the top, world class training, subconscious learning techniques, pragmatism and the ability to galvanise people into action means people achieve the results they want – and that's guaranteed!

Additionally I write and present leadership programmes for a leading entertainment company, am the UK Director for the Centre for International Business Coaching. (*www.internationalbusinesscoaching.com*) as well as joint owner of Who's Who Mentor.

Relevant qualifications include:

- Certified Master Coach, Behavioural Coaching Institute
- Member, International Coaching Council (ICC)
- B.Sc. (Hons) Psychology
- Studied NLP, (neuro-linguistic programming);
- Accredited coach, Sportsmind Institute of Australia
- Member, International Coaching Federation (ICF)

I am married, with three children, and my interests include sports, music (particularly jazz) and family activities.

Please feel free to contact me:

Tel: +44 (0)1932 267597 Mobile: +44 (0)7968 763312
E-mail: malcolmnicholson@aspecture.com
Web: www.aspecture.com
LinkedIn: www.linkedin.com/in/malcolmnicholson
Twitter: @aspecture

Kathleen Ann O'Grady

Raised on Long Island, New York, my professional development began at Nassau Community College. Having nearly failed my senior year of high school, I was prompted by my professor to enroll in the Honors program. I listened, and went on to exceed all expectations, graduating at the top of my class.

Following this experience, I transferred to The University of Massachusetts at Amherst where I majored in Communication. Thinking I would follow in my father's footsteps and work for NBC Studios in New York City, I enrolled in courses relating to film and media. I soon realized that my true passion was interpersonal communication and branding, and shifted my academic focus.

When I entered the work world, I held various executive level support positions in sales, real estate, global investment, hedge fund, research & development, and non-profit industries. My intention was to develop a polished professional business sense and corporate organizational intuition. I achieved this goal through partnering with executive talent and establishing a renewed self-awareness.

After witnessing the great benefits and dramatic impact of coaching, and reflecting on my varied observations of leadership, I embarked on my career as a professional coach with a focus on authentic communication and branding.

Authentic communication is a critical component of every professional and personal exchange; thus, I am driven to empower others in order to enhance their authenticity in both the business and personal realm. As a coach, I act as a catalyst for people to discover, rediscover, and embrace their authentic genius. I lead by example and show others that they can be whomever they choose to be, at any given moment. Authenticity is not a predetermined set of characteristics or personality; it is a constant layering of relationships and experiences that result from our conscious ability to choose who we are — each day.

I launched Raleigh Coaching, LLC as a vehicle for my creative energy. Raleigh Coaching works with small business owners and individual leaders within organizations, to inspire the creation of authentic brands. I find that there is a significant difference between recognizing people for their achievements and recognizing them for their potential. Achievements are of the past; potential is infinite. For me, branding is not simply the base-coat to a marketing strategy; it is a vision of authentic distinction—one that leads to people doing what they love and being financially rewarded in the process. It is all about creating contagious success.

I have a Bachelor of Arts in Communication from The University of Massachusetts at Amherst (UMass) and later completed The Business Coaching Certificate Program at North Carolina State University (NCSU). I then earned the distinction of Associate Certified Coach (ACC) through the International Coach Federation (ICF), and most recently became an Energy Leadership Index Master Practitioner (ELI-MP) at the Institute for Professional Excellence in Coaching (iPEC). To show my commitment to the continued quality and ethical standards of the professional coaching field, I serve as President of the 2010-2011 Board of Directors for the Raleigh-Area Chapter of the International Coach Federation (ICF-RAC).

Raleigh Coaching, LLC in based Raleigh, North Carolina
and is on the web at www.RaleighCoaching.com.
Email: Kathleen@RaleighCoaching.com
Skype: RaleighCoach
Twitter: @RaleighCoaching
LinkedIn: www.linkedin.com/in/kathleenogrady

Steve Roche

Steve is a writer, trainer and professional coach... passionate about encouraging people to live their lives in the way they choose, for the greatest success and happiness.

Following a successful business career he has spent many years in the personal development area, becoming one the most experienced coaches in the UK. In the early 90s Steve trained in the practical psychology of change, becoming a Master Practitioner and NLP Certified Coach.

Steve has found that relating successfully to others and the world around us begins with acceptance of ourselves and our situation. Some of the biggest underlying issues for those who come to coaching are about building confidence and self-belief, and learning to be congruent with themselves.

As a director of Suffolk Coaching Zone (SCZ), Steve provides personal coaching to groups and individuals, trains people in Coaching Skills at Foundation and Advanced levels, and runs workshops on a range of personal development topics.

Suffolk Coaching publishes a monthly email newsletter "Interesting Times", which covers news, events and latest thinking in the coaching world. The SCZ website also has details of trainings and workshops, free resources, and our Coaching Fitness Check.

Steve is also:

A leading contributor to 'Alchemy for Managers', the online source of management expertise. His topics include Presentations, Business Writing, Action Learning, Meetings and Facilitation. A free trial is available from the People Alchemy website.

A teacher of 'Co-Counselling', a way of working that gives people personal and emotional support within a peer network, as a cost-free alternative to professional counselling. His popular book "What's on Top?" is an easy-read introduction to the subject.

A facilitator of 'Action Learning', an powerful and exciting form of group coaching. He has also written an introductory book that explains Action Learning.

Steve is also the author of the following books: *"What's on Top?"(Introduction to Co-Counselling) http://bit.ly/bADxuD and "Action Learning: Effective Change Through the Power of Group Coaching" http://bit.ly/97HLfl*

Contact Steve directly at steve.roche@btinternet.com or via:
Suffolk Coaching Zone www.suffolk-coaching.com
People Alchemy www.peoplealchemy.co.uk
Coaching at IBC www.ipswichbuddhistcentre.org.uk/main.html

Karen Skehel

I am a holistic business coach, coaching supervisor and founder of Walk on Waves coaching. I bring over 25 years of business and personal development experience to my coaching and supervision clients. I am also a holistic entrepreneur, creating businesses and projects in the holistic field that focus on helping others. Since 2001, when I first started coaching, I have moved through various incarnations as a coach in order to meet the wide-ranging needs of my clients. Today, I split my time between coaching entrepreneurs, other business leaders and their teams on both their business and personal needs; providing transformational supervision to both executive coaches and non-executive coaches who are serious and committed to their own personal and professional development, and developing new holistic businesses and projects.

My background spans advertising sales and marketing, commercial radio and sales promotion, and counselling and group facilitation. I founded and ran my own successful marketing agency and I have led personal development workshops in relationships, coaching and in "emotional intelligence". I have coached in front of 1.5 million people on ITV's most popular day time programme, and have also appeared on ITV2. My tips for success in business have been broadcast on radio to 25 markets in the US. For four years, I wrote for Natural Health Magazine as The Soul Doctor and The Life Coach, addressing readers' life challenges. I have pioneered the use of self-healing coaching to help people reduce or overcome the symptoms of long-standing or so called incurable conditions. I have developed a new alternative therapy called "Chikara", and a feel-good workshop programme *www.theinnerspa.co.uk* to replenish body, mind and spirit.

I hold a Management Sciences degree (BSc Hons) and a Diploma in Group Facilitation (Emotional Intelligence). I am a certified counsellor (CCST) and a certified coach (at both foundation level and mastery levels) and hold a Diploma in Supervision.

My greatest passion in working with coaches is in the area of supervision where change is often transformational and multi-dimensional. Supervision I describe as "coaching in Technicolor". In 2010, I founded The Association of Coaching Supervisors to raise the profile of coaching supervision amongst both coaches and buyers of coaching. My greatest passion in working with entrepreneurial leaders is helping the amazing become phenomenal. My greatest passion in working as a holistic entrepreneur is to create and develop innovative concepts that will help more people in unusual and extraordinary ways.

**Find out more at www.wow-coaching.co.uk
and www.coachingsupervisor.co.uk and at
www.associationofcoachingsupervisors.com**

PaTrisha-Anne Todd

Your personal power is greater than anything you can imagine. LCSi-Education provides the resources to ignite your creativity through training and real-world experience. Clarity of vision with The Six Step Coaching Model provides instant insight and personal empowerment to Live Life by Design.

I am the founder of LCSi - Life Coach School International, an online educational entity offering the official Cosmic Soul Coaching Diploma, based upon the metaphysical Universal Laws.

In my private coaching practice, I've been privileged to meet and work with entrepreneurs, millionaires, TV and film stars and politicians. In 2006, I was flown to New York and to Texas to visit with President George Bush Sr. I have trained like-minded, vibrant, dynamic individuals to achieve satisfaction and financial freedom through their work with the principles of the Law of Attraction. Personal

Development is a growing industry and I'd be delighted to share with you my free Be - Do - Have System which I've used throughout my professional, thirty year career, living my lifestyle by design.

I remember my "journey" beginning as a young girl attending school in South London. At school I was bullied because 'I was ill. I quickly learned to keep away from people who thought inside the box or deliberately caused me heartache. Unknowingly, I was building my own foundation in self worth and personal empowerment. Cosmic Energy and Law of Attraction guided me to grow and realise my ambition to become the People Millionaire.

Today, my disability does not hinder me. I build my immune system by eating the best food in season, participating in activities that keep me vital and maintaining a positive mental attitude. You can too!

Please visit my web site and have a look around. If you would like to know more, complete the CALL BACK 24 form and I'll contact you personally.

I'm very fortunate to have the opportunity to help many individuals. Can I help you? Or perhaps you know someone who would like more information to Live Life by Design? If so, please share this with them. Looking forward... www.lcsi-education.com

Resources

Books

Anderson, Hans Christian (1844) *The Ugly Duckling*

Arbinger Institute (January 2010) *Leadership and Self Deception: Getting Out of the Box*

Ballard, J. G. (March, 2005) *Empire of the Sun*

Barber, Judy (November 2005) *Good Question! The Art of Asking Questions to Bring About Positive Change*

Bird, Tom and Cassell, Jeremy (December 2009) *Brilliant Selling*

Chopra, Deepak (November 1994) *7 Spiritual Laws of Success*

de Freitas, Sandra (May 2008) *Does This Blogsite Make My Wallet Look Fat?*

Devalia, Arvind (November 2005) *Get the Life You Love and Live It*

Fortgang, Laura Berman (April 2009) *The Little Book of Meaning: Why We Crave It, How We Create It*

Gerber, Michael (January 2001) *The E-Myth (Revisited): Why Most Small Businesses Don't Work and What to Do About It*

Goleman, Daniel (September 2006) *Emotional Intelligence: Why it can matter more than IQ*

Katie, Byron (December 2003) *Loving What Is: Four Questions That Can Change Your Life*

Kaszina, Annie, *The Woman You Want To Be (www.emotionalabuserecoverynow.com/twywtb.htm)*

Kiyosaki, Robert T. (January 2010) *Rich Dad, Poor Dad*

Kline, Nancy (November 1998) *Time to Think: Listening to Ignite the Human Mind*

Lee, Andrea J. (November 2005) *Multiple Streams Of Coaching Income*

Martin, Curly (November 2001) *The Life Coaching Handbook*

McNamara, Hannah (August 2007) *Niche Marketing for Coaches: A Practical Handbook for Building a Life Coaching, Executive Coaching or Business Coaching Practice*

Miskimin, David (January 2006) *The Coaching Parent: Help your children realise their potential by becoming their personal success coach*

Parfitt, Jo (May, 2008) *Career in Your Suitcase*

Pick, Marcelle (April 2009) The Core Balance Diet: 4 Weeks to Boost Your Metabolism and Lose Weight for Good

Verstegen, Mark and Williams, Pete (April 2005) *Core Performance: The Revolutionary Workout Program to Transform Your Body & Your Life*

Robbins, Tony (1988) *Unleash the Power Within*

Sapolsky, Robert (August 2004) *Why Zebras Don't Get Ulcers*

Sherman, S. and Freas, A., (2004), *Wild West of Coaching*

Smart, J.K. (2002) *Real Coaching and Feedback: How to Help People Improve Their Performance*

Whitmore, John (October 2009) *Coaching for Performance: Growing Human Potential and Purpose*

Williams, Patrick and Davis, Deborah (October 2007) *Therapist as Life Coach: An Introduction for Counselors and Other Helping Professionals*

Online Resources

harvardbusinessonline.hbsp.harvard.edu/hbsp/hbr/articles/article.jsp?articleID=R0411E&ml_action=get-article&print=true

O'Donovan, Gerard, How Coaching Can Improve Your Life, *www.noble-manhattan.com*, Free Reports

Noble Manhattan Life Coach Programme, available at *www.noble-manhattan.com/Practitioner.php*

www.getcoachingleads.com available through Noble Manhattan Coaching

Noble Manhattan Business Building Day: details available at *www.noble-manhattan.com/building_business.php*

International Institute of Coaching, *www.internationalinstituteofcoaching.org*

International Coach Federation, *www.coachfederation.org*

The Corporate and Executive Coaching Organisation, *www.cecoach.com*

"Enhancing Attitudes, Behaviors and Techniques", Sandler Sales Institute, *www.sandlerinternational.com*

The Association of Coaching Supervisors, available at *www.associationforcoaching.com/home/index.htm*

Worldwide Coaching Support Groups, *www.coaching-support.com*

JigsawBox, *www.JigsawBox.com*

Take Action, Get Clients, *www.takeactiongetclients.com*

The Chartered Institute of Personnel and Development (CIPD), *www.cipd.co.uk*

Pryor, (February 2008) CIPD People Management publication, *"Coaches are hired to help the client get results... As a client am I in this for me or the organisation?"*

Living Life by Design, *www.livinglifebydesign.wordpress.com*

Robbins, Tony Unlimited Power course, *www.motivationalmagic.com*

Newcastle College's Diploma in Business Performance Coaching, available at *www.flexible-elearning.co.uk/advanced-diploma-performance-coaching.html*

James, Tad Time Line Therapy, available at *www.timelinetherapy.net*

Corporate Coach U International (CCUI), *www.coachinc.com/CCU*

Myers Briggs Inventory (MBTI I & Step II), *www.myersbriggs.org*

The London Coaching Group, *www.londoncoachinggroup.co.uk*

Coaching at Work Magazine, *www.coaching-at-work.com*

The Ambassadors Programme, *www.ambassadorprogramme.com*

The Inspirational Women's Network in partnership with Lloyds TSB, *www.iwn.realbusiness.co.uk*

Pinky Lilani OBE, creator of the network and founder of the Asian Women of Achievement Awards and Women of the Future Awards, *www.spicemagic.com*

The Kids Company, *www.thekidco.com*

Eurocoachlist, *www.eurocoachlist.com*

Fraser Clarke business coaching course, *www.fraserclarke.com*

Hippocrates Health Institute in Florida, *www.hippocratesinst.org*

Alexander Technique (AT), *www.alexandertechnique.com*

Turner, Rachel, and Niland, John, Coach U workshop, *www.coachu.com*

Money Gym, *www.themoneygym.com*

The Artist's Way, *www.theartistsway.com*

Additional Resources

CIPD Research, *Taking the Temperature of Coaching*, Source Coaching At Work, Vol 4, Issue 6, 2009

Miskimin, D. (August 2007) *Assignment - Executive Coaching FINAL V1.0.doc*, submitted as part of Diploma in Corporate and Executive Coaching, Cheshire

Sherman S. and Freas A. (01 November 2004) *"The Wild West of Executive Coaching"*, Harvard Business Review

Passmore, J. & Marianetti, O. (2007). *"The role of mindfulness in coaching"*, The Coaching Psychologist 3 (3): 131-137

Passmore, J. and Marianetti, O. (2008) *Mindfulness*

Goffee R. and Jones G. (March 2007) *"Leading Clever People - How do you manage people who don't want to be led and may be smarter than you?"* Harvard Business Review

Grant, A. and Green, J. (2001) *It's your life. What are you going to do with it? Coach Yourself: Make Real Change in Your Life*

Lee, G. (2003) *"Leadership Coaching: From personal insight to organisational performance"*, Chartered Institute of Personnel & Development

Schwarz, Jeffrey and Rock, David (August 2009) *The Neuroscience of Leadership*

Lightning Source UK Ltd.
Milton Keynes UK
01 April 2011

170243UK00002B/28/P